GUMAYRAH LEARNING HUB - NAEEM

LEARN TAJWEED
Simplify Your Qur'an journey

Fashina Omobolaji Naeemah

CONTENTS

- CONTENTS 2
- FOREWORD 7
- INTRODUCTION 8
- DEDICATION 9
- ACKNOWLEDGMENT 10
- TOWARDS QUR'AN REFLECTION 11
- BENEFITS FROM THE REFLECTION OF THE QUR'AN 13
- TAJWEED 16
- HURUFUL HIJAI) THE ARABIC ALPHABET 20
  - HOW TO PRONOUNCE 20
- SIMILAR SOUNDING LETTERS 24
- ARABIC ALPHABETS CHART (HURUFUL HIJAI) LETTER NAMES & SOUNDS 25
- TAJWEED 26
  - TAJWEED IS DIVIDED INTO 4 GROUPS: 26
- MAKHARIJ AL HUROOF 27
- TAJWEED 1: MAKHARIJ AL HUROOF 28
- HOW TO PINPOINT THE MAKHRAJ OF A LETTER 29
- IMPORTANCE OF MAKHARIJ 30
- MAKHARIJ AL HUROOF 31
- MAKHARIJ AL HUROOF 32
- POINTS OF ORIGIN (ARTICULATION) OF THE LETTERS 33
- STRUCTURE OF THE TONGUE: 4 MAIN AREAS 38
- SOUNDS OF THE LETTERS OF THE LIPS 42
- SIFAT AL HUROOF 45
- TAJWEED 2) SIFAT AL HUROOF 46
  - IMPORTANCE OF CORRECT APPLICATION OF THE SIFAT (CHARACTERISTICS) 47
- SIFAT AL HUROOF (PERMANENT & TEMPORARY ATTRIBUTES) 49
- PERMANANT ATTRIBUTES (LAZIMAH) THAT HAVE OPPOSITE

CHARACTERISTICS 50

HAMS - JAHR (CONTINUATION OR STOPPAGE OF BREATH) 50
PERMANANT ATTRIBUTES (LAZIMAH) THAT HAVE OPPOSITE CHARACTERISTICS 51
SHIDDAH-TAWASSUT-RAKHAWAH STOPPAGE & CONTINUATION OF SOUND) 51
PERMANANT ATTRIBUTES (LAZIMAH) THAT HAVE OPPOSITE CHARACTERISTICS 52
ISTI'LAA - ISTEFAAL (HEAVINESS & LIGHTNESS) 52
PERMANANT ATTRIBUTES (LAZIMAH) THAT HAVE OPPOSITE CHARACTERISTICS 53
ITBAAQ - INFITAAH (CLOSURE & OPENING OF THE INSIDE OF THE MOUTH) 53
PERMANANT ATTRIBUTES (LAZIMAH) THAT HAVE OPPOSITE CHARACTERISTICS 54
ISMAAT - IDHLAQ (PRONOUNCED WITH EFFORT & EASE) 54

PERMANENT ATTRIBUTES (LAZIMAH) WITHOUT OPPOSITES 55

PERMANENT ATTRIBUTES (LAZIMAH) WITHOUT OPPOSITES 59

SUMMARY OF PERMANANT ATTRIBUTES 60
(LAZIMAH) WITH THE OPPOSITES 60
SUMMARY OF PERMANANT ATTRIBUTES (LAZIMAH) WITHOUT OPPOSITES 61

SIFAAT OF QALQALAH 68

PERMANENT ATTRIBUTES (LAZIMAH) WITHOUT OPPOSITES 69

THE QUALITY (SIFAAT) OF QALQALAH 69
TWO TYPES OF SUKUN 70

THE LEVELS OF QALQALAH 72

REASON FOR QALQALAH 73
READING QALQALAH 75

EXERCISING THE TONGUE 76

& REPETITION 76

TAJWEED 3: EXERCISING THE TONGUE & REPETITION 77

SIMILAR SOUNDING LETTERS LEAD TO SIMILAR SOUNDING WORDS 78
THE THREE LEVELS OF SPEED IN RECITING THE HOLY QUR'AN 79

THE THREE LEVELS OF SPEED IN RECITING THE HOLY QUR'AN 82

HOW DIACRITICS CONTROL WORDS 83

AHKAM AL HUROOF 84

TAJWEED 4: AHKAM AL HUROOF 85

THE RULES OF LAAM 88

AHKAM AL HUROOF: 1) RULES OF LAAM 89

4 TYPES OF LAAM SAAKIN 89
4 TYPES OF LAAM SAKIN – FURTHER DIVIDED 90

LAAM SAKIN: 1) LAAM AT TA'REEF (SUN & MOON LAAM) 91

LAAM SAKIN: 1) LAAM AT TA'REEF (EXAMPLES OF EACH LETTER) 92
LAAM SAKIN: 2) LAAM AL FI'IL 93
UNDERSTANDING HEAVY AND LIGHT LETTERS THE ARABIC ALPHABET 94
THE RULE OF LAAM: 4) LAAM AL LAFDHIL JALALI 95
THE RULE OF LAAM: 4) LAAM AL LAFDHIL JALALI 97

THE RULES OF NUN SAKIN ن and TANWEEN 98

RULES OF NUN SAKIN AND TANWEEN 99
RULES OF NUN SAKIN AND TANWEEN 100
THE FOUR RULES OF NUN SAKIN AND TANWEEN 101
THE LETTERS RELATED TO THE NUN SAKIN AND TANWEEN RULES 102
NUN SAKIN AND TANWEEN 103
RULE 1: IDH'HAAR (to say CLEARLY) 103
NUN SAKIN AND TANWEEN: RULE 2 IDH'GHAAM (To Merge or Join) 106

TYPE 1 – IDH'GHAAM MA'AL GHUNNAH – Merging with Nasal Sound – LETTERS يمنو also known in acronym as YAMNU letters 108

NUN SAKIN AND TANWEEN: RULE 2 IDH'GHAAM (To Merge or Join) 109

NUN SAKIN AND TANWEEN 111

RULE 3: IKHFAA (to Hide or to Conceal) 111
NUN SAKIN AND TANWEEN: RULE 3 IKHFAA (To Hide or Conceal) 112
NUN SAKIN AND TANWEEN .... Error! Bookmark not defined.
RULE 4: IQLAB/QALB (to Change or Convert) .... Error! Bookmark not defined.
NUN SAKIN AND TANWEEN: RULE 4 IQLAB (To Change or Convert) 115
NUN SAKIN AND TANWEEN: RULE 4 IQLAB (To Change or Convert) 116
NUN SAKIN AND TANWEEN SUMMARY 117
RULES OF NUN SHADDAH AND MEEM SHADDAH 118

WHAT IS GHUNNAH? 119

RULES OF NUN SHADDAH AND MEEM SHADDAH 120
THE RULES OF MEEM SAKIN مْ 121

- THE 3 RULES OF MEEM SAKIN 122
- MEEM SAKIN: RULE 2 - IKHFAA SHAFAWI (To hide or conceal) 124
- MEEM SAKIN: RULE 3 – IDH'HAAR SHAFAWI (To recite clearly) 125
- THE RULES OF MEEM SAKIN IN BRIEF 127

THE RULES OFOTHER IDH'GHAM 128
- THE RULES OF OTHER IDH'GHAM 129
- WHY IDH'GHAM 130
- RULES OF OTHER IDH'GHAM – 1.) IDH'GHAM MUTAMAATHILAYN 133
- RULES OF OTHER IDH'GHAM – 2.) IDH'GHAM MUTAJAANISAYN 134
- RULES OF OTHER IDH'GHAM – 3.) IDH'GHAM MUTAQAARIBAYN 136
- RULES OF OTHER IDH'GHAM – 4.) IDH'GHAM MUTABAA'IDAIN 139

THE RULES OF NUN QUTNI 140
- NUN QUTNI (THE SMALL ن) 141
- THE RULES OF RAA ر 144
- THE 8 RULES OF RAA TAFKHEEM RELATED TO FAT-HA & DHAMMA 146
- THE RULES OF RAA TAFKHEEM 147
- THE 4 RULES OF RAA TARQEEQ RELATED TO KASRA 148
- THE RULES OF RAA TARQEEQ 149
- (Light – Empty Mouth Pronounciation) 149
- THE 2 EXCEPTION RULES OF RAA TAFKHEEM RELATED TO KASRA 150
- CERTAIN WORDS WHERE BOTH TAFKHEEM AND TARQEEQ IS ALLOWED 151

AHKAM AL MUDOOD (THE RULES OF MADDAH) 154
- DURATION OF ELONGATION OF MADDAH 155
- THE 9 TYPES OF MUDOOD 155
- BREAKDOWN OF THE 9 TYPES OF MUDOOD 156
- TYPES OF MADD: 1.) MADD AL ASLIYYA OR AT-TABEE 158
- NATURAL OR ORIGINAL MADD 158
- WHAT IS A VOWEL COUNT OR LENGTHENED FOR 2, 4, 6 HARAKA MEAN? 159
- MADD AL FAR'I: MADD CAUSED BY OTHER FACTORS 161
- Madd Al Far'i: Maddah Caused by Hamza 165

THE 14 HURUFUL MUQATT'TA'AAT 169
- DIVISION OF THE 14 HURUFUL MUQATT'TA'AAT ACCORDING TO THEIRPROLONGATION 171
- THE MADD AL-HARFI IN THE HURUFUL MUQATT'TA'AAT 172
- EXAMPLES OF MADD UL HARFEE MUTHAQQAL 173
- MADD AL FAR'I: MADDAH CAUSED BY SUKUN – 8.) MADD UL-LEEN 175

MADD AL FAR'I: MADDAH CAUSED BY SUKUN – 9.) MADD UL-ARIDH LISSUKUN 176

RULES OF HAA 177
RULES OF HAA 178

H A M Z A 181
HAMZATUL QAT'AA ء 183
HAMZATUL QAT'AAء 184
HAMZATUL WASL ا 186
THE RULE OF HAMZATUL WASL: SKIPPED IN CONTINOUS RECITATION 188
HAMZATUL WASL PRONOUNCED IN VERBS – Easy to remember 193
HAMZATUL WASL FOLLOWED BY ANOTHER HAMZA 194

AL-WAQF (THE STOP) 195
DIVISIONS OF THE STOP 197
THE SYMBOLS OF WUQUF 198
SUMMARY OF THE SYMBOLS OF WUQUF 200
THE RULES OF WUQUF 202
RULES OF WAQF (STOPPING RULES) 203
EXAMPLES FOR RULES OF WAQF (STOPPING RULES) 205
AS – SAKT (ARABIC) or س (The Breathless Pause) 207
AL-IBTIDAA (The Beginning or Starting) 208
AL-WAQF WITH HAMZATUL WASL 209

SOME EXCEPTIONS FOUND IN THE HOLY QUR'AN 210
SOME EXAMPLES FOR PRACTICE 212

TERMINOLOGY FREQUENTLY USED IN TAJWEED 216

FOREWORD

As a teacher of the Quran, I have always had issues with students skipping class because they find it difficult to understand.

I have also come to realize that many students think the concepts of *tajweed* are exclusive to the rules of nun *saakinah* and *tanween* only, hence they have the notion that once they know the rules of nun saakinah and *tanween*, they have understood the whole concept of *tajweed*.

All these and more are among the setbacks students encounter when it comes to the area of *tajweed* which I have come to realize and, in a bid, to help my students excel more, I thought of different ways to make learning and understanding *tajweed* easier for them.

To get the best for them, I spoke with a more experienced colleague in the field and he suggested the compilation of these rules in a language students would understand easily, such that they would comprehend and put into effective practice these rules when it comes to recitation of the glorious Qur'an and that is what gave birth to this book.

I ask Allāh to accept this from me as an act of *Ibaadah*.

INTRODUCTION

This book is compiled with great passion to aid an easier understanding of the rules of *tajweed*. I also shared my thoughts on the need to improve our connections with Allāh (سُبْحَانَهُ وَتَعَالَى) through reflections in this amazing book.

It is going to be an exemplarily beautiful experience in your Qu'ran learning journey.

DEDICATION

To my daughter, because of whom everything makes sense.

ACKNOWLEDGMENT

All praises to Allāh (سُبْحَانَهُوَتَعَالَى) Who has blessed my tiny efforts and made me grow exponentially and still making me grow more. Thereafter, I am grateful to my parents who nurtured me to greatness, may Allāh (سُبْحَانَهُوَتَعَالَى) reward you Dad, and may Allāh (سُبْحَانَهُوَتَعَالَى) prolong your life Mummy.

I am grateful to my siblings, may Allāh (سُبْحَانَهُوَتَعَالَى) answer all your *Du'a* and keep you firm on Khayr.

Moreover, I am grateful to Ustādh Saboor Aboo Israaeel Kewdirorunwiyy who planted the seed of this book in my head.

To Brother Yūnus Olukodo of SYO BYTES, who took it upon himself to bring this manuscript to life, I am grateful. It was indeed a hard work.

To my bread and butter, Umm Aadam, I love you and I am honored to be in your tribe of women. I admire your strength, my sweetheart.

Dear MBM, meeting you was nothing short of Allah's grace, thank you so much for being awesome and also sharing the awesomeness with the world.

I am full of gratitude to Sis Juwayriyyah Oyiza. For some reason or the other, she sees the best in me, and she doesn't fail to remind me of my awesomeness.

I am always in awe of your support, Sis Lateefah Abifarin, and my dearest Zou, you are indeed a pillar to lean on.

My favorite lawyer, Fatimah Usman, may you continue to thrive in goodness and wellness. A prayer answered is what you are to me, I love you Allāh (سُبْحَانَهُوَتَعَالَى).

That said, Allāh (سُبْحَانَهُوَتَعَالَى) has blessed me so much that I can continue to type and type and still I won't be able to express all on this page.

To everyone that has crossed my path, one way or the other, you've all been of amazing impact on my life and success, I am wholeheartedly grateful to you all.

May Allāh (سُبْحَانَهُوَتَعَالَى) reward you all abundantly and never leave you to your affairs in the blink of an eye. *Amin.*

TOWARDS QUR'AN REFLECTION

If you know me before now, you'd know I have always been a fan of reflection; I enjoy savoring the world of the Qur'an and being mesmerized by its beauty. I allow my mind to wonder as to why it's a beautiful world albeit transient.

Equally, reflection is always a way of calming myself, which explains why I am obsessed with reflecting on the Qur'an. I have always thought of myself as a special breed but the world broke me and I tarried away from nature, wallowing in despair. Guess what gave me my footing back? *TADABURR*. What I am trying to say is that the solution for everything you are looking for is in the Quran and you won't get it until you ponder on the Words of Allāh.

What is *TADABURR*? it simply means a time out of our day-to-day activities to meditate and ponder on the meaning of the verses of the Quran. *Tadaburr* is to contemplate and brood upon the Qur'an to gain enlightenment and feels an increase in *eeman*, have deep insights into Allāh's nature and attributes.

"He is Allāh(سُبْحَانَهُوَتَعَالَى); there is no god but He, Knower of the unseen and the seen; He is the Most Gracious, the Most Merciful."

هُوَ ٱللَّهُ ٱلْخَالِقُ ٱلْبَارِئُ ٱلْمُصَوِّرُ لَهُ ٱلْأَسْمَاءُ ٱلْحُسْنَىٰ يُسَبِّحُ لَهُ مَا فِى ٱلسَّمَٰوَٰتِ وَٱلْأَرْضِ وَهُوَ ٱلْعَزِيزُ ٱلْحَكِيمُ

"He is Allāh; there is no god but He, the Sovereign, the Holy, the Most Perfect, the Granter of security, the Watcher over all, the Almighty, the Compeller, the Supreme." Surah Hashr.[1]

One thing I found astonishing in the Qur'an is the synergy Allāh(سُبْحَانَهُوَتَعَالَى) has put between Him, us, and the Qur'an, such that reading the Qur'an and trying to decipher the message feels like a personal conversation with the Creator. The manner of approach to which Allāh (سُبْحَانَهُوَتَعَالَى) relates helped us sort of achieve self-realization and invariably have a strong bond with Allāh (سُبْحَانَهُوَتَعَالَى). The most powerful one made it easy for us to worship him. Allāh (سُبْحَانَهُوَتَعَالَى) doesn't just give us a concept and expects us to fill in the gaps; he took us through the concept with explicit explanations using parables to help

---
[1] *Surah Al-Hashr, Qur'an Chapter 59, Verse 24.*

us understand better. This makes me laugh at those who walk around the Earth with pride saying they owe no one explanation. The One who created us sent down the prophet and revealed the Qur'an to explain to us the concept of Islam in clear terms.

إِنَّ ٱللَّهَ لَا يَسْتَحْىِۦٓ أَن يَضْرِبَ مَثَلًا مَّا بَعُوضَةً فَمَا فَوْقَهَا ۚ فَأَمَّا ٱلَّذِينَ ءَامَنُوا۟ فَيَعْلَمُونَ أَنَّهُ ٱلْحَقُّ مِن رَّبِّهِمْ ۖ وَأَمَّا ٱلَّذِينَ كَفَرُوا۟ فَيَقُولُونَ مَاذَآ أَرَادَ ٱللَّهُ بِهَٰذَا مَثَلًا ۘ يُضِلُّ بِهِۦ كَثِيرًا وَيَهْدِى بِهِۦ كَثِيرًا ۚ وَمَا يُضِلُّ بِهِۦٓ إِلَّا ٱلْفَٰسِقِينَ ۝

"Verily, Allāh is not ashamed to set forth a parable even of a mosquito or so much more when it is bigger (or less when it is smaller) than it. And as for those who believe, they know that it is the Truth from their Lord, but as for those who disbelieve, they say: "What did Allāh intend by this parable?" By it He misleads many, and many He guides thereby. And He misleads thereby only those who are Al-Fasiqun (the rebellious, disobedient to Allāh)." [2]

مَثَلُ ٱلَّذِينَ ٱتَّخَذُوا۟ مِن دُونِ ٱللَّهِ أَوْلِيَآءَ كَمَثَلِ ٱلْعَنكَبُوتِ ٱتَّخَذَتْ بَيْتًا ۖ وَإِنَّ أَوْهَنَ ٱلْبُيُوتِ لَبَيْتُ ٱلْعَنكَبُوتِ ۖ لَوْ كَانُوا۟ يَعْلَمُونَ ۝

The parable of those who take protectors other than Allāh is that of the spider, who builds (to itself) a house; but truly the flimsiest of houses is the spider's house; - if they but knew.[3]

Another thing that stands out is the way *Allāh* kept repeating himself over and over again and never deviating from the central theme of the *Quran* which is MONOTHEISM.

---

[2] *Surah Al-Baqarah, Qur'an Chapter 2, Verse 2.*
[3] *Surah Al-'Ankabut, Qur'an Chapter 29, Verse 41.*

BENEFITS FROM THE REFLECTION OF THE QUR'AN

Irrespective of whether you believe it or not, gaining the full benefit of pondering and reflecting on the Qur'an requires you to empty your mind of every preconceived notion and bias so as not to project such ideas on the book.

Reflecting on the Qur'an is a direct command from Allāh, we are directed to ponder on the holy book for that's how we would reap the fruits.

This is the Blessed Book that We have revealed to you, (O Muhammad), that people with understanding may reflect over its verses and those with understanding derive a lesson. Q37:49

The Quran has been called a blessed Book in the sense that it is highly useful for man.

Most of us have restricted ourselves to just reading the Qur'an while it is a very good rewardable act of worship; reading the Qur'an requires a deep commitment to reflect and digest the Message Allāh wants us to get. This brings me to this question:

What does the Qur'an mean to you?
How do you ponder upon the Qur'an?
What mesmerizes you about the Qur'an?

What sort of relationship do you have with the Quran?
For me, once I reflected on a particular portion of the Qur'an, I always wish I had pondered on the verse before as I know it would have prevented some misbehavior in the past. Before reflecting on surah *al-mutoffifn*, I had always been on the defensive side when my deen or mode of dressing is insulted or humiliated. But after understanding the last verses of that surah, all I do is laugh at their silliness because Allāh has defended me. What better defense do I have for myself against the word of *Allāh*?

فَٱلۡيَوۡمَ ٱلَّذِينَ ءَامَنُواْ مِنَ ٱلۡكُفَّارِ يَضۡحَكُونَ ﴿٣٤﴾

Verily, those who committed crimes used to laugh at those who believed. Are not the disbelievers paid for what they used to do; meaning, `will the disbelievers be recompensed for their mockery and belittlement against the believers, or not. This means that they surely will be paid in full, completely, and perfectly (for their behavior).[4]

---
[4] *Surah Al-Mutaffifin, Quran chapter 83, Verse 34*

Tadabur is akin to having a good relationship with the Qur'an as it illuminates the heart and exposes the reader to the best source of continuous learning. As far as I am concerned, the Qur'an is the most important and complete self-development Book ever and one can only benefit from it by constantly digesting the lesson. The Qur'an is full of abundant blessings and knowledge and advice for those that reflect the Qur'an.

يَطُوفُ عَلَيْهِمْ وِلْدَانٌ مُّخَلَّدُونَ ۝

"And We have indeed made the Qur'an easy to understand and remember: then is there any that will receive admonition" [5]

Amazing to me is the synergy of the beneficial relationship we can have with the Qur'an that inspires arrays of emotions depending on where and why you are reading. Allāh(سُبْحَانَهُ وَتَعَالَى) has made the Qur'an a companion and guideline for us where we can find assurances, acknowledgments of our struggle, patience for our trials, solutions, and hopes for our worries and addresses our fears, but we can only tap into those benefit through tadaburr/Qur'an.

وَلَقَدْ نَعْلَمُ أَنَّكَ يَضِيقُ صَدْرُكَ بِمَا يَقُولُونَ ۝

"We certainly know that your heart is truly distressed by what they say" [6]

وَأَصْبَحَ فُؤَادُ أُمِّ مُوسَىٰ فَارِغًا ۖ إِن كَادَتْ لَتُبْدِي بِهِ لَوْلَا أَن رَّبَطْنَا عَلَىٰ قَلْبِهَا لِتَكُونَ مِنَ الْمُؤْمِنِينَ ۝

"On the other hand, the heart of Moses' mother was sorely distressed. Had We not strengthened her heart that she might have full faith (in Our promise), she would have disclosed the secret" [7]

وَكُلًّا نَّقُصُّ عَلَيْكَ مِنْ أَنبَاءِ الرُّسُلِ مَا نُثَبِّتُ بِهِ فُؤَادَكَ ۚ وَجَاءَكَ فِي هَـٰذِهِ الْحَقُّ وَمَوْعِظَةٌ وَذِكْرَىٰ لِلْمُؤْمِنِينَ ۝

"And each [story] We relate to you from the news of the messengers is that by which We make firm your heart. And there has come to you, in this, the

---

[5] Surah Al-Waqi'ah, Qur'an Chapter 54, Verse 17.
[6] Surah Al-Hijr, Qur'an Chapter 15, Verse 97.
[7] Surah Al-qasas, Qur'an Chapter 28, Verse 10.

truth and an instruction and a reminder for the believers'[8]

وَنَزَعْنَا مَا فِى صُدُورِهِم مِّنْ غِلٍّ تَجْرِى مِن تَحْتِهِمُ ٱلْأَنْهَـٰرُ وَقَالُوا۟ ٱلْحَمْدُ لِلَّهِ ٱلَّذِى هَدَىٰنَا لِهَـٰذَا وَمَا كُنَّا لِنَهْتَدِىَ لَوْلَآ أَنْ هَدَىٰنَا ٱللَّهُ

We shall strip away all rancor from their hearts, and rivers shall flow beneath them, and they shall say: 'All praise be to Allāh Who has guided us on to this. Had it not been for Allāh Who granted us guidance, we would not be on the Right Path.[9]

Reflecting on the Quran also helps to reaffirm our place with Allāh, helping us to be steadfast and knowing the One whom we worship is indeed the Most Powerful and the only One whom we seek help from. "Surely Allāh defends those who believe. Certainly, Allāh has no love for the perfidious, the thankless" [10]
"Whereas those who strive against Our Signs, seeking to profane them, they are the friends of the Fire!"[11]

READ THE QURAN
REFLECT s
PONDER.

---

[8] *Surahul Hud, Qur'an Chapter 11, Verse 120.*
[9] *Surah Al-Araf, Qur'an Chapter 7, Verse 43.*
[10] *Surah Al-Hajj, Verse 38*

[11] Surah Al-Hajj, Verse 51

TAJWEED

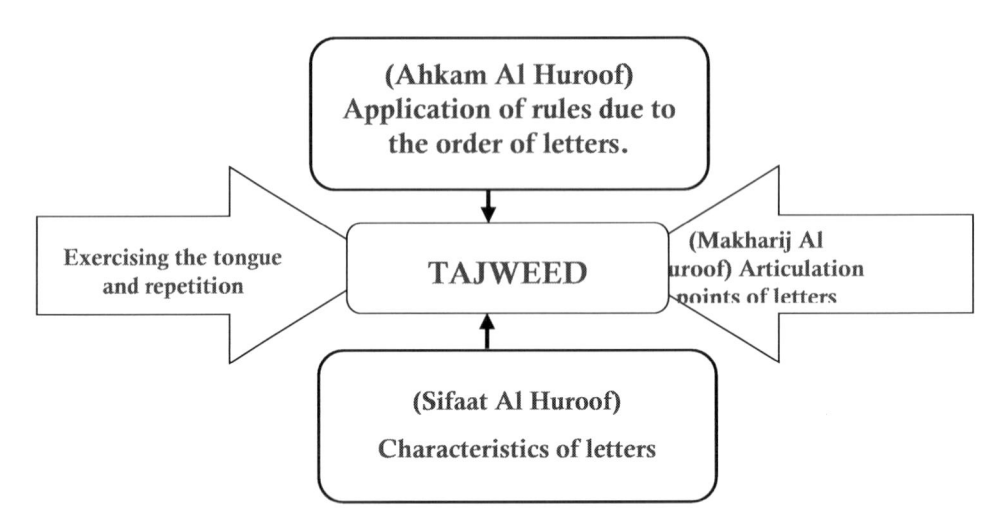

```
                    ┌──────────────────────────┐
                    │   (Ahkam Al Huroof)      │
                    │ Application of rules due │
                    │   to the order of letters.│
                    └──────────────────────────┘
                                 ↓
  ⟶ Exercising the tongue  →  TAJWEED  ←  (Makharij Al
      and repetition                      Huroof) Articulation
                                          points of letters  ⟵
                                 ↑
                    ┌──────────────────────────┐
                    │   (Sifaat Al Huroof)     │
                    │ Characteristics of letters│
                    └──────────────────────────┘
```

Qur'an reading is the recitation of the Qur'an according to Tajweed&Tarteel as taught by the Prophet Muhammad (Peace and Blessings of Allah be upon him). It is one of the Sciences from U'loom Al Qur'an (sciences of the Qur'an) Linguistic Definition: The word Tajweed comes from the root word Jawada which means 'to improve' or 'to make better', though linguistically, it means "to beautify something".

Applied Definition: Tajweed is to give every letter its right with its description and its origination.

Tajweed refers to rules governing pronunciation during Qur'an recitation; such as prolongation, merging, conversion, distinctness, accuracy, commas, pauses and stopping rules. This allows the reciter to emphasise the accent, phonetics, rhythms, fluency and

temper, where and how to pause, where the pronunciation should be long or short, where letters should be sounded together (harf to harf) and where they should be kept separate, and so on.

When asked about the meaning of Tarteel, `Ali (رَضِيَ اللَّهُ عَنْهُ) replied, "It means the Qur'an should be recited with Tajweed and with due observance to the rules of Waqf (pausing to take a breath in the recitation of Qur'an, with the intention of continuing).

❖ Tajweed helps the reciter to avoid making mistakes when reciting

قَلْبٌ   كَلْبٌ

Example: (means: Heart) (means: Dog)
- ❖ It is very important and a personal obligation on each individual to learn Tajweed.
  They have to know the Makharij, Sifaat and Ahkam.

- ❖ It is said in the Holy Qur'an in SuratulMuzzamil 73:4
  "……. *And recite the Qur'an in slow, measured rhythmic tones*"

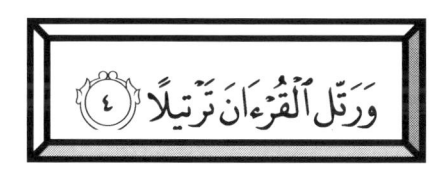

$$\text{وَرَتِّلِ ٱلْقُرْءَانَ تَرْتِيلًا ﴿٤﴾}$$

The benefit of reciting the Holy Qur'an with *Tajweed* is preserving our tongue frommistakes (LAHN) whenreading the Glorious Qur'an.

The Science of Beautifying the Noble Qur'an

التجويد

A scholar was once asked *"When a person is reciting Qur'an, is it obligatory to observe and listen to it?"*

The scholar replied, "Yes! When Qur'an is being recited to you (near you), it is compulsory upon you to listen to it and be silent."

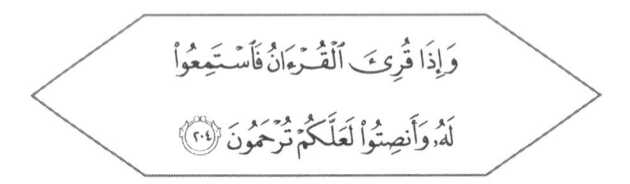

$$\text{وَإِذَا قُرِئَ ٱلْقُرْءَانُ فَٱسْتَمِعُوا۟ لَهُۥ وَأَنصِتُوا۟ لَعَلَّكُمْ تُرْحَمُونَ ﴿٢٠٤﴾}$$

"And when the Qur'an is recited, then listen to it and remain silent, that mercy may be shown to you." [12]

Ali (رضي الله عنه) said that there is a hundred *Hasanah* (reward) for each letter of the Holy Qur'an that the reciter recites in prayer while standing up, fifty while sitting down, twenty-five with Wudhoo while not praying, and ten without Wudhoo.

This narration explains the importance of the Holy Qur'an and its words:

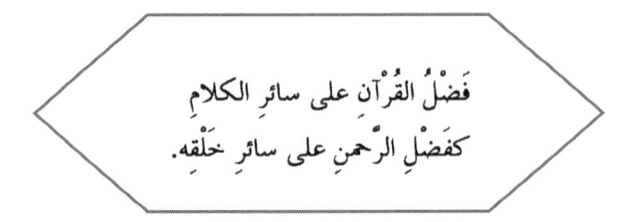

$$\text{فَضْلُ القُرْآنِ على سائِرِ الكلامِ كَفَضْلِ الرَّحمنِ على سائِرِ خَلْقِه.}$$

---

[12] Surah Al-A'raf, Verse 204

Abu Sa'id (رَضِيَٱللَّهُعَنْهُ) reported: The Messenger of Allah (صَلَّىٱللَّهُعَلَيْهِوَسَلَّمَ) said, "The superiority of the words of Allah over all other words is like the superiority of Allah over His creation."[13]

---

[13] Sunan al-Tirmidhī 2926

HURUFUL HIJAI) THE ARABIC ALPHABET

HOW TO PRONOUNCE

HOW TO PRONOUNCE	NAME AND PHONETIC SOUND	ARABIC ALPHABET
Tongue is flat in the mouth and the sound comes from the centre of the mouth	Name: Alif Sound: (a) as in Umbrella	ا
Mouth and lips together. One dot below the letter	Name: Baa' Sound: (b) as in Balloon	ب
Tongue touches the roots of the upper teeth. Two dots above the letter	Name: Taa' Sound: (t) for Teddy	ت
Tongue is placed between and behind the upper teeth. Three dots above the letter	Name: Thaa' Sound: (th) for Thumb	ث
Pronounced as 'Ja' sound Ja has one dot in the tummy	Name: Jiim Sound: (j) for Jam	ج
Pronounced from the middle of the throat while pushing air out, with a strong and sustained expulsion of breath.	Name: Haa' Sound: (h) for Hello Lightly	ح

Distinctive sound like when you are clearing the throat. A grating sound. Dot on head (place finger on head)	Name: Khaa' Sound: (Kh) for Khadija, Khaleel., sound from the Throat	خ
Pronounced as 'Da' sound	Name: Daal Sound: (d) for Daddy	د
Keeping the tongue flat in the mouth between the teeth	Name: Dhaal Sound: (dh) for The, This	ذ
Strongly rolled as in Spanish and somewhat rounded as 'rau' in 'raucous'	Name: Raa' Sound: (r) for Rabbit	ر
Pronounced as 'Z' sound	Name: Zaa' Sound: (z) for Zahra	ز
Sound: (Sa) for Sun, Smile	Name: Seen Sound: (s) for Sun, Smile	س
Place finger on the lips. Shhhh	Name: Sheen Sound: (sh) for Shirt	ش
Emphatic 's' pronounced with the tip of the tongue touching the roots of the upper front teeth whistling sound and tongue is curved.	Name: Saad Sound: (ṣ) for Swafiya	ص

Pronounced with the tongue pressing hard against the upper teeth andpalate, with a full mouth.	Name: Daad Sound: (d) for though, that	ض
Tongue touches roots of the upper teeth and is a heavy sound and tongueis curved	Name: Taa' Sound: (t) for Twahir	ط
Raise tongue between the teeth and bring it down with force	Name: Zaa' Sound: (z) for Dhohr	ظ
Normally transliterated by an open Inverted comma	Name: `Ayn (') Heavy sound 'Ali. Place hand on throat	ع
Pronounced as 'Gh' exactly as the sound made in gargling. Care should taken not to pronounce as simply 'Ga'	Name: Ghayn (gh) for Green	غ
Pronounced as 'Fa' Taught as loop with one dot	Name: Faa' Sound: (f) for Fatima	ف
A guttural sound pronounced from the back of the throat. It is a heavy 'Qa'. Taught as loop with two dots	Name: Qaaf Sound: (q) for Qasim or Qamar (Moon).	ق
	Name: Kaaf	

Pronounced as 'ka'. Tongue in centre of the mouth	Sound: (k) for Kite	ك
Pronounced as 'La'	Name: Laam	ل
	Sound: (l) for Lemon	
Pronounced as 'Ma'	Name: Miim	م
	Sound: m	
Explain that it is different to 'Fa' as it does not have a loop. Pronounced as 'Na'	Name: Nuun	ن
	(n) for Nose	
Pronounced as 'Wa'	Name: Waaw	و
	Sound: (w) for Wow, Water	
Prounounced as a normal 'Ha' from the chest. Said heavily – place hand on chest.	Name: Haa'	ه
	Sound: (h) for Hot	
Pronounced as 'Ya'	Name: Yaa'	ي
	Sound: (y) for Yippee, Yay, Yellow	

SIMILAR SOUNDING LETTERS

There are some similar sounding letters in Arabic, which if not pronounced Correctly change the meaning of the word completely.

ARABIC LETTER	SOUND
أ ع ء	A Ayn Alif
ت ط	Tta Taa
ث س ص	Saad Sin Thaa'
هـ ح	Ḥa Ha
ك ق	Qaf Kaf
ز ذ ظ ض	Daad Zaad Dhaal Zaay
خ غ	Ghayn Khaa'

ARABIC ALPHABETS CHART (HURUFUL HIJAI) LETTER NAMES & SOUNDS

ج	ث	ت	ب	ا
Jiim (ja)	The (th)	Taa (ta)	Baa' (b)	Alif (a-Light)
ر	ذ	د	خ	ح
Raa (r)	Dhaal (dh)	Daal (d)	Khaa' (kh)	Haa' (h Light)
ض	ص	ش	س	ز
Daad (d)	Saad (s)	Shiin (sh)	Sin (sa)	Zaay (z)
ف	غ	ع	ظ	ط
Faa' (f)	Ghayn (gha)	Ayn (heavy)	Taa (zha)	Taa' (t)
ن	م	ل	ك	ق
Nuun (n)	Miim (m)	Laam (l)	Kaaf (k)	Qaaf (q)
ل + ا = لا	ي	ه	و	
(Laa) LamAlif= Alif+ Lam	Yaa' (ya)	Haa (heavy)	Waaw (w)	

TAJWEED

TAJWEED IS DIVIDED INTO 4 GROUPS:

1. **Makharij Al Huroof** – Pinpointing the point of articulation of each letter. Makharij Al Huroof is divided into the 5 areas of human speech were the sound originates from.
2. **Sifat Al Huroof** – Defining the certain qualities or characteristics of each letter, which distinguishes it from other sounds. Sifat Al Huroof is divided into 2 areas which show the qualities and attributes of the Arabic Alphabet letters.
3. **Exercising the tongue & repetition**.
4. **Ahkam Al Huroof** – Explaining the rules and the changes which occur to the pronunciation of the letters, when combined with others. Ahkam Al-Huroof is divided into 11 areas that show us the Tajweed rules applied when reciting the Holy Qur'an

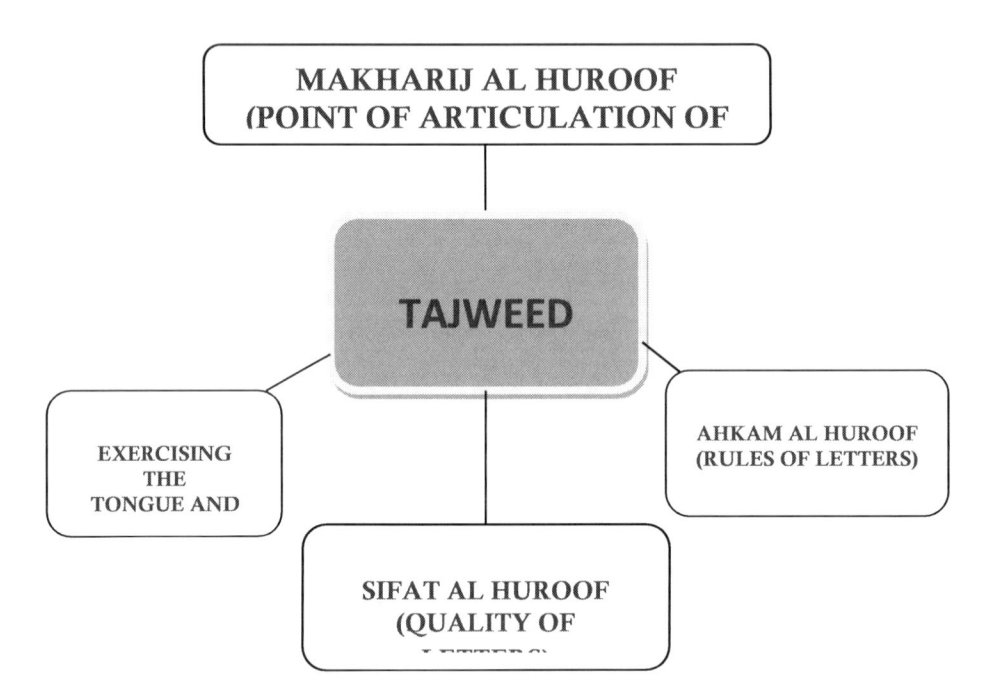

```
                MAKHARIJ AL HUROOF
               (POINT OF ARTICULATION OF
                         |
                         |
                      TAJWEED
                    /         \
                   /           \
   EXERCISING                   AHKAM AL HUROOF
      THE                      (RULES OF LETTERS)
   TONGUE AND
                    SIFAT AL HUROOF
                     (QUALITY OF
```

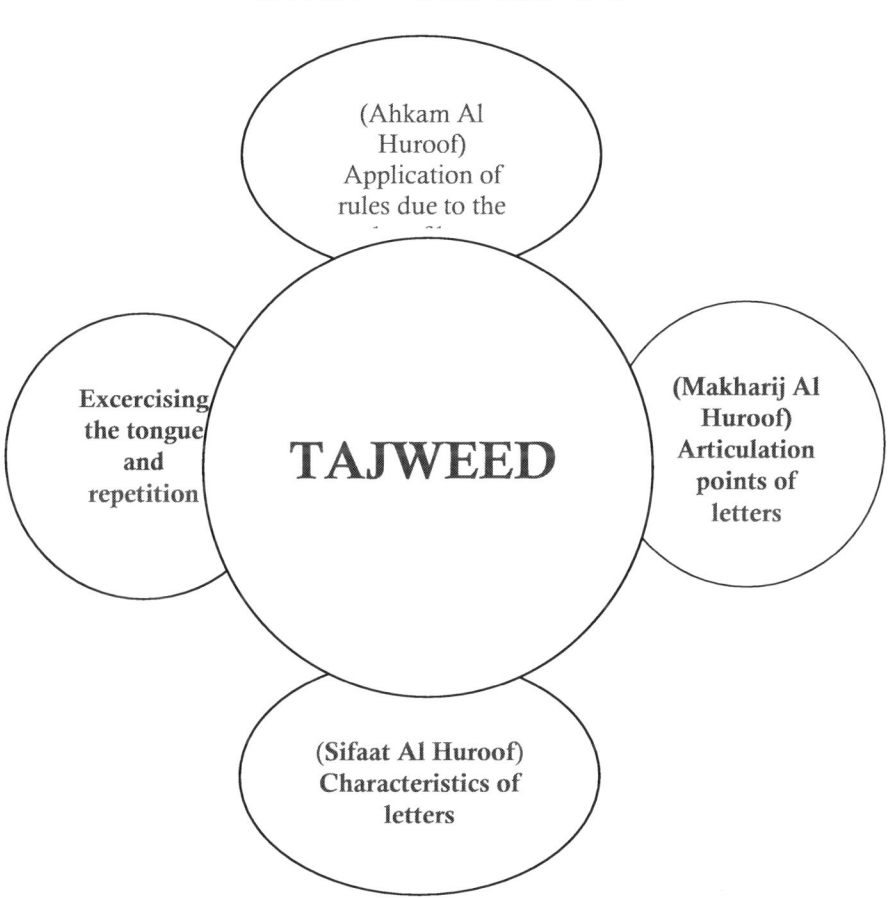

MAKHARIJ AL HUROOF

TAJWEED

- (Ahkam Al Huroof) Application of rules due to the...
- (Makharij Al Huroof) Articulation points of letters
- (Sifaat Al Huroof) Characteristics of letters
- Excercising the tongue and repetition

TAJWEED 1: MAKHARIJ AL HUROOF

MAKHARIJ

Originates from the word Makhraj which means to Exit. The applied meaning is where the letters come from

HUROOF

Originates from the word Harf which means letter. Each letter is a sound that relies on a specific Makhraj or point

MAKHARIJ AL HUROOF

MEANS Proper pronunciation of each letter from their point of origin or point of articulation

ARTICULATION POINTS

- ❖ Articulation point is the place where a letter is pronounced from, making its sound different from the sound of other letters.
- ❖ Each Quranic letter has a different articulation point.
- ❖ A letter is only a sound that relies on a specific articulation point.
- ❖ 5 major speech areas of the human body are used to pronounce different letters.
- ❖ From the 5 major areas, there are 17 different articulation points used to pronounce the 28 original letters and the 3 lengthened letters.

HOW TO PINPOINT THE MAKHRAJ OF A LETTER

❖ Place a Sukun on the letter and before that put a Hamza with Fat-ha, Kasra or Dhamma

❖ Say the letter and where the sound stops, that is the Makhraj point.

Example: The makhraj point of the letter Meem and Ha

The makhraj point of Meem is when the 2 lips join together. Notice the sound stops at the makhraj point.	أُمْ	إِمْ	أَمْ
	UM	IM	AM
The makhraj point of the letter Ha is articulated from the middle of the throat. Notice the sound stops at the makhraj point.	أُحْ	إِحْ	أَحْ
	UH	IH	AH

IMPORTANCE OF MAKHARIJ

Pronouncing each letter of the Arabic language in its correct Makharij is very important,
as mispronouncing a letter can completely change the meaning of the word.

Example 1:

Letter (Harf)	ص	Letter (Harf)	س
Word	صيف	Word	يفس
Meaning	Sword	Meaning	Summer

Example 2:

Letter (Harf)	ق	Letter (Harf)	
Word	قلب	Word	كلب
Meaning	Heart	Meaning	Dog

MAKHARIJ AL HUROOF

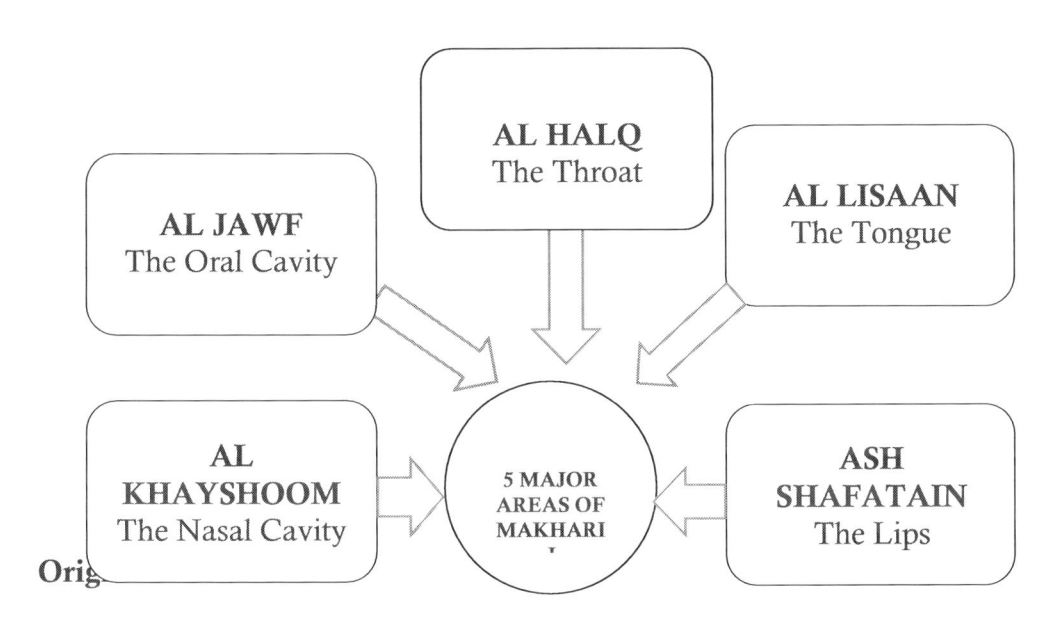

- **AL JAWF** — The Oral Cavity
- **AL HALQ** — The Throat
- **AL LISAAN** — The Tongue
- **AL KHAYSHOOM** — The Nasal Cavity
- **ASH SHAFATAIN** — The Lips

5 MAJOR AREAS OF MAKHARIJ

- اَلْخَيْشُوْمُ
- اَلْجَوْفُ
- اَلشَّفَتَانِ
- اَلْحَلْقُ
- اَللِّسَانُ

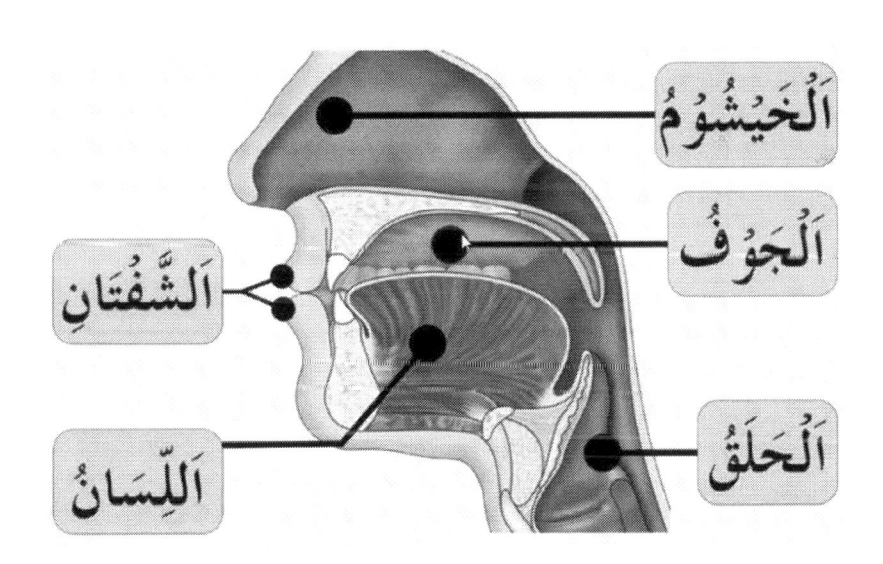

MAKHARIJ AL HUROOF

The 5 major areas of pronounciation originate from the human speech zone. These arefurther divided into 17 points of articulation

5 MAJOR AREAS	ARTICULATION POINTS	NUMBER OF LETTERS
1. **AL JAWF** – THE ORAL CAVITY The empty space in the chest, throat and mouth	1	3 lengthened letters
2. **AL HALQ** – THE THROAT These letters are pronounced from the upper, middle and lower part of the throat	3	6
3. **AL LISAAN** – THE TONGUE	10	18
4. **ASH SHAFATAIN** – THE LIPS	2	4
5. **AL KHAYSHOOM** THE NASAL CAVITY From the hole of the nose towards the inside of the mouth	1	Ghunnah of the letter Nun and Mee

The diagram below shows the 5 areas of Makharij and the letters that originate from them.

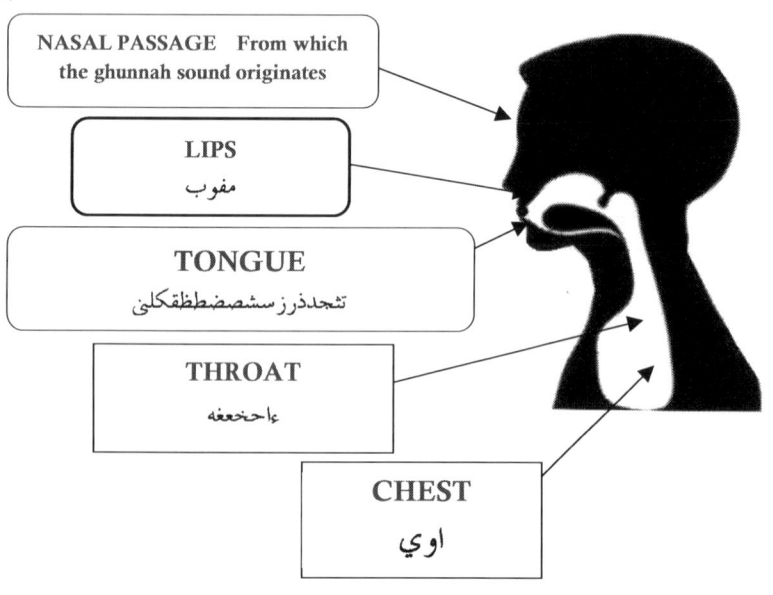

NASAL PASSAGE From which the ghunnah sound originates

LIPS
مفوب

TONGUE
تشجدذرزسشصضطظقكلنى

THROAT
ءاحخععغه

CHEST
اوي

POINTS OF ORIGIN (ARTICULATION) OF THE LETTERS

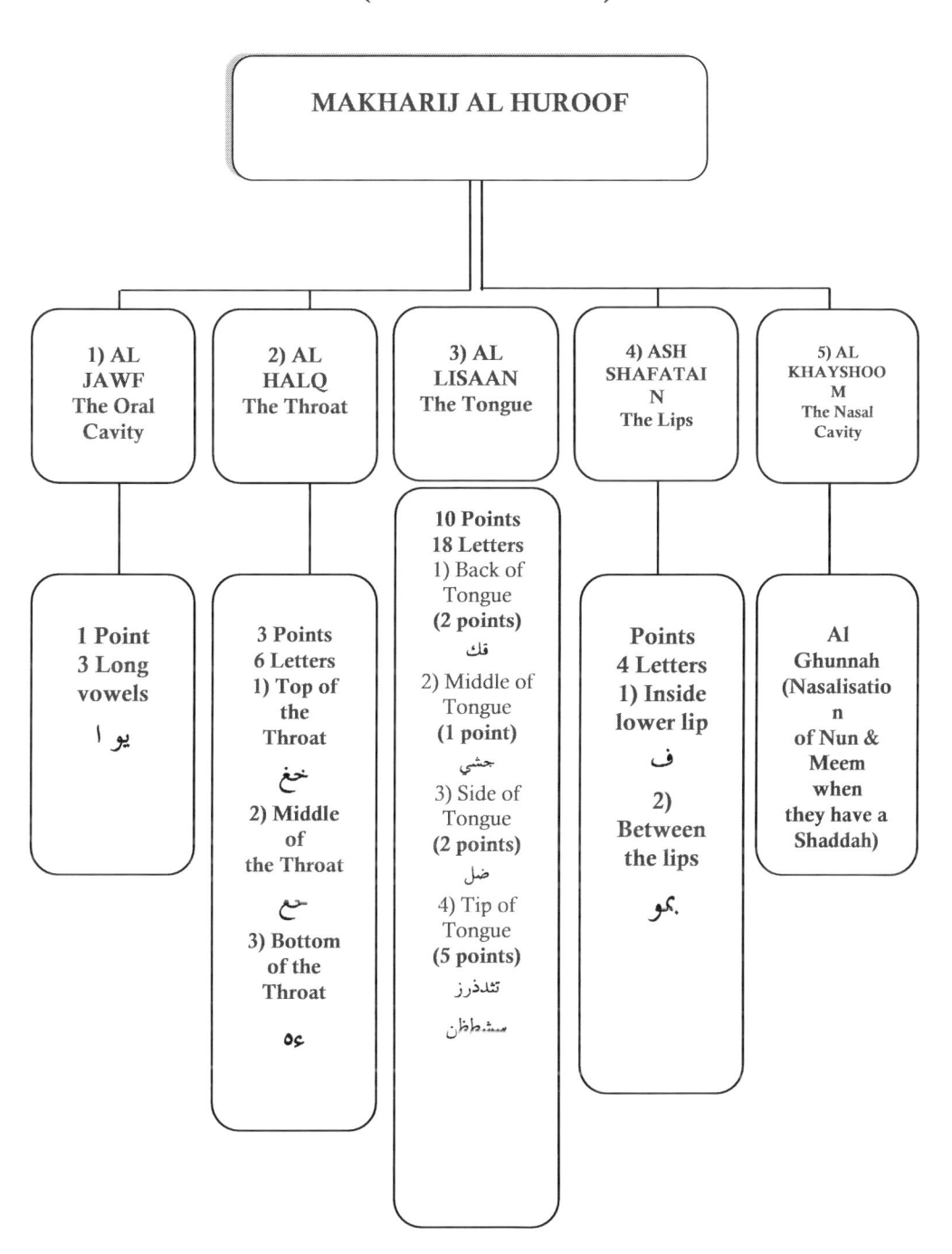

MAKHARIJ AL HUROOF

1) AL JAWF - The Oral Cavity

1 Point
3 Long vowels

و ي ا

2) AL HALQ - The Throat

3 Points
6 Letters

1) Top of the Throat

خ غ

2) Middle of the Throat

ح ع

3) Bottom of the Throat

ه ء

3) AL LISAAN - The Tongue

10 Points
18 Letters

1) Back of Tongue **(2 points)**

ق ك

2) Middle of Tongue **(1 point)**

ج ش ي

3) Side of Tongue **(2 points)**

ض ل

4) Tip of Tongue **(5 points)**

ت د ذ ر ز

س ش ط ظ ن

4) ASH SHAFATAIN - The Lips

Points
4 Letters

1) Inside lower lip

ف

2) Between the lips

ب م و

5) AL KHAYSHOOM - The Nasal Cavity

Al Ghunnah (Nasalisation of Nun & Meem when they have a Shaddah)

1. AL JAWF – THE ORAL CAVITY – 1 Articulation point and 3 long vowels

- ❖ The empty space in the mouth and throat is a place and an articulation point at the same time.
- ❖ The three Madd letters (lengthened letters) originate from this non-specific area.
- ❖ These letters finish with the stopping of the sound (that stops with the air). These letters of Alif, Waw and Ya, do not have a specific space that they finish at, like other letters do. Instead, these letters finish with the stopping of the sound.
- ❖ The letters of Al-Jawf are similar to the vowel sounds in English and are known as the Original Madd (Madd al-Asli).
- ❖ The Long Vowel sounds are produced by a relatively free flow of air, they are also called **Al-Huroof Al-Maddiyya**.

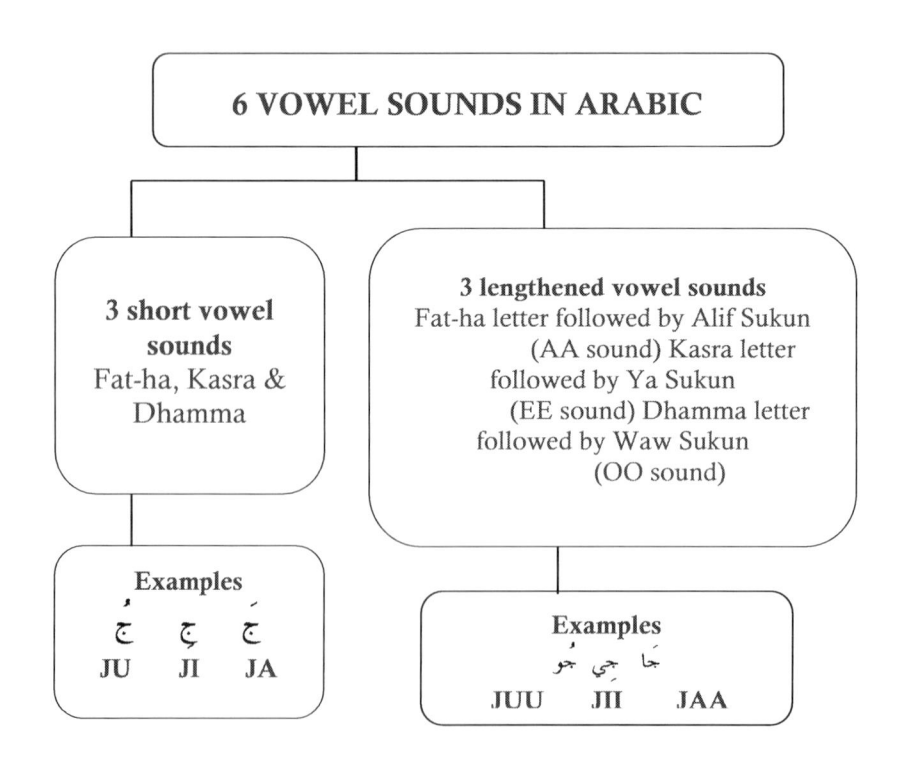

6 VOWEL SOUNDS IN ARABIC

3 short vowel sounds
Fat-ha, Kasra & Dhamma

Examples
جُ جِ جَ
JU JI JA

3 lengthened vowel sounds
Fat-ha letter followed by Alif Sukun (AA sound) Kasra letter followed by Ya Sukun (EE sound) Dhamma letter followed by Waw Sukun (OO sound)

Examples
جَا جِي جُو
JUU JII JAA

1. **AL JAWF – THE ORAL CAVITY – continued**
The lengthened sounds have to be extended for 1 second

Fat-ha letter followed By Alif Sukun	Kasra letter followed by Ya Sukun	Kasra letter followed by Ya Sukun
جَا – حَا – خَا KHAA- HAA - JAA	جِي – حِي – خِي KHII- HII - JII	جُو – حُو – خُو KHUU- HUU - JUU
اهْدِنَا	دِين	مَغْضُوب
عَذَابٌ	مُسْتَقِيم	كَفَرُوا
بِهِمَا	الَّذِين	قَالُوا
لِسَعْيِهَا	مُحِيطٌ	يَعْلَمُون
فِيهَا	حَسِيبًا	نُورٌ

2. **AL HALQ – THE THROAT – 3 Articulation points and 6 Letters**

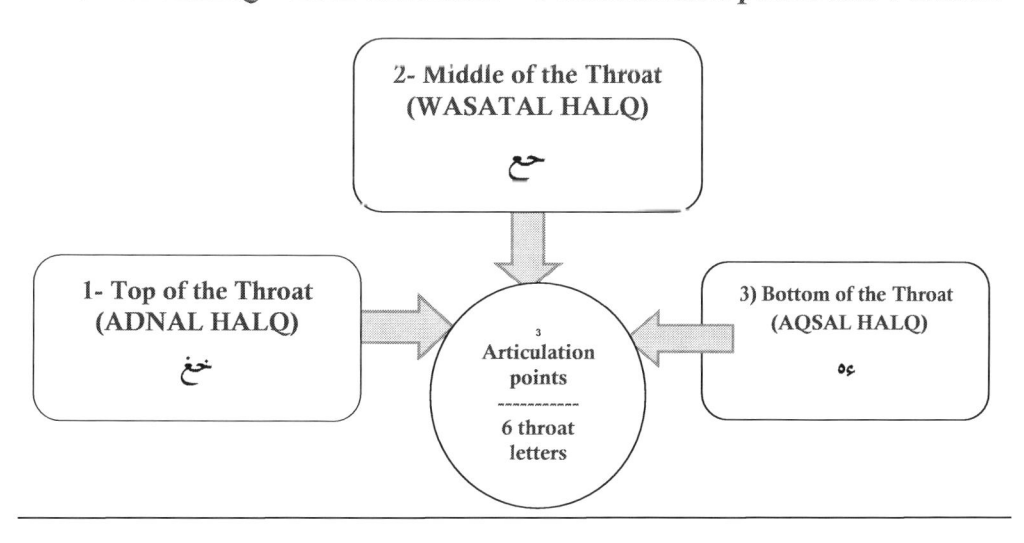

- **2- Middle of the Throat (WASATAL HALQ)** ح ع
- **1- Top of the Throat (ADNAL HALQ)** خ غ
- **3) Bottom of the Throat (AQSAL HALQ)** ء ه

3 Articulation points — 6 throat letters

Articulation From	Letter	Detail	Makhraj Point
1. Top of the Throat (AdnalHalq)	خ	'kha' scratching sound	خَأ
	غ	As if water is being gargled 'ghh'	غَأ
2. Middle of the Throat (WasatalHalq)	ح	Imagine having eaten spicy food 'Hha' (middle of throat squeezed)	حَأ
	ع	As if one wants to bite a fruit 'Aa' (middle of throat squeezed)	عَأ
3. Bottom of the Throat (AqsalHalq)	ه	Ha similar to the 'H' in word He	هَأ
	ءأا	Hamza equal to the 'A' letter in English (apple)	ءَأ

2. AL HALQ – THE THROAT – continued

Bottom of throat	ء	يومئذ	ء إذا	شيءٌ	إذا جاء
	ه	اهدنا	همزة	عليهم	أثقالها
Middle of throat	ع	بعد	أعوذ	سمعهم	أنعمت
	ح	محفوظ	حور	جحيم	الحمد
Top of throat	غ	يعني	غفر	صغير	غضب
	خ	أخلاق	خروج	بخل	خسر

- ❖ The Throat letters are also known as Hurooful Halqi.
- ❖ Care should be taken on how they are pronounced, as similar sounding lettersfrom the same articulation point can change the meaning of the word

Similar sounding letters ء (Hamza) and ع (Ayn)		
Word	أليم	عليم
Meaning	Painful	All Knowing
Add (عذابٌ) meaning 'punishment'	عذاب أليم	عذاب عليم
Final meaning	Painful punishment	All Knowing punishment

1. AL LISAAN – THE TONGUE – 10 Articulation points and 18 Letters

This is the widest part of the speech area and it contains different parts like tongue, teeth and so on. The tongue touches different parts of the mouth to articulate different letters.

Articulation points of Al-Lisaan	The 18 Letters of the tongue
Ten	ص ث ظ ذ ت د ط ل ن ر ج ش ي ك ق ض س ز

STRUCTURE OF THE TONGUE: 4 MAIN AREAS

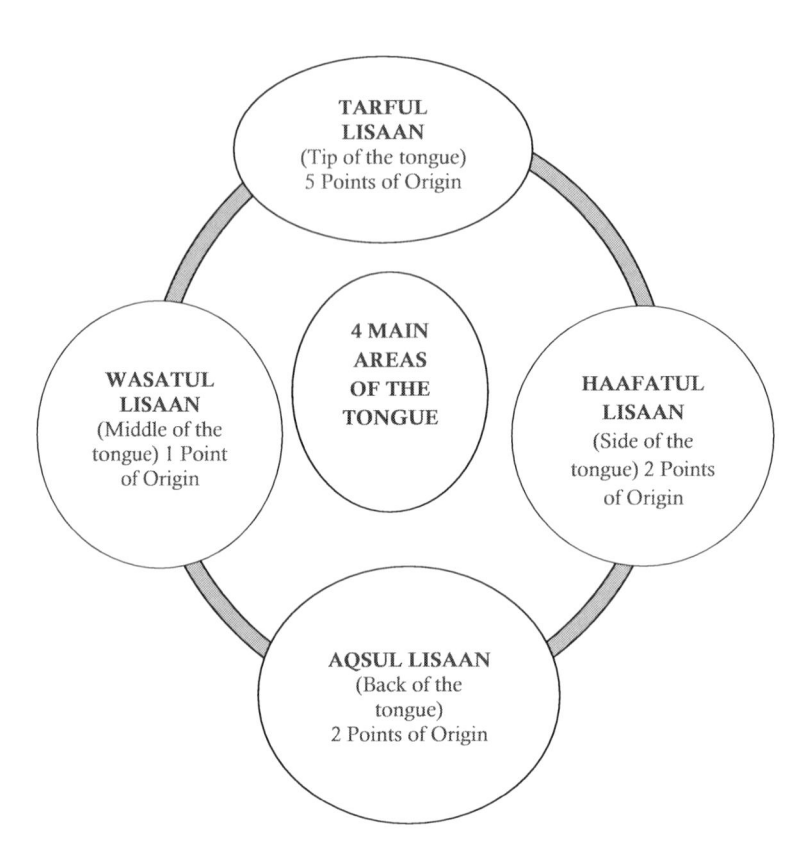

- **TARFUL LISAAN** (Tip of the tongue) 5 Points of Origin
- **HAAFATUL LISAAN** (Side of the tongue) 2 Points of Origin
- **AQSUL LISAAN** (Back of the tongue) 2 Points of Origin
- **WASATUL LISAAN** (Middle of the tongue) 1 Point of Origin

4 MAIN AREAS OF THE TONGUE

3 AL LISAAN – THE TONGUE – continued

Huroof Al-Lisaan – are 18 tongue letters that exit from 10 articulation points and are divided into 4 parts of the tongue

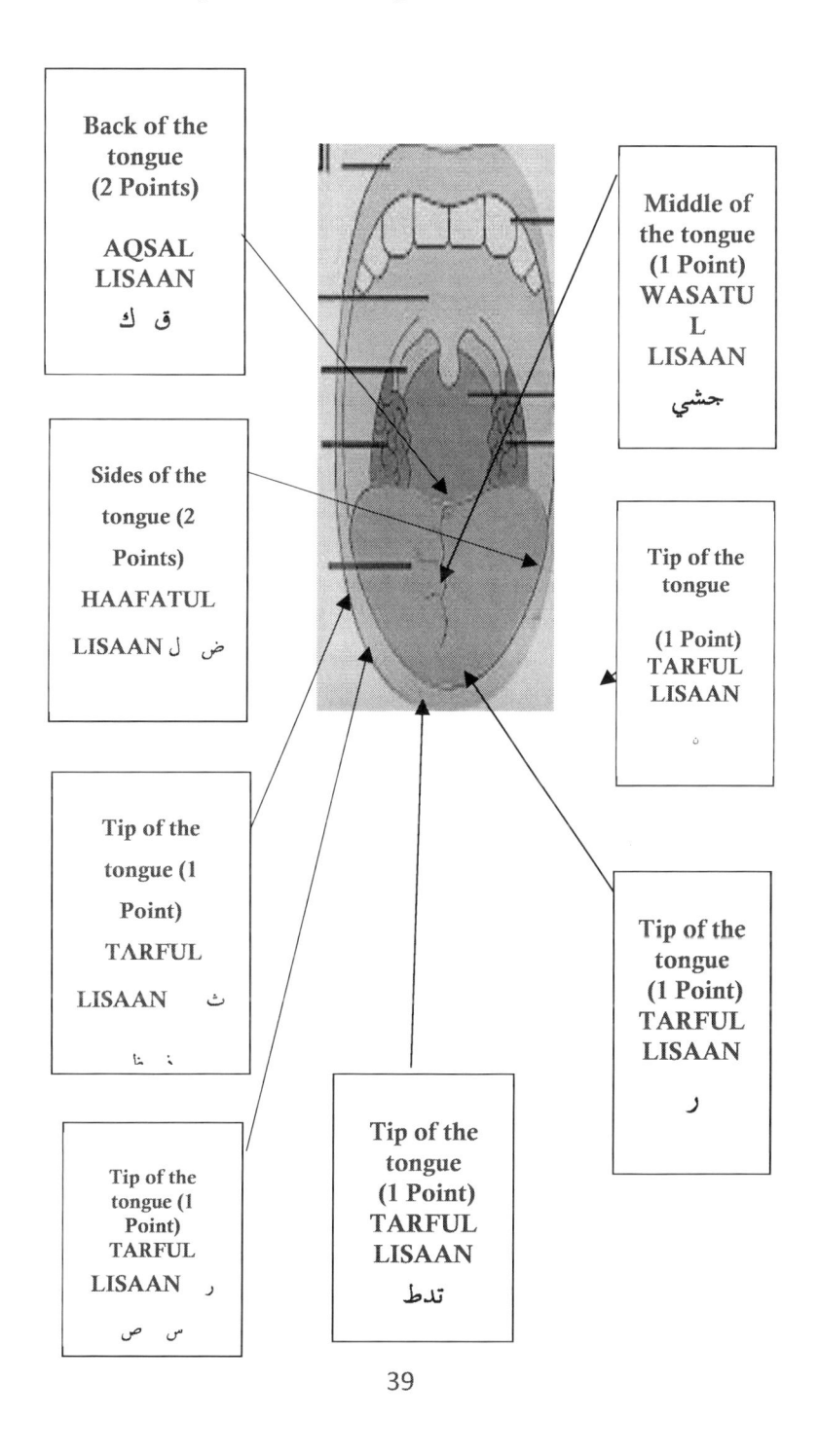

Back of the tongue (2 Points)
AQSAL LISAAN
ق ك

Middle of the tongue (1 Point)
WASATUL LISAAN
ج ش ي

Sides of the tongue (2 Points)
HAAFATUL LISAAN ض ل

Tip of the tongue (1 Point)
TARFUL LISAAN
ن

Tip of the tongue (1 Point)
TARFUL LISAAN ث
ذ ظ

Tip of the tongue (1 Point)
TARFUL LISAAN
ر

Tip of the tongue (1 Point)
TARFUL LISAAN ر
س ص

Tip of the tongue (1 Point)
TARFUL LISAAN
ت د ط

AL LISAAN - 10 ARTICULATION POINTS	18 LETTER/S
BACK OF THE TONGUE - (AQSAL LISAAN) 1. Heavy letter, pronounced when the root of the tongue, touches the soft part of the upper palate (closer to the back of the tongue)	ق
2. Light letter, pronounced when the root of the tongue, touches the sides of the lower palate (closer to the mouth) eg. Cake in English	ك
MIDDLE OF THE TONGUE - (WASATUL LISAAN) 3. The centre of the tongue, touches the upper palate directly above it. 3 letters originate from this point.	ج ش ي
SIDE OR EDGE OF THE TONGUE - (HAAFATUL LISAAN) 4. The upturned sides of the back of the tongue are raised to meet the edges of the top back teeth. Arabic is also known as the language of Dhaad ض this is a unique and difficult letter to pronounce.	ض
5. Originates from the front edge of the tongue, touching the back gums of the upper 6 teeth eg. Like in English	ل
TIP OF THE TONGUE - (TARFUL LISAAN) 6. Articulated from the top part of the tip of the tongue, touching the roots of the upper incisors (top front teeth). 3 letters originate from this point.	ط د ت
7. Articulated from between the tip of the tongue and the plates of the upper and lower incisors. This leaves a small gap between the tongue and incisors (hence the whistle sound). 3 letters originate from this point	ص س ز
8. Articulated from the tip of the tongue touching the roots of the upper incisors. (Note: In Al Khayshoom, the letter Nun is only a Ghunnah – Nasal sound, its actual pronunciation is made with the tongue)	ن
9. When the tip of the tongue touches the gums of the upper incisors – we must very slightly roll the tongue.	ر
10. Articulated when the top of the tip of the tongue touches the edges of the top 2 incisors (part of the tongue will stick out)	ذ ظ ث

2. ASH SHAFATAIN – THE LIP LETTERS – 2 Articulation points and 4 Letters

Shafataan means the lips

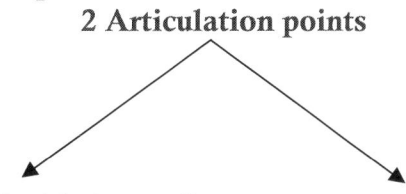

2 Articulation points

1) Between the lips   2) Inside lower lip

Huroofal Shafataan means the letters of the lips

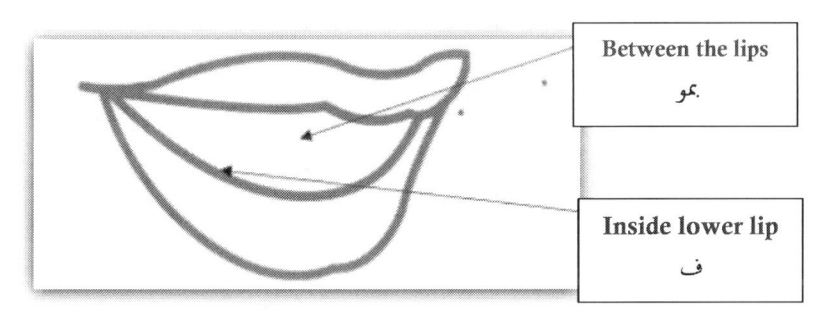

Between the lips
بو

Inside lower lip
ف

Between the lips	و	م	ب
	وأ	أم	بأ
The Sound	AW	AM	AB
	Both the lips have to meet to make the above sounds AND for the letter WAAW, we round both the lips		
Inside the lower lip	ف		
	فأ (a unique letter) The sound of this letter is AF		

SOUNDS OF THE LETTERS OF THE LIPS

To make the sound of a letter, we put a Sukun on the letter and a Hamza Fat-ha before it.

3. ASH SHAFATAIN – THE LIP LETTER continue

Al-Huruf al Shafawiyyah – The Labial Letters

ف This letter is sounded when the edges of the front two teeth touch the wet portion of the bottom lip and separate

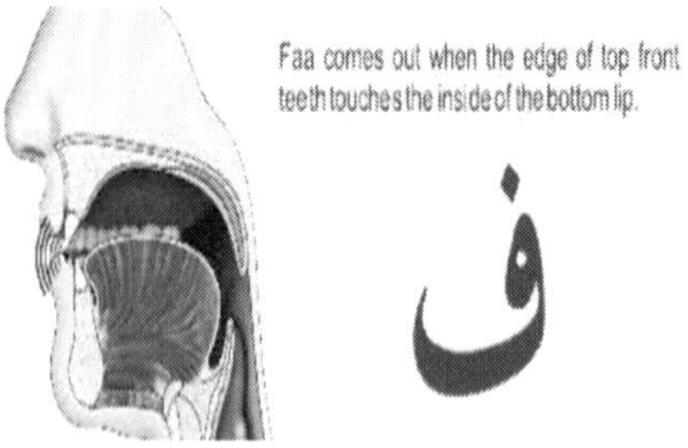

Faa comes out when the edge of top front teeth touches the inside of the bottom lip.

ب This letter is sounded when the wet portion of the lips open from a closed position

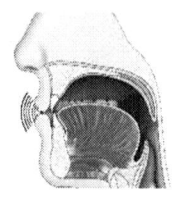

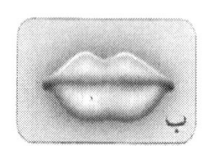

م This letter is sounded when the dry portion of the lips open from a closed position

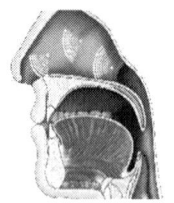

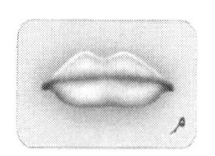

و The un-lengthened Waw is articulated by forming a circle of the two lips without the two lips meeting completely

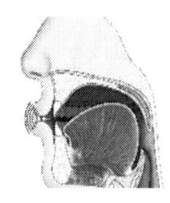

4. AL KHAYSHOOM: AL-GHUNNAH – Nasalisation – continued

When we find 'Nun' or 'Meem' with a Shaddah, then we lengthen for 2 seconds with a Nasal sound. This Ghunnah is a very clear 'n' sound, it comes automatically when we lengthen the Nun shaddah or Meem shaddah.

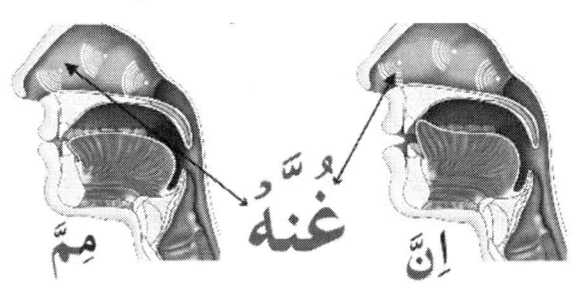

مِّ غنّه اِنَّ

Try to pronounce the sound of Nun or Meem, by holding your nose and feel the vibration.
The simplest and most common type of Ghunnah is with Nun and Meem when they
appear with a Shaddah. We hold the Ghunnah sound in our nose for 2 counts.

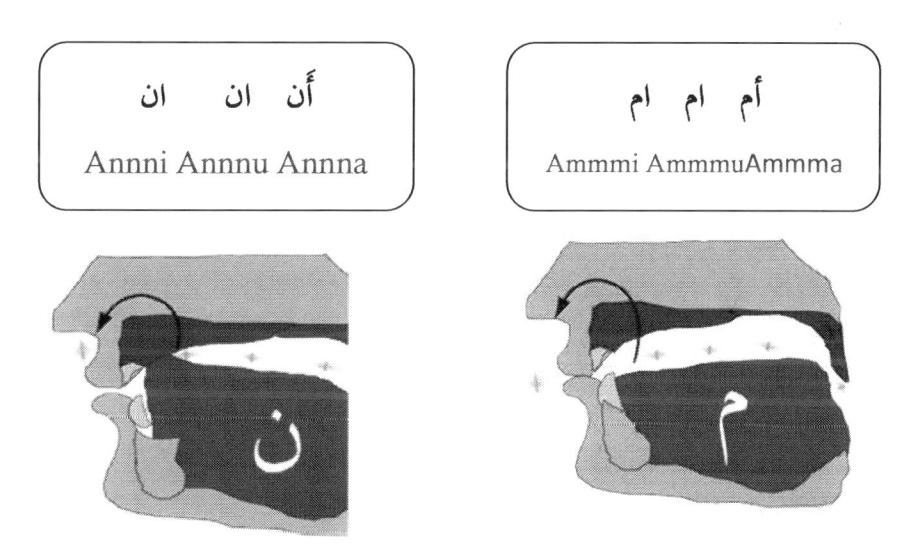

أنّ انّ انّ
Annni Annnu Annna

أمّ امّ امّ
Ammmi Ammmu Ammma

5. AL KHAYSHOOM: AL-GHUNNAH – Nasalisation – continued

When we find 'Nun' or 'Meem' with a Shaddah, then we lengthen for 2 seconds with a Nasalsound. This Ghunnah is a very clear 'n' sound, it comes automatically when we lengthen theNun shaddah or Meem shaddah.

ن		م	
Jinn-na-ti	جَنَّتِ	Falamm-ma	فَلَمَّا
Jahann-na-ma	جَهَنَّمَ	Amm-ma	عَمَّ
	إن الذين		عبد من
	كأنّ		ضاحكا من
	أعين الناس		قوّمًا مّا
	والناس		سحرٌ مبين
	من النار		نفسٌ ماذا
	ولكن		منهم مقتصد

SIFAT AL HUROOF

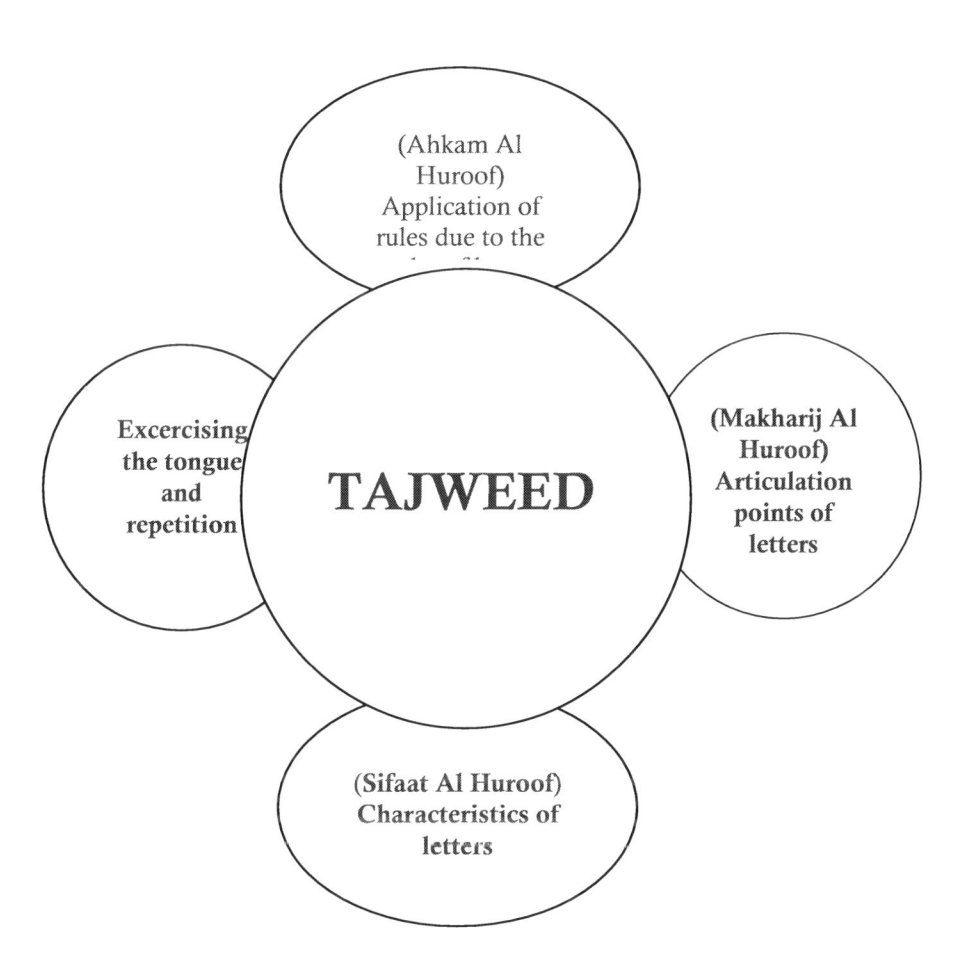

TAJWEED

- (Ahkam Al Huroof) Application of rules due to the ...
- (Makharij Al Huroof) Articulation points of letters
- (Sifaat Al Huroof) Characteristics of letters
- Excercising the tongue and repetition

TAJWEED 2) SIFAT AL HUROOF

DEFINITION: These are the specific qualities and characteristics that occur in a letter, when it reaches its articulation point and differentiates it from other letters.

Makharij Al Huroof– Point of origin where the letters are articulated from is permanent and the letters are also permanent.

Sifat Al Huroof is all about **how** the letters are pronounced. The letters change according to the situation. If the letter is articulated properly, but not pronounced correctly with its correct characteristic, then this letter might change to sound like another letter.

IMPORTANCE OF CORRECT APPLICATION OF THE SIFAT (CHARACTERISTICS)

SIFAT AL HUROOF

- Teaches the various timings of Sakin letters (Very important aspect for good recitation)
- To learn which letters flow with the sound and which letters floe without sound
- To learn which letters flow with the air and which ones without the air
- To learn which letters have a Nasalisation (Ghunnah) and which letters have an Echo (Qalqalah)
- To differentiate between the common letters in the Makhraj makes the letter clearer, giving it, its due right
- To beautify the recitation and the pronounciation
- To recognize the Strong and the Weak letters
- To recognize the Light and Heavy letters

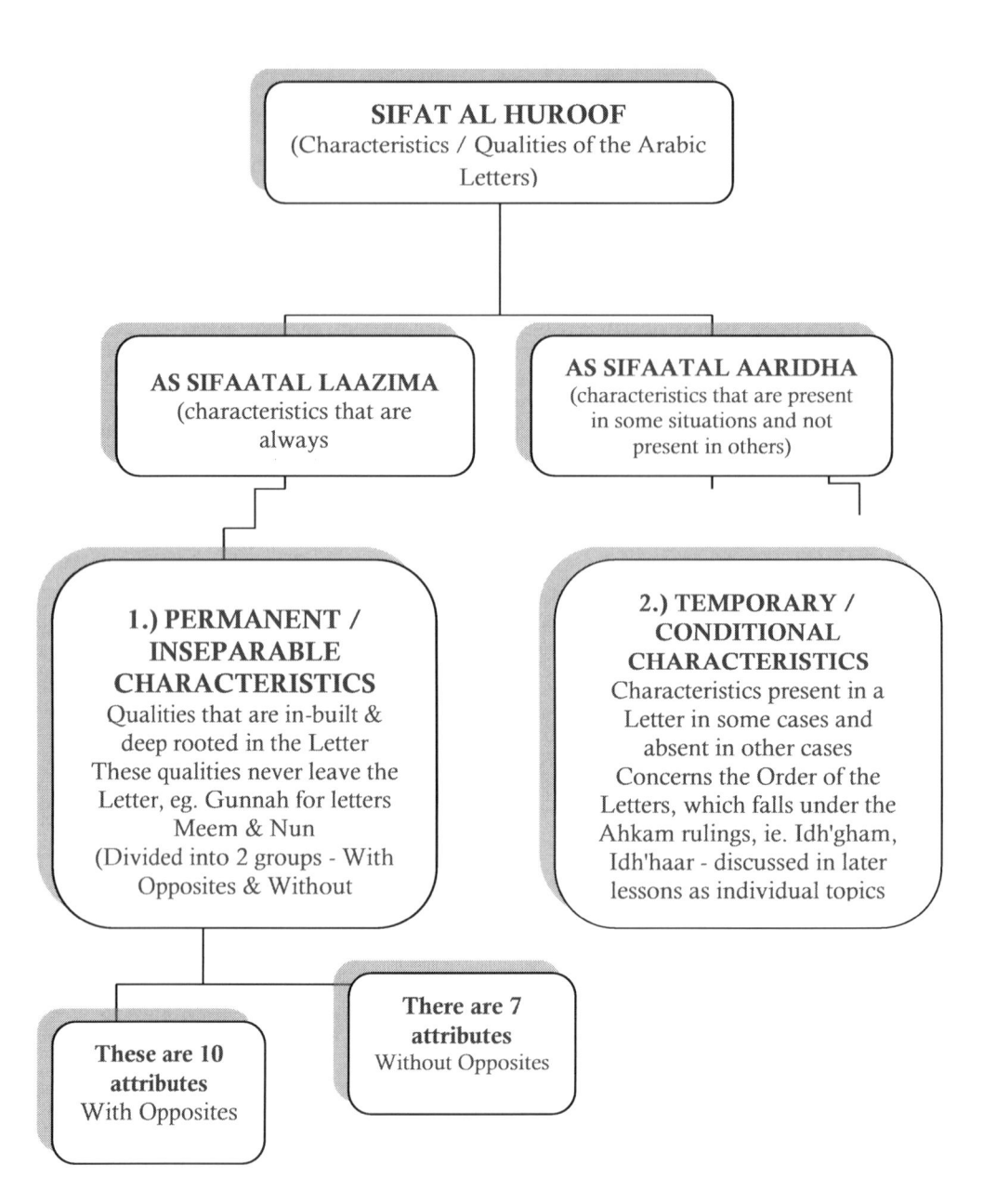

```
                    SIFAT AL HUROOF
              (Characteristics / Qualities of the Arabic
                           Letters)
```

- **AS SIFAATAL LAAZIMA** (characteristics that are always
- **AS SIFAATAL AARIDHA** (characteristics that are present in some situations and not present in others)

1.) PERMANENT / INSEPARABLE CHARACTERISTICS
Qualities that are in-built & deep rooted in the Letter. These qualities never leave the Letter, eg. Gunnah for letters Meem & Nun
(Divided into 2 groups - With Opposites & Without

2.) TEMPORARY / CONDITIONAL CHARACTERISTICS
Characteristics present in a Letter in some cases and absent in other cases. Concerns the Order of the Letters, which falls under the Ahkam rulings, ie. Idh'gham, Idh'haar - discussed in later lessons as individual topics

These are 10 attributes With Opposites

There are 7 attributes Without Opposites

SIFAT AL HUROOF (PERMANENT & TEMPORARY ATTRIBUTES)

PERMANENT ATTRIBUTES

also known as **SIFAT AL LAZIMAH, DHATIYYA** or **MUQAWWIMAH**

CHARACTERISTICS OF PERMANENT ATTRIBUTES

1.) They are an intergral part of the letter **(Dhatiyyah)**

2.) They constitute the letter ie. make up of the letter **(Muqawwimah)**

3.) They are inseparable from the letter **(Lazimah)**

4.) Without any one of these qualities, the letter will either be pronounced as just another letter or will become a non-Arabic letter or just a sound

TEMPORARY ATTRIBUTES

also known as **SIFAT AL AARIDHA, MUHASSINAH** or **MAHALLIYYAH**

CHARACTERISTICS OF TEMPORARY ATTRIBUTES

1.) They do not form an integral part of the letter **(Aaridha)**

2.) They do not constitute the letter, ie. the letter will be pronounced without them

3.) They are not present in the letter all the time at every place **(Mahalliyyah)**

4.) Their purpose is only to add to the beauty of recitation **(Muhassinah)**

5.) They change according to the arrangement of the letters

10 Attributes with Opposites
Hams-----------------Jahr
Shiddah---Tawassut---Rakhawah
Isti'laa-----------Istifaal
Itbaaq--------Infitaah
Ismaat---------Idhlaq

7 Attributes without Opposites
As - Safeer, Al - Qalqalah, Al - Leen, Al - Inhiraf, Al - Takreer, Al - Istitaalah and Al - Tafash-shee

PERMANANT ATTRIBUTES (LAZIMAH) THAT HAVE OPPOSITE CHARACTERISTICS

HAMS - JAHR (CONTINUATION OR STOPPAGE OF BREATH)

ATTRIBUTES	THEIR OPPOSITE ATTRIBUTES
HAMS – Continuation of Breath • The softness o these letters allow for breathing to continue freely when pronouncing them. • Air flows with the letter due to the weakness of its origin, causing weakness in its reliance on its makharij • Amount of air depends on theMakhraj of the letter • Letters ك and ت have least airescaping compared to the other 8 letters	**JAHR – Stoppage of Breath** • Imprisonment of the breathwhenpronounced. • Air does not flow with the letter dueto the strength of its origin, causingit to rely greatly on its makharij • The rest of the letters have this quality
11 LETTERS تحخهسشصفكهة	**18 LETTERS** All the letters, excluding Hams Letters ءبجدذرزضططظعغقلمنوي
When Hams letters are pronounced with aSakin, air flows from the mouth	When Jahr letters are pronounced with a Sakin, air does not flow from the mouth
NOTE: Letters can have the same Makharij (Point of Origin), but different Sifaat (Quality). Eg. خ and غ both originate from the top of the throat, but their Sifaat arenot the same خ(air) غ(no air)	

PERMANANT ATTRIBUTES (LAZIMAH) THAT HAVE OPPOSITE CHARACTERISTICS

SHIDDAH-TAWASSUT-RAKHAWAH STOPPAGE & CONTINUATION OF SOUND)

ATTRIBUTES		THEIR OPPOSITE ATTRIBUTES
Shiddah - Strength **The Strong Letters** • Imprisonment of the Sound of the letter due to complete reliance on the articulation point • The articulation point is closed completely • No running of sound • This is when the letters are Sakin, which causes a strong stoppage of the sound	**TAWASSUT In Between The Moderate Letters** • This is moderation between Shiddah & Rakhawah. The sound of the letter is not stopped, nor is it allowed to continue. • This is when the letters are Sakin	**RAKHAWAH** **The Soft Letters** • The continuation of the sound of the letter, when pronouncing it due to weakness in reliance of the articulation point. • There is no collision and the sound is soft. • This is when the letters are Sakin
8 LETTERS قطدجتبء ك	**5 LETTERS** نملعر	**16 LETTERS** ةشسزذخحث يهوفغظضص

PERMANANT ATTRIBUTES (LAZIMAH) THAT HAVE OPPOSITE CHARACTERISTICS

ISTI'LAA - ISTEFAAL (HEAVINESS & LIGHTNESS)

ATTRIBUTES		THEIR OPPOSITE ATTRIBUTES
ISTI'LAA **Letters of Elevation** • The elevation of the back of the tongue towards the roof of the mouth, when pronouncing a letter • Thick sound • Known as Heavyletters **(Tafkheem)** (Heavy letters – Full mouth) With Isti'laa, the tongue isjust raised, whereas forItbaaq, there is actualcontact	PART TIME HEAVY & PART TIME LIGHT LETTERS— الر • In the name ofAllāh (discussedelsewhere in thisbook – Lafdhil Jalali) • Rules of ر(discussed elsewhere in this book) • Regarding letter ا(Pronouncing changes according to itsposition)	**Letters of Lowering** • Keeping the tongue lowered from theroof of the mouthwhile pronouncing aletter • Flat sound • Known as Light letters (**Tarqeeq**) (Light letters – Empty mouth Includes rest of the letters except ل and ر , which have their own rules
7 LETTERS خصضغطقظ	**2 SITUATIONS FOR LETTER ا (ALIF)** When it is heavy OR when it is light	**21 LETTERS** ءبتثجحدذ رزسشعفك لمنوهي

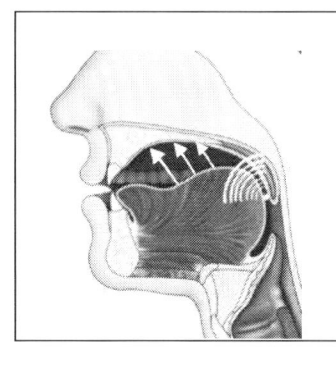

When Alif appears after a Heavy letter, it is **pronounced Heavily** eg. قَالَ When Alif appears after a Light letter, it is **pronounced Lightly** eg. مَالَ

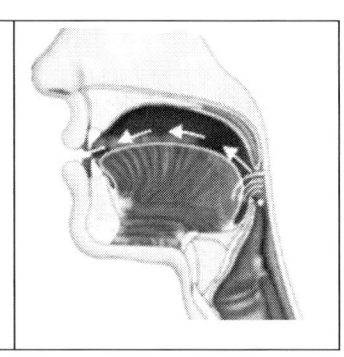

PERMANANT ATTRIBUTES (LAZIMAH) THAT HAVE OPPOSITE CHARACTERISTICS

ITBAAQ - INFITAAH (CLOSURE & OPENING OF THE INSIDE OF THE MOUTH)

ATTRIBUTES	THEIR OPPOSITE ATTRIBUTES
ITBAAQ – Adhesion • Closure between parts of the tongue and the upper palate of the mouth when pronouncing these 4 letters • The compression of the sound between the tongue and the mouth • These letters are also Isti'laa letters (Heavy letters) • NOTE: Every Itbaaq letter is an Isti'laa letter, but every Isti'laa letter is not a letter of Itbaaq	**INFITAAH - Separation** • Keeping the tongue separated from the roof of the mouth while pronouncing a letter • The absence of the compression of the sound • All letters of the Arabic Alphabet, apart from the 4 letters of Itbaaq
4 LETTERS ظ ط ض ص	**24 LETTERS** ر ذ د خ ح ج ث ت ب ء ل ك ق ف غ ع ش س ز ي و هـ ن م

PERMANANT ATTRIBUTES (LAZIMAH) THAT HAVE OPPOSITE CHARACTERISTICS

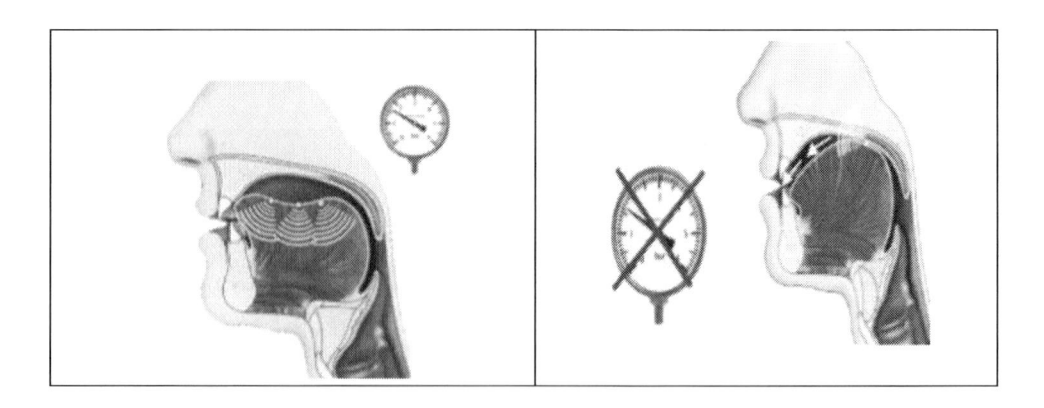

ISMAAT - IDHLAQ (PRONOUNCED WITH EFFORT & EASE)

ATTRIBUTES	THEIR OPPOSITE ATTRIBUTES
ISMAAT – The Hard Pronounced • The articulation of the letters with utmost strength and stability from their makharij, without which the letter will not be articulated • Effort is put in reciting these letters. • Includes all letters excluding Idhlaq letters	**IDHLAQ - Fluency** • Purity in Speech • The articulation of the letters with utmost ease from the sides of the tongue or lips as if they are slipping away • Lightly Pronounced letters
22 LETTERS زذدخحججثتء عظطضصشس	**6 LETTERS** برفلمن

The Qualities of the letters
صفات الحروف

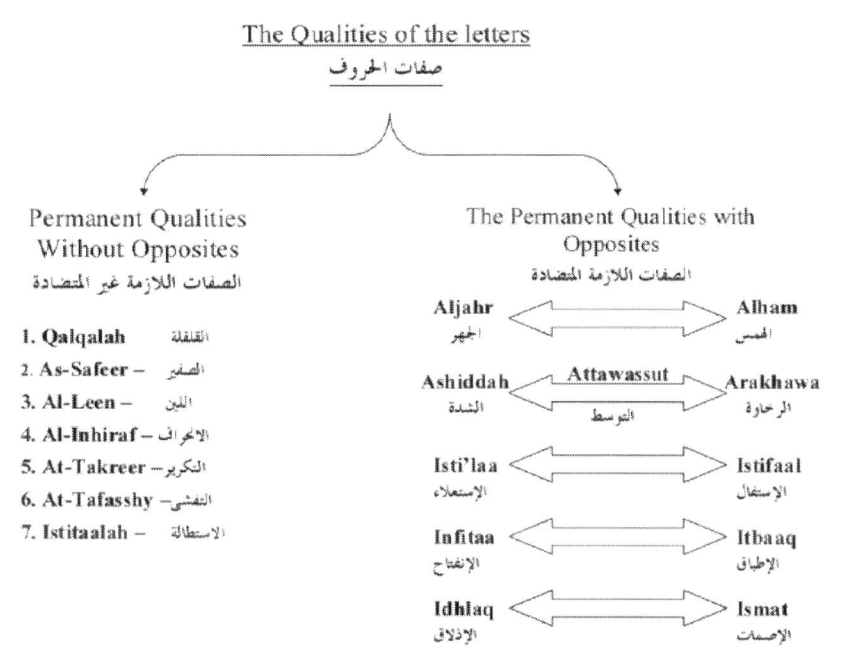

Permanent Qualities Without Opposites
الصفات اللازمة غير المتضادة

1. Qalqalah — القلقلة
2. As-Safeer — الصفير
3. Al-Leen — اللين
4. Al-Inhiraf — الانحراف
5. At-Takreer — التكرير
6. At-Tafasshy — التفشي
7. Istitaalah — الاستطالة

The Permanent Qualities with Opposites
الصفات اللازمة المتضادة

Aljahr الجهر	⟷	Alham الهمس
Ashiddah الشدة	⟷ Attawassut التوسط ⟷	Arakhawa الرخاوة
Isti'laa الإستعلاء	⟷	Istifaal الإستفال
Infitaa الإنفتاح	⟷	Itbaaq الإطباق
Idhlaq الإذلاق	⟷	Ismat الإصمات

PERMANENT ATTRIBUTES (LAZIMAH) WITHOUT OPPOSITES

1. **AS-SAFEER – WHISTLING**: صسز It is the natural occurrence of a whistle like sound emitted while pronouncing the letters. The sound resembles that of a bird when these letters are pronounced. The sound emerges from the tip of the tongue and upper front teeth. Note: The letter ز has a more buzzing sound than the whistling sound in س and ص

2. **AL-QALQALAH – ECHOING**: قطبجد This is the most important of the non-opposite qualities. The letters possessing this quality are called Muqalqalah. The letters in this group are pronounced with an echoing quality. It is the vibration of the Makharij, a breaking of tension or release with the emergence of the letter when accompanied by Sukoon. Qalqalah is discussed at length in another chapter.

3. **AL-LEEN – SOFTNESS**: وي These letters are pronounced without difficulty. The letters are articulated from its makharij with a natural ease and softness present in the letter. The letters are Waw Sakinah with a Fat-ha before it and Ya Sakinah with a Fat-ha before it.

4. **AL-INHIRAF – INCLINATION**: The inclination to move the makhraj of one letter to the other during pronounciation. لر Leaning away from one point of articulation to another. Technically it is the 'slight deviation of the tongue towards the makhraj of Raa while pronouncing Laam, and towards its back and towards Laam while pronouncing Raa.'

5. **AL-TAKRIR – REPETITION**: رTechnically means the trilling of the tongue while pronouncing the letter رthat causes the letter to be pronounced more than once.(we must **abstain** from this quality so that the letter is pronounced only once)

6. **AL-TAFASH-SHEE – SPREAD**: شSpreading the sound of the letter startingfrom its articulation point, until it collides with the inner plates of the top teeth.

7. **AL-ISTITAALAH – PROLONGATION**: ضThe stretching of the sound over the entire tongue when pronouncing the letter. The prolongation of the sound throughout its makhraj from its beginning till the end.

2 EXTRA PERMANENT ATTRIBUTES (WITHOUT OPPOSITES)

8. **GHUNNAH – NASAL SOUND**: This is the sound coming from the nasal passagewhen pronouncing the two letters نand مNasal sound is retained when:-

   a) مand نcarry a Shaddah أمَّه ثمَّ إنّماً

   b) Idghaam of مin مaccompanied by a vowel.منهما كم من وهم

   c) Idghaam of نin four letters of ن و م ي

   مَنْ يَشَاء، مِنْ مَالٍ، مِنْ وَلِيٍّ، مِنْ نَفْسٍ

   d) All the Ikhfaa. Ikhfaa of نnext to the rest of the letters, and Ikhfaa of مnext to the letter ب

   منكم أنزل أنتم به من بعد (مم بعد)

Note: These are explained in detail in chapters of rules of Idghaam, rules of Noon Sakinand Tanween and rules of Meem Sakin. The amount of nasal sound retained from minimum 1 to maximum 5 is:

a) مand نcarrying a vowel. (This is a quality - Sifaat)

أمِنَ غَنَمُ

b) مْ and نْ have the rule of Idhaar. (This is a quality - Sifaat) غَمْرَةٍ مِنْهَا

c) مْ and نْ have the rule of Ikhfaa. (This is a rule – Ahkam) أَمْ بِهِ كُنْتُمْ

d) نْ has the rule of Idghaam (half Idghaam). (This is a rule – Ahkam)

مِنْ وَلِيٍّ   طَلْعٌ نَضِيدٌ

e) مْ and نْ carrying a Shaddah. (This is a rule - Ahkam) اِنَّمَامِمَّا

Note: These are explained in detail in chapters of rules of Idghaam, rules of Noon Sakin and Tanween and rules of Meem Sakin.

9) **NABRAH – DOMINATION OR COMMAND**: Hamza is said to be Athqal Al-Huroof, the heaviest of all letters. It has a special sharpness and heaviness which makes it dominate and have superiority over the rest of the letters. It is glottal stop. This quality of Hamza sometimes results in Hamza taking different rules in the recitation of the Holy Qur'an which affect its heaviness.

The rules of Hamza are:-

a) **TAS-HEEL – TO MAKE EASY**: This means to pronounce Hamza softly without taking into consideration its quality of strength and domination or its being a glottal stop. In the recitation of 'Aasim by the narrator Hafs, there is only one word which takes this rule, in Surah Fussilat, Ayah 44 ءَ

أَعْجَمِيٌّ

The second Hamza is pronounced softly, in the middle between the sound of Hamza and the long vowel of Alif.

b) **TABDEEL – TO CHANGE**: This means changing the second Hamza to the long vowel of Alif. This rule has been set out in the writing of the Holy Qur'an.

Example: ءَأَمَنُوا is changed into ءَامنوا

c) **HATHF – TO ELIMINATE**: This is another rule for Hamza. It means omitting Hamza from the word. In the recitation of 'Aasim by the narrator Hafs, there is only one word which practically takes this rule, in Surah Hujuraat, Ayah 11:

بِئْسَ الِاسْمُ

The letters ل and س are accompanied by Sukoon, as the rule of the joining of two letters with Sukoon (Noon Sakin with Kasra is added), in here ل takes a Kasra. The Hamza after the letter ل is omitted. When stopping at the word بِئْسَ the second word can be read in two ways, either as اَلِسْمُ or لِسْمُ

PERMANENT ATTRIBUTES (LAZIMAH) WITHOUT OPPOSITES

AS - SAFEER (WHISTLING)
صس

AL - LEEN (SOFTNESS) Pronounced without difficulty

AL - QALQALAH (ECHOING) Letters of Vibration - Qutubjad Letters
قطبجد

AL - ISTITAALAH (PROLONGATION) Stretching the sound over the entire tongue

AL - TAKREER (REPETITION) Fast Vibration

AL - INHIRAF (INCLINATION) Move the Makhraj of one letter to ل ر

AL-TAFASH-SHEE (SPREAD) Sound spread in the mouth

SUMMARY OF PERMANANT ATTRIBUTES (LAZIMAH) WITH THE OPPOSITES

QUALITY NAME & DEFINITION	NO OF LETTERS	ALPHABETS
Hams Continuation of breath	11	ةكفصشسخحثت
Jahr– Stoppage of breath	18	غعظططضزردجبء يونملق
Shiddah– Strong stoppage of sound	8	كقطدجتبء
Tawassut– In between stoppage and continuation of sound	5	نملعر
Rakhawah– Continuation of sound	16	ظضصشسزذحخث ةيهوفغ
Isti'laa– Elevated – Back of tongue rises to palate pronounced heavily	7	قغظطضصخ
Istefaal– Lowness Tongue low from palate (pronounced lightly)	21	سزردحجتثبء يهونملكفعش
Itbaaq– Covered – Centre of tongue rises to palate	4	ظطضص
Infitaah– Open – Tongue separated from palate		سزذدحخجشتبء يوهنملكقففغعش
Ismaat– Pronounced with effort		شسزذدحخجحثتء وهكقغعظططضص ي

Idhlaq– Fluency – Smooth and easy to pronounce	6	نملفرب

SUMMARY OF PERMANANT ATTRIBUTES (LAZIMAH) WITHOUT OPPOSITES

QUALITY NAME & DEFINITION	NO OF LETTERS	ALPHABETS
Safeer – Whistling – Sound like a bird	3	زسص
Qalqalah – Echoing – Breaking of tension or release	5	دجبطق
Leen – Softness – pronounced without difficulty	2	يو
Inhiraf – Inclination – Move makharij of one into another	2	لر
Takrir – Repetition – Prounouncing the letter more than once (not recommended)	1	ر
Tafashshee – Spread – Spreading around the sound of the word in the mouth once (not recommended)	1	ش
Istitaalah – Prolongation – Stretching sound over entire tongue.	1	ض
Ghunnah – Nasal Sound – Comes from the Nasal passage	2	نم
Nabrah – Domination – Command and Sharpness, the heaviest of all letters	1	ء

PERMANENT QUALITIES OF INDIVIDUAL LETTERS

أ	JAHR – Stoppage of Breath
	SHIDDAH – Strong letters
	ISTEFAAL – Light letters
	ISMAAT – Read with effort
	INFITAAH – Separation of tongue and upper palate
ب	JAHR – Stoppage of Breath
	SHIDDAH – Strong letters
	ISTEFAAL – Light letters
	INFITAAH – Separation of tongue and upper palate
	IDHLAQ – Smooth - Read with ease
	QALQALAH – Echoing or Vibration
ت	HAMS – Continuation of Breath
	SHIDDAH – Strong letters
	ISTEFAAL – Light letters
	INFITAAH – Separation of tongue and upper palate
	ISMAAT – Read with effort
ث	HAMS – Continuation of Breath
	RAKHAWAH – Soft letters
	ISTEFAAL – Light letters
	INFITAAH – Separation of tongue and upper palate
	ISMAAT – Read with effort
ج	JAHR – Stoppage of Breath
	SHIDDAH – Strong letters
	ISTEFAAL – Light letters
	ISMAAT – Read with effort
	INFITAAH – Separation of tongue and upper palate
	QALQALAH – Echoing or Vibration
ح	HAMS – Continuation of Breath
	RAKHAWAH – Soft letters
	ISTEFAAL – Light letters
	INFITAAH – Separation of tongue and upper palate
	ISMAAT – Read with effort

خ	HAMS – Continuation of Breath
	RAKHAWAH – Soft letters
	ISTI'LAA – Heavy letters
	INFITAAH – Separation of tongue and upper palate
	ISMAAT – Read with effort
د	JAHR – Stoppage of Breath
	SHIDDAH – Strong letters
	ISTEFAAL – Light letters
	ISMAAT – Read with effort
	INFITAAH – Separation of tongue and upper palate
	QALQALAH – Echoing or Vibration
ذ	JAHR – Stoppage of Breath
	RAKHAWAH – Soft letters
	ISTEFAAL – Light letters
	INFITAAH – Separation of tongue and upper palate
	ISMAAT – Read with effort
ر	JAHR – Stoppage of Breath
	TAWASSUT – In Between stoppage & continuation of breath
	ISTEFAAL – Light letters
	INFITAAH – Separation of tongue and upper palate
	IDHLAQ – Smooth - Read with ease
	TAKREER – Avoid trilling of the tongue when reading letter RA
	INHIRAF – Incline – Move makharij of one into another
ز	JAHR – Stoppage of Breath
	RAKHAWAH – Soft letters
	ISTEFAAL – Light letters
	INFITAAH – Separation of tongue and upper palate
	ISMAAT – Read with effort
	AS SAFEER – Whistling – Sound like a bird

س	HAMS – Continuation of Breath
	RAKHAWAH – Soft letters
	ISTEFAAL – Light letters
	INFITAAH – Separation of tongue and upper palate
	ISMAAT – Read with effort
	AS SAFEER – Whistling – Sound like a bird
ش	HAMS – Continuation of Breath
	RAKHAWAH – Soft letters
	ISTEFAAL – Light letters
	INFITAAH – Separation of tongue and upper palate
	ISMAAT – Read with effort
	TAFASHSHEE – Spreading the sound in the mouth
ص	HAMS – Continuation of Breath
	RAKHAWAH – Soft letters
	ISTI'LAA – Heavy letters
	ITBAAQ – Adhesion of tongue and upper palate
	ISMAAT – Read with effort
	AS SAFEER – Whistling – Sound like a bird
ض	JAHR – Stoppage of Breath
	RAKHAWAH – Soft letters
	ISTI'LAA – Heavy letters
	ITBAAQ – Adhesion of tongue and upper palate
	ISMAAT – Read with effort
	ISTITAALAH – Prolongation – Stretching the sound
ط	JAHR – Stoppage of Breath
	SHIDDAH – Strong letters
	ISTI'LAA – Heavy letters
	ITBAAQ – Adhesion of tongue and upper palate
	ISMAAT – Read with effort
	QALQALAH – Echoing or Vibration
ظ	JAHR – Stoppage of Breath
	RAKHAWAH – Soft letters
	ISTI'LAA – Heavy letters
	ITBAAQ – Adhesion of tongue and upper palate
	ISMAAT – Read with effort

ع	JAHR – Stoppage of Breath
	TAWASSUT – In Between stoppage & continuation of breath
	ISTEFAAL – Light letters
	INFITAAH – Separation of tongue and upper palate
	ISMAAT – Read with effort
غ	JAHR – Stoppage of Breath
	RAKHAWAH – Soft letters
	ISTI'LAA – Heavy letters
	INFITAAH – Separation of tongue and upper palate
	ISMAAT – Read with effort
ف	HAMS – Continuation of Breath
	RAKHAWAH – Soft letters
	ISTEFAAL – Light letters
	INFITAAH – Separation of tongue and upper palate
	IDHLAQ – Read with ease
ق	JAHR – Stoppage of Breath
	SHIDDAH – Strong letters
	ISTI'LAA – Heavy letters
	INFITAAH – Separation of tongue and upper palate
	ISMAAT – Read with effort
	QALQALAH – Echoing or Vibration
ك	HAMS – Continuation of Breath
	SHIDDAH – Strong letters
	ISTEFAAL – Light letters
	INFITAAH – Separation of tongue and upper palate
	ISMAAT – Read with effort
ل	JAHR – Stoppage of Breath
	TAWASSUT – In Between stoppage & continuation of breath
	ISTEFAAL – Light letters
	INFITAAH – Separation of tongue and upper palate
	IDHLAQ – Read with ease

	INHIRAF – Incline – Move makharij of one into another
م	JAHR – Stoppage of Breath
	TAWASSUT – In Between stoppage & continuation of breath
	ISTEFAAL – Light letters
	INFITAAH – Separation of tongue and upper palate
	IDHLAQ – Read with ease
	GHUNNAH – Nasal Sound from the Nasal passage
ن	JAHR – Stoppage of Breath
	TAWASSUT – In Between stoppage & continuation of breath
	ISTEFAAL – Light letters
	INFITAAH – Separation of tongue and upper palate
	IDHLAQ – Read with ease
	GHUNNAH – Nasal Sound from the Nasal passage
و	JAHR – Stoppage of Breath
	RAKHAWAH – Soft letters
	ISTEFAAL – Light letters
	INFITAAH – Separation of tongue and upper palate
	ISMAAT – Read with effort
	LEEN – Softness – pronounced without difficulty
ه	HAMS – Continuation of Breath
	RAKHAWAH – Soft letters
	ISTEFAAL – Light letters
	INFITAAH – Separation of tongue and upper palate
	ISMAAT – Read with effort
ء	JAHR – Stoppage of Breath
	SHIDDAH – Strong letters
	ISTEFAAL – Light letters
	INFITAAH – Separation of tongue and upper palate
	ISMAAT – Read with effort

ي	JAHR – Stoppage of Breath
	RAKHAWAH – Soft letters
	ISTEFAAL – Light letters
	INFITAAH – Separation of tongue and upper palate
	ISMAAT – Read with effort
	LEEN – Softness – pronounced without difficulty
ة	HAMS – Continuation of Breath
	RAKHAWAH – Soft letters

SIFAAT OF QALQALAH

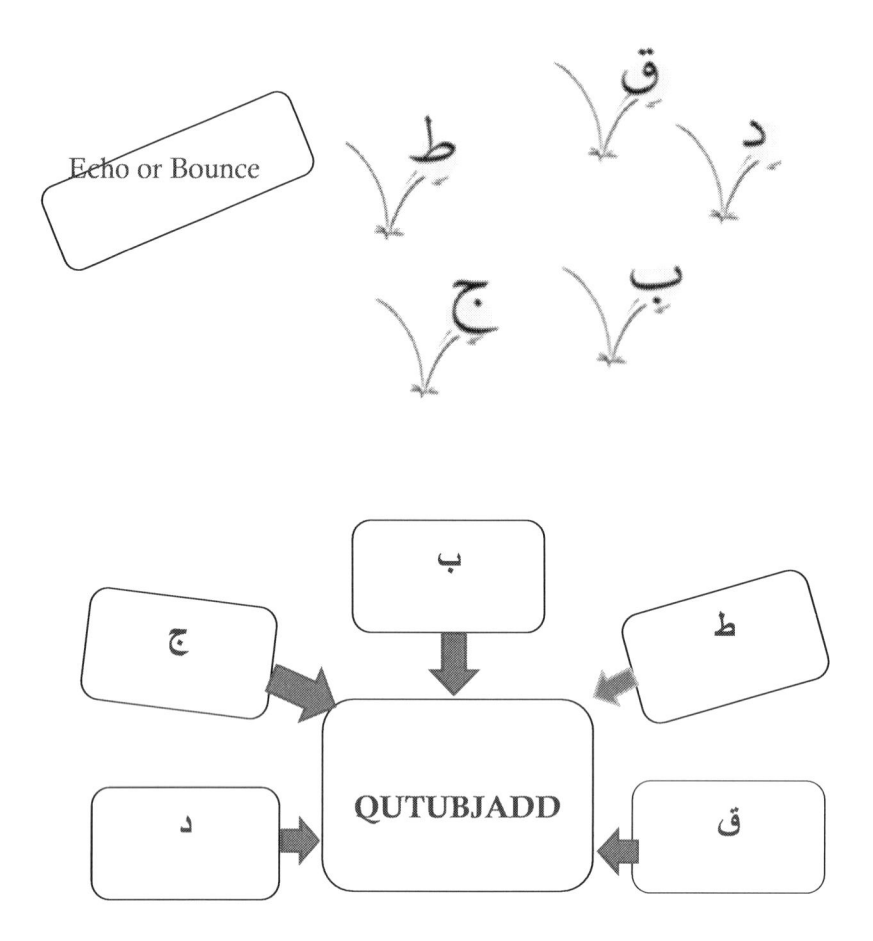

Echo or Bounce

ق د
ط
ج ب

QUTUBJADD

ب ج ط د ق

PERMANENT ATTRIBUTES (LAZIMAH) WITHOUT OPPOSITES

THE QUALITY (SIFAAT) OF QALQALAH

When Arabic letters are read with a Sukun, the sound of the letter is completed. There are 5 letters that when they are pronounced with a Sukun, their sound is not completed and they are therefore read with a Vibration or Echo, so as to complete the sound.

DEFINITION: To pronounce with an **Echoing or Bouncing sound**, when the letter carries a SUKOON only. The characteristic of Qalqalah is found in the following five letters, when they carry a Sukoon. They are known by the acronym **QUTUBJAD.**

ق ط ب ج د   قُطْبُجَدْ

1. The 5 letters of Qalqalah are read with an Echo when they carry a Sukun, or stopping or pausing at the end of a sentence, or even when they appear in the middle of a sentence.
2. Example: (قْ) try and say the word 'AQ', it is a little difficult as the back of the tongue and back of the throat come together. The sound is stuck and does not fully come out, therefore it is read with an echo, so as to release the sound, 'AQQ'
3. When the sound is pronounced with an echo, separation takes place between the 2 points of articulation, therefore the sound is completed.
4. Since an additional sound is being made, care must be taken that a Sakin letter should not sound doubled (Mushaddad - as if it is carrying a Shaddah) or voweled (Mutaharrik – as if it has a fat-ha or a Dhamma)

أُطْ	إطْ	أَطْ	أُقْ	إِقْ	أَقْ
أُجْ	إجْ	أَجْ	أُبْ	إِبْ	أَبْ

أُدْ	إِدْ	أَدْ

TWO TYPES OF SUKUN

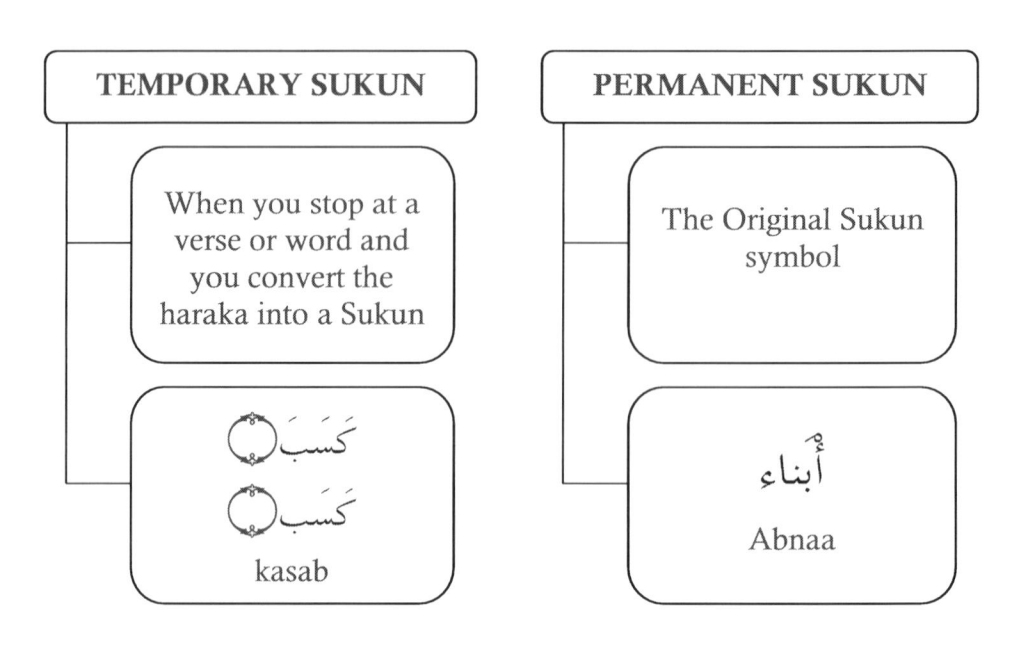

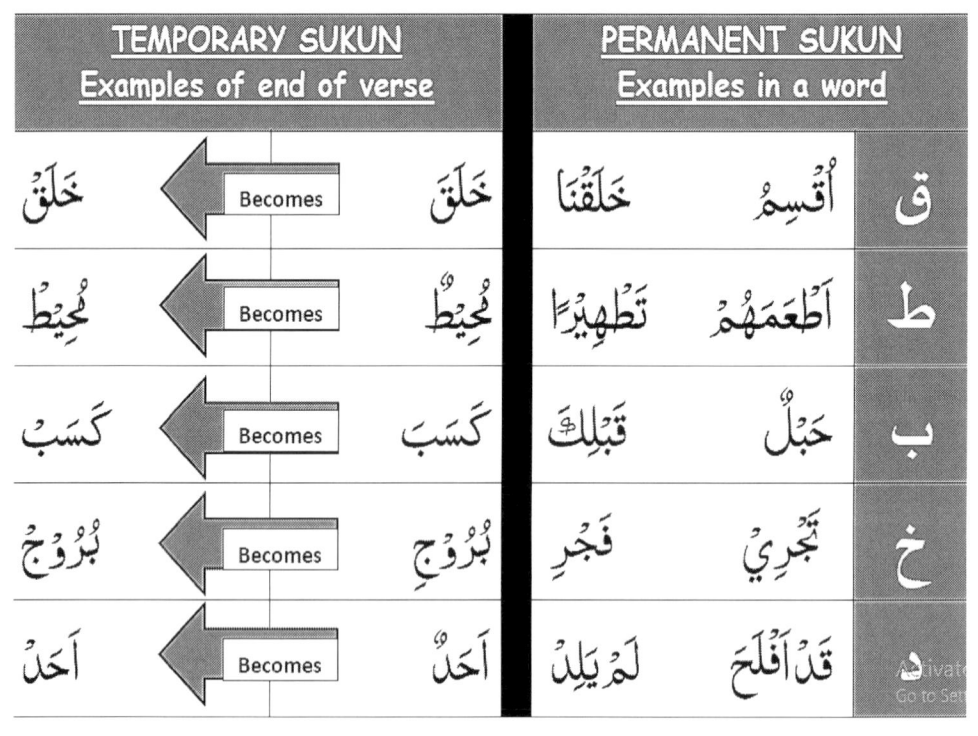

TEMPORARY SUKUN

When you stop at a verse or word and you convert the haraka into a Sukun

كَسَبُ
كَسَبْ

kasab

PERMANENT SUKUN

The Original Sukun symbol

أَبْناء

Abnaa

	PERMANENT SUKUN — Examples in a word		TEMPORARY SUKUN — Examples of end of verse	
ق	أُقْسِمُ	خَلَقْنَا	خَلَقَ → Becomes →	خَلَقْ
ط	أَطْعَمَهُمْ	تَطْهِيرًا	مُحِيطٌ → Becomes →	مُحِيطْ
ب	حَبْلٌ	قَبْلِكَ	كَسَبَ → Becomes →	كَسَبْ
خ	تَجْرِي	فَجْرٍ	بُرُوجٍ → Becomes →	بُرُوجْ
د	قَدْ أَفْلَحَ	لَمْ يَلِدْ	أَحَدٌ → Becomes →	أَحَدْ

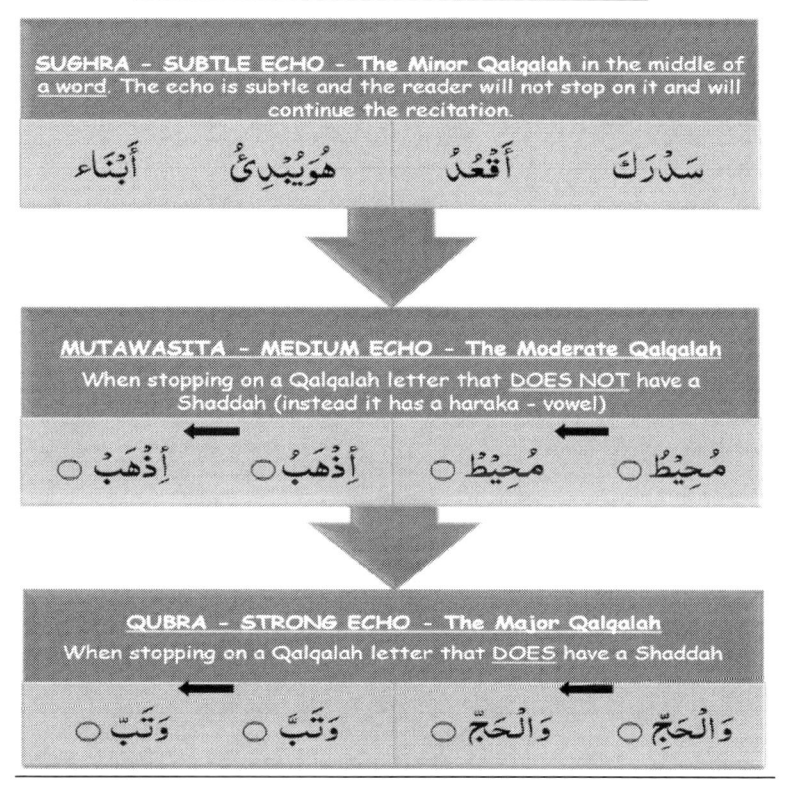

LEVELS OF QALQALAH

SUGHRA - SUBTLE ECHO - The Minor Qalqalah in the middle of a word.
The echo is subtle and the reader will not stop on it and will continue the recitation.

سَدْرَكَ   أَقْعُدُ   هُوَيُبْدِئُ   أَبْنَاء

MUTAWASITA - MEDIUM ECHO - The Moderate Qalqalah
When stopping on a Qalqalah letter that **DOES NOT** have a Shaddah (instead it has a haraka - vowel)

مُحِيطٌ ○   مُحِيطٌ ○   اِذْهَبْ ○   اِذْهَبْ ○

QUBRA - STRONG ECHO - The Major Qalqalah
When stopping on a Qalqalah letter that **DOES** have a Shaddah

وَالْحَجِّ ○   وَالْحَجِّ ○   وَتَبَّ ○   وَتَبَّ ○

THE LEVELS OF QALQALAH

The degrees of Qalqalah refer to the strength of the vibration in the non-vowelled letter depending on its position in a word, while the division into levels takes into consideration the strength of the inherent qualities of the Qalqalah letters.

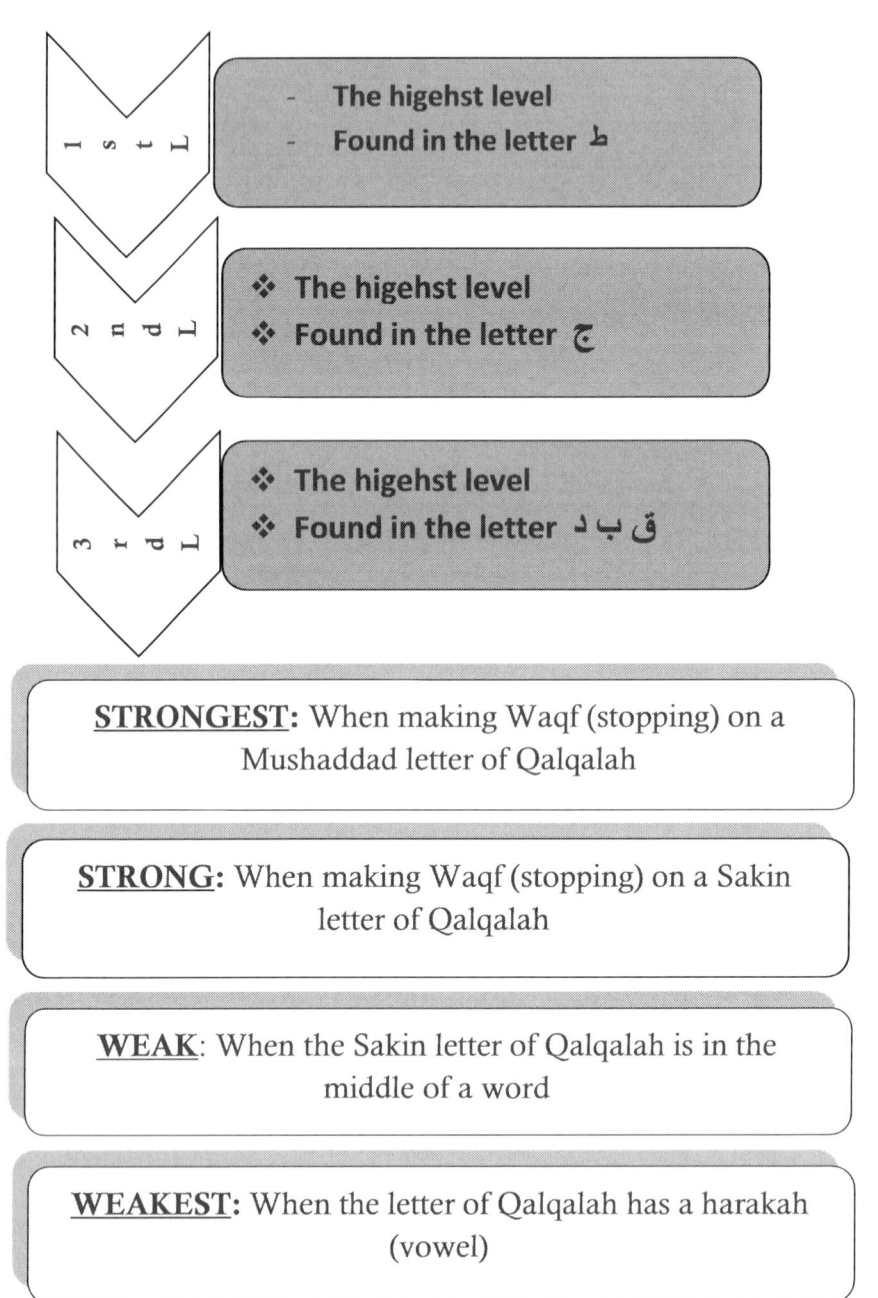

1st Level
- The higehst level
- Found in the letter ط

2nd Level
- The higehst level
- Found in the letter ج

3rd Level
- The higehst level
- Found in the letter ق ب د

STRONGEST: When making Waqf (stopping) on a Mushaddad letter of Qalqalah

STRONG: When making Waqf (stopping) on a Sakin letter of Qalqalah

WEAK: When the Sakin letter of Qalqalah is in the middle of a word

WEAKEST: When the letter of Qalqalah has a harakah (vowel)

REASON FOR QALQALAH

The reason that these 5 letters have this quality of Qalqalah is because they have the qualities of strength or force and the quality of audibility.

When the letter has the quality of strength or force, the sound and air is completely cut off and the letter is trapped in its Makhraj, hence it is not heard when
pronounced. But these 5 letters have the quality of audibility, so they should be heard when pronounced.

The only way it can be heard is to break the tension and
release the Makhraj, to give Qalqalah to the letter. TheQalqalah is necessary for these 5 letters because they have the attributes of Jahr (stoppage of the flow of breath) and Shiddah (stoppage of the flow of sound), so without Qalqalah, there would be no sound.

IDENTIFYING THE QALQALAH

1. Look for one of the letters of Qalqalah

دجبطق

2. Ask yourself: Does it have a Permanent or Temporary Sukun?
3. What level of Qalqalah is it? Subtle, Medium or Strong?

SURAH LAHAB

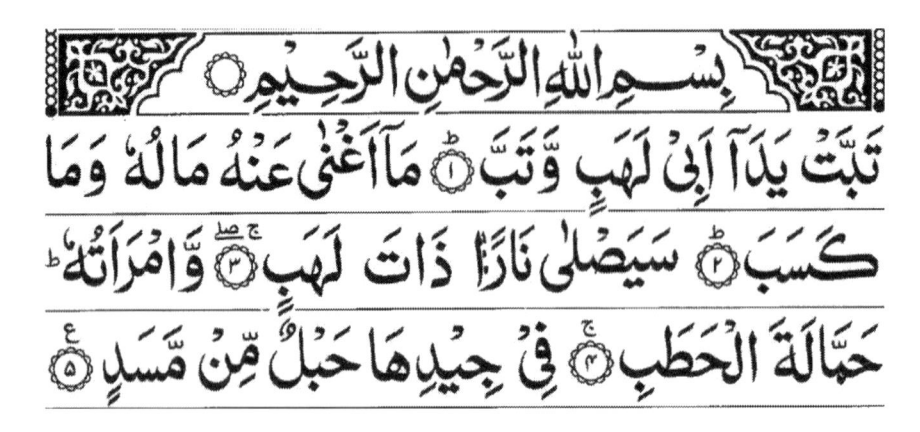

بِسْمِ اللَّهِ الرَّحْمَٰنِ الرَّحِيمِ

تَبَّتْ يَدَا أَبِي لَهَبٍ وَتَبَّ ۝١ مَا أَغْنَىٰ عَنْهُ مَالُهُ وَمَا كَسَبَ ۝٢ سَيَصْلَىٰ نَارًا ذَاتَ لَهَبٍ ۝٣ وَامْرَأَتُهُ حَمَّالَةَ الْحَطَبِ ۝٤ فِي جِيدِهَا حَبْلٌ مِّن مَّسَدٍ ۝٥

READING QALQALAH

﴿ مُقْتَدِرٍ ﴾	﴿ بِمِقْدَارٍ ﴾	﴿ أَقْبَلَ ﴾	ق
﴿ يُطْعِمُنِي ﴾	﴿ بِقِطْعٍ ﴾	﴿ شَطَرَ ﴾	ط
﴿ يُبْدِئُ ﴾	﴿ قِبْلَةً ﴾	﴿ سَبْحًا ﴾	ب
﴿ تُجْزَوْنَ ﴾	﴿ عِجْلًا ﴾	﴿ وَجْهَكَ ﴾	ج
﴿ يُدْرِيكَ ﴾	﴿ سِدْرَةٍ ﴾	﴿ وَشَدَدْنَا ﴾	د

NOTE: If any of the Qalqalah appear with Sukoon, it will be read with an Echoing sound, whether it be in the middle of a word or at the end.

If the letter of Qalqalah comes at the end of a word and you stop on it, it will be pronounced with a strong echoing sound, and if the letter has a Shaddah it will be pronounced even stronger.

أُقْسِمُ	بِمِقْدَارٍ	يَقْضِ
نُطْعِمُ	بِقِطْعٍ	أَطْهَرُ
يُبْعَثُونَ	حَسِبْتَ	أَبْصِرْ
مُجْرِمِينَ	حِجْرٌ	أَجْرًا
يُدْخِلُ	سِدْرٍ	عَدْلٍ

EXERCISING THE TONGUE & REPETITION

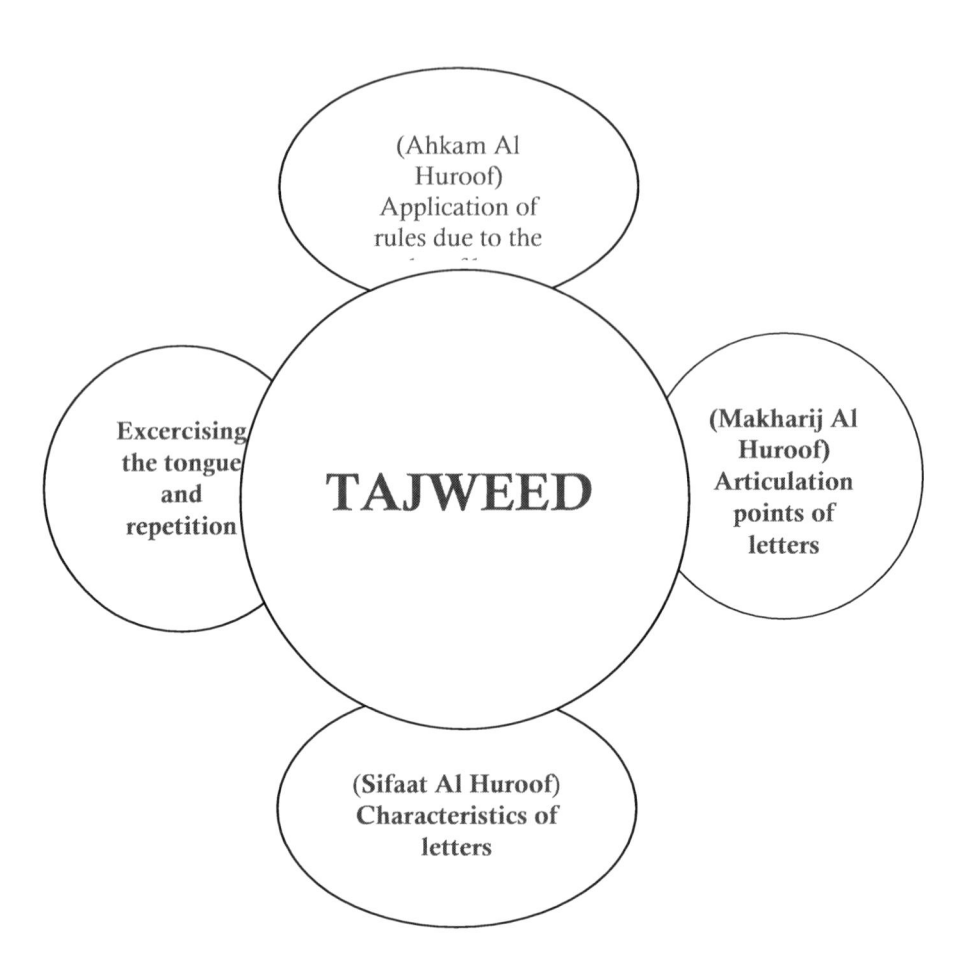

- **TAJWEED**
  - (Ahkam Al Huroof) Application of rules due to the ...
  - (Makharij Al Huroof) Articulation points of letters
  - (Sifaat Al Huroof) Characteristics of letters
  - Excercising the tongue and repetition

TAJWEED 3: EXERCISING THE TONGUE & REPETITION

Recitation of the Holy Qur'an requires one to be informed about the letters, vowels, how letters are connected and the various rules of Tajweed, etc. Most important is how topronounce the letters and this involves the mouth and in particular the tongue.

There are certain mistakes that are consistent, therefore, one has to train the parts of the tongue, so that the letters are pronounced correctly, otherwise the meaning of the
word changes, which should be avoided completely.

The letters that occur in Arabic, are not common in other languages. Letters can have similar sounds to other languages, but they have different articulation points. Letters that sound similar to the untrained ear, can be very different in pronunciation.

The Qur'an is the word of Allāh(سُبْحَانَهُ وَتَعَالَى), revealed to man as a guidance and we have to be extremely careful to read it as best as we can.

Below are some letters that sound similar to each other. Read them correctly and notice how different parts of the tongue are used to pronounce them, even though they sound similar.

اَ	-	عَ	ثَ	-	سَ
حَ	-	هَ	ثَ	-	شَ
جَ	-	زَ	سَ	-	شَ
يَ	-	زَ	صَ	-	سَ
خَ	-	غَ	تَ	-	طَ
خَ	-	قَ	ذَ	-	ظَ
غَ	-	قَ	ظَ	-	ضَ

SIMILAR SOUNDING LETTERS LEAD TO SIMILAR SOUNDING WORDS

Some similar pairs of letters from the Arabic Alphabet, when put together, form similar sounding words. So extra care must be taken to pronounce each letter correctly.

Below are some pairs of words which illustrate this point. Notice some of the letters may be different but the words sound the same

حَلَقَ – هَلَكَ	قَلْب – كَلْب
تَابَ – طَابَ	رَكَدَ – رَقَدَ
تِيْنٌ – طِيْنٌ	قَصَدَ – كَسَدَ
ذَلِيْلٌ – ظَلِيْلٌ	دَرْب – ضَرْب
سَبٌّ – صَبٌّ	بَعَدَ – بَعْضَ
سَبَحَ – صَبَحَ	دَلَّ – ضَلَّ

THE THREE LEVELS OF SPEED IN RECITING THE HOLY QUR'AN

1. **TAHQEEQ** – Reciting the Holy Qur'an slowly and with serenity, whilepondering the meaning. Reciting with deeper concentration and observing theTajweed rules. This is a slowness without elongation. There is a possibility that when reciting slowly, one may lengthen a letter overits limit. This results in Tamteet, elongation, which is a mistake. Tamteetmeans giving rise to letters of Madd from the harakaat. Therefore, the reciterhas to be extra careful when reciting with Tahqeeq.The reading level of Tahqeeq is usually for beginners in order to train thetongue to recite the letters according to their nature and quality and topractice the rules of recitation.

Advantages: Less Tajweed mistakes are made
Disadvantages: Less verses are recited. Time spent to recite one Juz is about one and a half to two hours.
This type of recitation is usually recited in gatherings and meetings when there is a special programme.

2. **TAHDEER (or Hadr)** – It is a swift method of reciting the Holy Qur'an withobservation of the rules of Tajweed. The reader then must be careful not tocut off the lengthened letters, and not to shorten the vowels to the pointthat the reading is not correct.When reading with Hadr, there is a danger of reducing the timing of theletters and inserting one into another. The letters must be pronouncedcorrectly with their due rights. Therefore, there is no problem with recitingthe Qur'an with speed, on the condition that there is no Idh'gham (merging ofsome letters into others) or reduction in the required timing('eating/swallowing' part of the letter) This level of reading is usually for the Haafizul Qur'an who has memorized the Qur'an. Therefore he is fully aware of the reading laws of Tajweed and due to repetition of his reading, he avoids mistakes

Advantages: More verses recited. Time spent to recite one Juz is about half an hour.
Disadvantages: Recitation mistakes are made easily. This type of recitation is usually recited in the month of Ramadhan in order to obtain greater rewards by reciting more verses of the Holy Qur'an - This should **not** be encouraged as it causes errors in recitation.

3. **TADWEER** – It is reciting the Holy Qur'an with an average speed, at a medium level which is in between the two levels of Tahqeeq and Tahdeer. In this level the rules of Tajweed are preserved and observed. It is a

moderated recitation that is neither fast as Al-Hadrand nor slow as Tahqeeq. Time spent to recite one Juz is about 1 hour.

During recitation of the Holy Qur'an, regardless of which speed is being used (Tahqeeq, Tahdeer or Tadweer) one must apply the rule of Tarteel to all of them.

TARTEEL is TajweedulHuroofwaMa'arifatulWuqoof– it is Tajweed of the letters and knowledge of the stops.

It is reciting the Holy Qur'an clearly, pronouncing the letters correctly one by one and applying the rules of Tajweed with understanding and thinking about what is recited. The intention for recitation must be seeking closeness to Allāh(Subhānahuwata'āla) and not for getting popularity, money or such like.

Tarteel also means reading the Holy Qur'an, as the Holy Prophet Muhammad (saw) used to recite as he was ordered by Allāh (Subhānahuwata'āla) in the following Ayah:

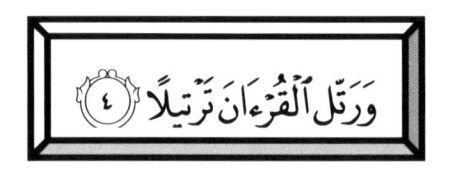

$$\text{وَرَتِّلِ ٱلۡقُرۡءَانَ تَرۡتِيلًا}$$

Rat-tilil Qur'an means pronounce each letter one by one. This means each letter is articulated individually. If we say 'Bismillah', we will hear the sound of the Ba, Seen and the Meem. We recite with Tarteel, whether we recite fast, slow or moderately.

When asked about the meaning of Tarteel, `Ali (رضي الله عنه) replied: "It means that the Qur'an should be recited with Tajweed and with due observance to the rules of Waqf (pausing or stopping at the end of the Verse)".

Tarteel is reciting the Holy Qur'an with an average speed, the same as Tadweer, but in addition to observing the rules of Tajweed and pronouncing the letters correctly, the reciter must have Tadabbur (a proper understanding and consideration of the Ayah recited).

Man HaqqaqahTilaawah (one who recites in Tahqeeq), must recite with Tarteel, andMan DawwaralTilaawah (one who recites in Tadweer), must recite with Tarteel, and Man HadaraTilaawah (one who recites in Hadr), must recite with Tarteel, articulating each letter individually.

The Prophet Muhammad (ﷺ) says: ألا
لا خير في قراءة لا تدبر فيها

"Truly, reciting without proper understanding is fruitless"

THE THREE LEVELS OF SPEED IN RECITING THE HOLY QUR'AN

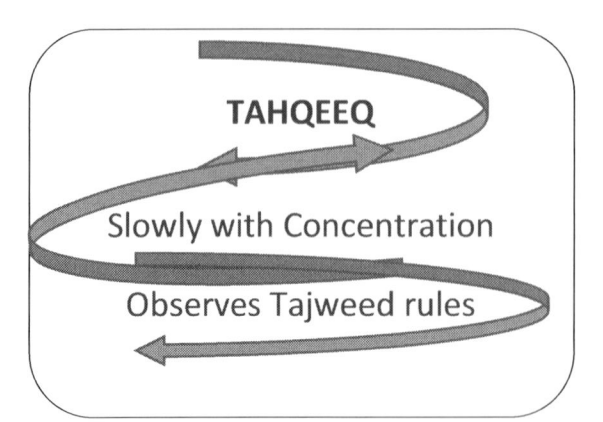

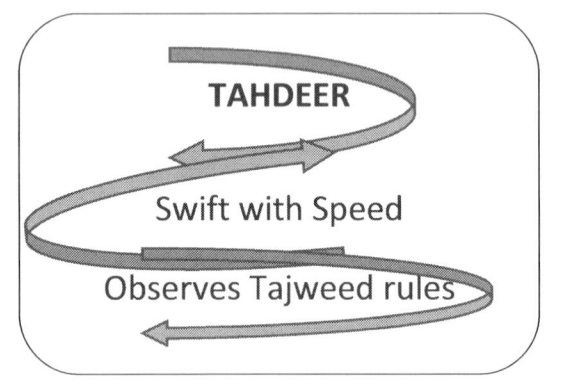

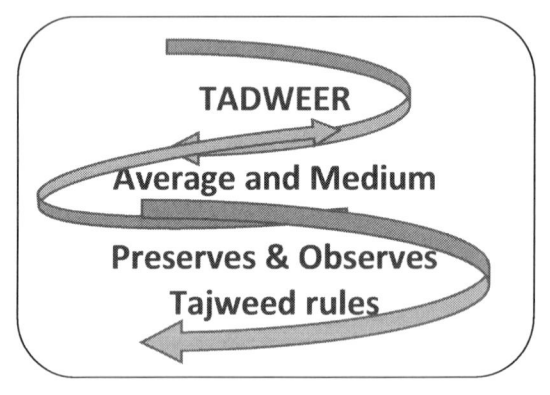

TAHQEEQ
Slowly with Concentration
Observes Tajweed rules

TAHDEER
Swift with Speed
Observes Tajweed rules

TADWEER
Average and Medium
Preserves & Observes Tajweed rules

HOW DIACRITICS CONTROL WORDS

Arabic Diacritics are actually called '**TASHKIL**' in Arabic. Simply put, they are signs written above or below letters to indicate how they are pronounced. A Diacritic can be a sign, mark, point or accent. In Arabic, the Diacritics or Tashkil are the short vowels of Fat-ha, Kasra and Dhamma, the lengthened long vowels and Tanween, Sukun and Shaddah.

Example: An Arabic word can have the same Three letters - in the example below we have the letters م : لس. By just changing the Diacritics, we can pronounce the words in so many different ways, each word with a different sound and meaning.

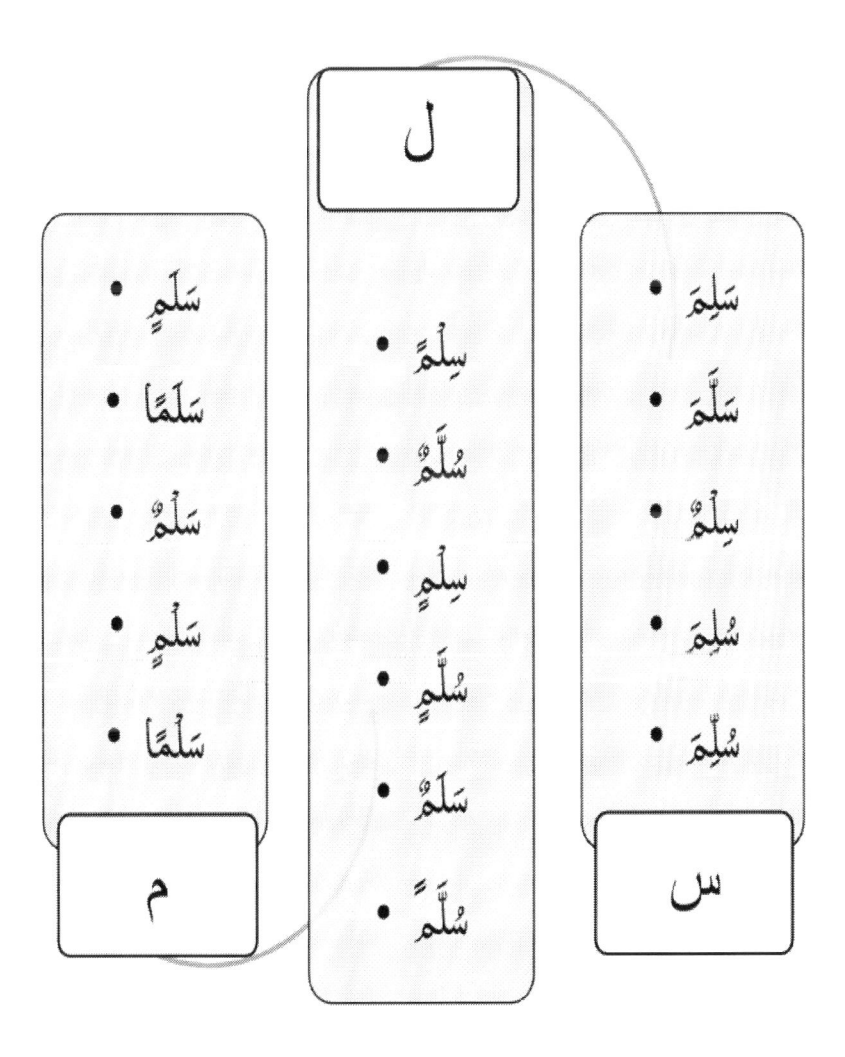

ل

م column	ل column (middle)	س column
• سَلِمٌ	• سَلِمٌ	• سَلِمَ
• سَلَمًا	• سِلْمٌ	• سَلَّمَ
• سَلَمٌ	• سُلَّمٌ	• سِلْمٌ
• سَلِمٌ	• سِلْمٍ	• سُلِمَ
• سَلَمًا	• سُلَّمٌ	• سُلِّمَ
	• سَلَمٌ	
	• سُلَّمٌ	

م		س

83

AHKAM AL HUROOF

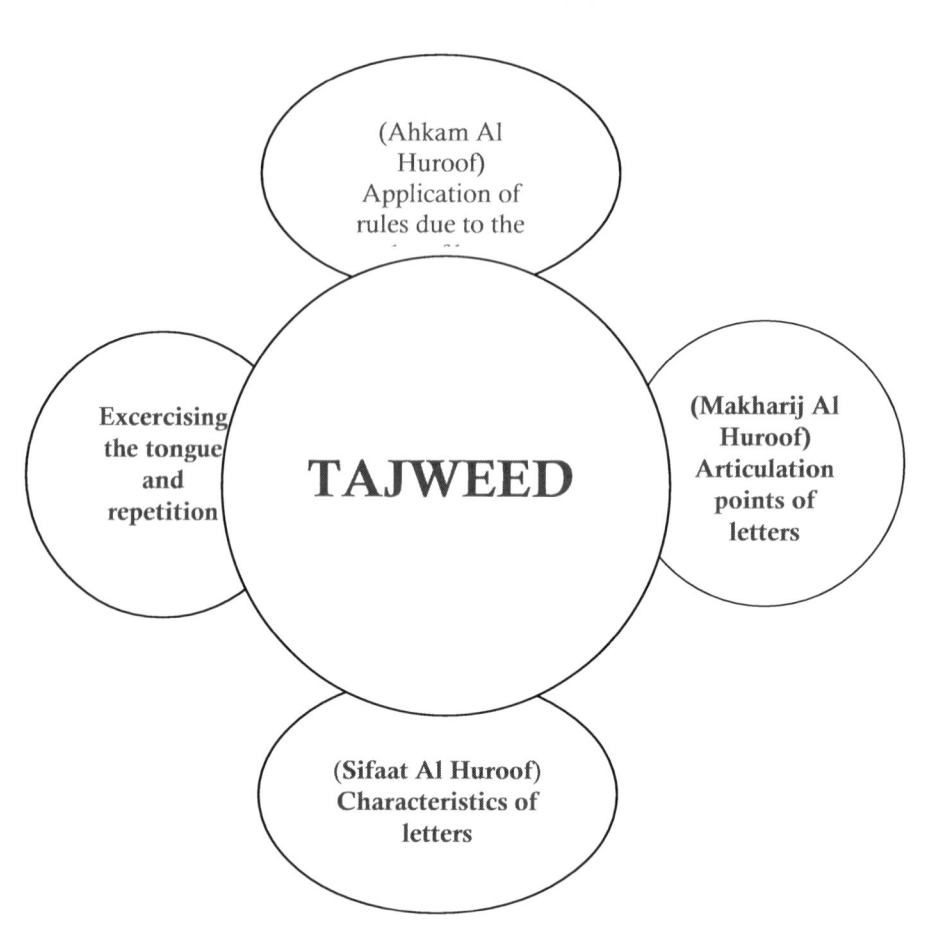

TAJWEED

- (Ahkam Al Huroof) Application of rules due to the ...
- (Makharij Al Huroof) Articulation points of letters
- (Sifaat Al Huroof) Characteristics of letters
- Excercising the tongue and repetition

TAJWEED 4: AHKAM AL HUROOF

AHKAM AL HUROOF – Rules of the letters – These are the changes which occur when a letter is combined with other letters. Each letter (Huruf) is given it's due right by applying the correct rules.

In Ahkam, we learn how to identify and apply the rules of Tajweed when reciting the Holy Qur'an. It is the knowledge of what rules change in the letters due to the order of letters.

The AHKAM rules are Eleven and each are further subdivided.

THE ELEVEN AHKAM RULES

i. The rules of LAAM

ii. The rules of NUN SAKIN AND TANWEEN

iii. The rules of NUN AND MEEMMUSHADDADAH

iv. The rules of MEEM SAKIN

v. The rules of OTHER IDHGHAM

vi. The rule of NUN QUTNI

vii. The rules of RAA

viii. The rules of MADDAH

ix. The rules of HAA

x. The rules of HAMZA

xi. The rules of WUQUF

TAJWEED

MAKHARIJ AL

MAKHARIJ

5 TYPES
1. AL JAWF -
2. The Oral Cavity AL HALQ - The Throat
3. AL LISAAN - The Tongue
4. ASHSHAFATAIN – The Lips
5. ALKHAISHOOM - The Nasal Cavity

SIFAT AL HUROOF

2 TYPES
1. DHATI
2. MAHA..

EXERCISING THE TONGUE

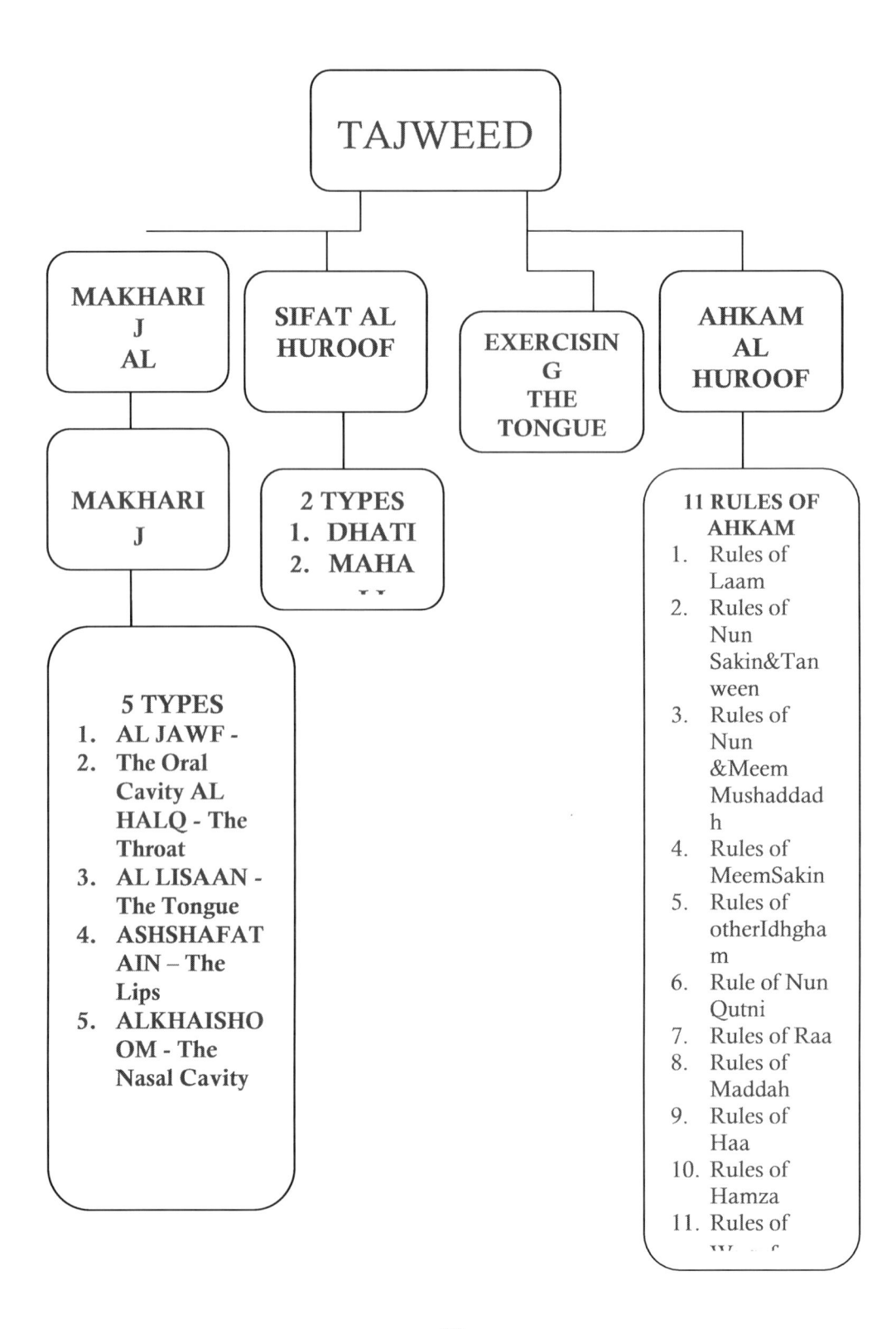

AHKAM AL HUROOF

11 RULES OF AHKAM
1. Rules of Laam
2. Rules of Nun Sakin&Tanween
3. Rules of Nun &Meem Mushaddadh
4. Rules of MeemSakin
5. Rules of otherIdhgham
6. Rule of Nun Qutni
7. Rules of Raa
8. Rules of Maddah
9. Rules of Haa
10. Rules of Hamza
11. Rules of W..f

Summarised Tajweed Rules

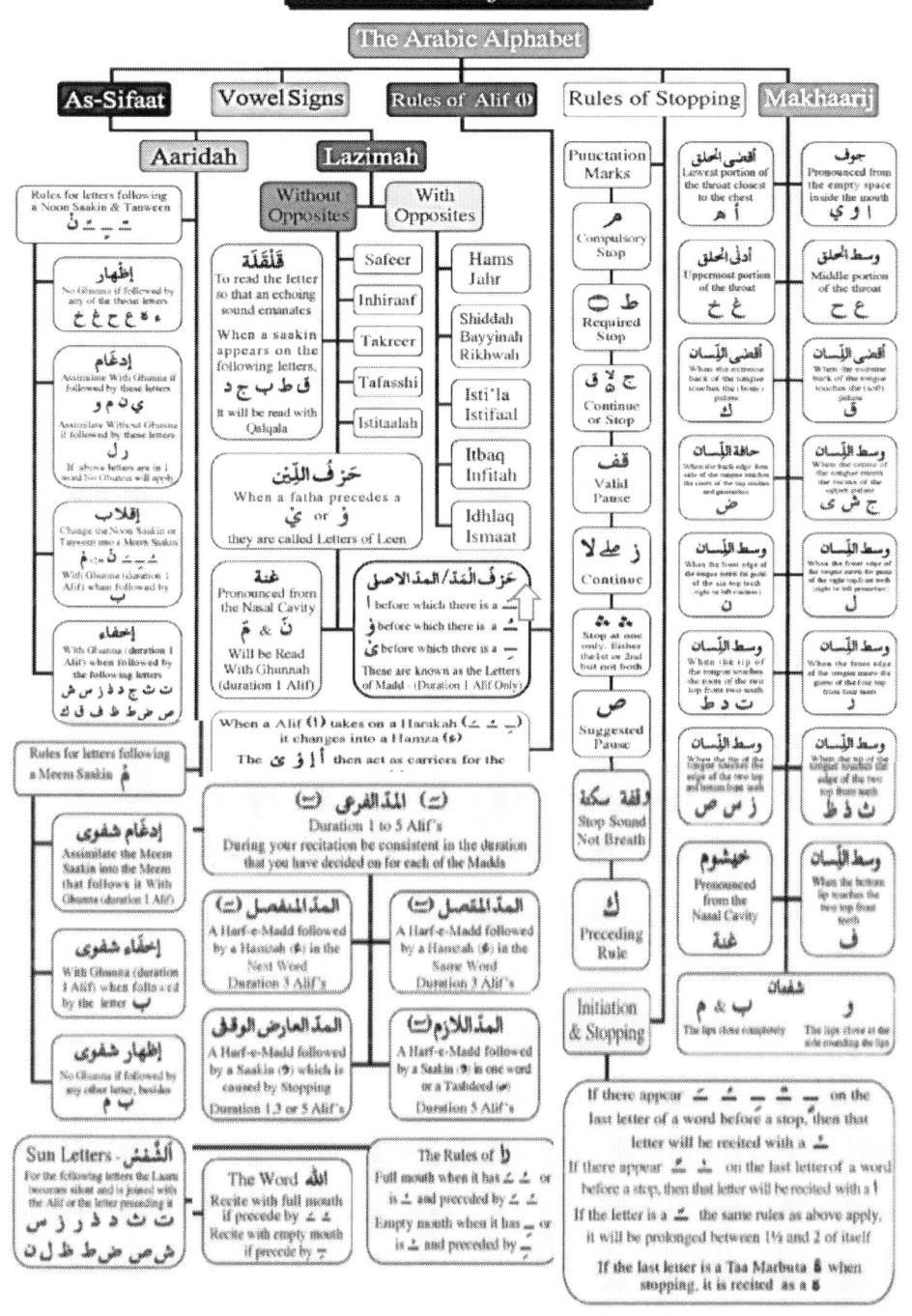

The Arabic Alphabet

As-Sifaat

Aaridah — Rules for letters following a Noon Saakin & Tanween ـًـٍـٌ ن

- **إظْهَار** — No Ghunna if followed by any of the throat letters: ء ه ع ح غ خ
- **إدْغَام** — Assimilate With Ghunna if followed by these letters: ي ن م و. Assimilate Without Ghunna if followed by these letters: ر ل. If above letters are in 1 word No Ghunna will apply.
- **إقْلَاب** — Change the Noon Saakin or Tanween into a Meem Saakin ـًمْـٍمْـٌمْ ن with Ghunna (duration 1 Alif) when followed by ب
- **إخْفَاء** — With Ghunna (duration 1 Alif) when followed by the following letters: ت ث ج د ذ ز س ش ص ض ط ظ ف ق ك

Rules for letters following a Meem Saakin مْ

- **إدْغَام شَفَوِي** — Assimilate the Meem Saakin into the Meem that follows it With Ghunna (duration 1 Alif)
- **إخْفَاء شَفَوِي** — With Ghunna (duration 1 Alif) when followed by the letter ب
- **إظْهَار شَفَوِي** — No Ghunna if followed by any other letter, besides ب م

Sun Letters - الشَّمْسِيّ — For the following letters the Laam becomes silent and is joined with the Alif or the letter preceding it: ت ث د ذ ر ز س ش ص ض ط ظ ل ن

Vowel Signs

Lazimah

Without Opposites

- **قَلْقَلَة** — To read the letter so that an echoing sound emanates. When a saakin appears on the following letters: ق ط ب ج د — It will be read with Qalqala

- **حَرْف اللَّين** — When a fatha precedes a و or ي they are called Letters of Leen

- **غُنَّة** — Pronounced from the Nasal Cavity نْ & مْ Will be Read With Ghunnah (duration 1 Alif)

- **حَرْف المَدّ / المَدّ الأصلي** — ا before which there is a ـَ ; و before which there is a ـُ ; ي before which there is a ـِ — These are known as the Letters of Madd - Duration 1 Alif Only

- When an Alif (١) takes on a Harakah (ـَ ـُ ـِ) it changes into a Hamza (ء). The ا و ى then act as carriers for the Hamza.

- **المَدّ الفَرْعِي** — Duration 1 to 5 Alif's. During your recitation be consistent in the duration that you have decided on for each of the Madds.

- **المَدّ المُنْفَصِل** — A Harf-e-Madd followed by a Hamzah (ء) in the Next Word — Duration 3 Alif's
- **المَدّ المُتَّصِل** — A Harf-e-Madd followed by a Hamzah (ء) in the Same Word — Duration 3 Alif's
- **المَدّ العَارِض الوَقْفِي** — A Harf-e-Madd followed by a Saakin (ـْ) which is caused by Stopping — Duration 1, 3 or 5 Alif's
- **المَدّ اللَّازِم** — A Harf-e-Madd followed by a Saakin (ـْ) in one word or a Tashdeed (ـّ) — Duration 5 Alif's

With Opposites

- Hams / Jahr
- Shiddah / Bayyinah / Rikhwah
- Isti'la / Istifaal
- Itbaq / Infitah
- Idhlaq / Ismaat

- Safeer
- Inhiraaf
- Takreer
- Tafasshi
- Istitaalah

The Word الله — Recite with full mouth if preceded by ـَ or ـُ. Recite with empty mouth if preceded by ـِ

The Rules of ر — Full mouth when it has ـَ or ـُ and preceded by ـَ or ـُ. Empty mouth when it has ـِ or is ـْ and preceded by ـِ

Rules of Alif (١)

Rules of Stopping

Punctuation Marks

- مـ — Compulsory Stop
- ط — Required Stop
- ج — Continue or Stop
- قف — Valid Pause
- ز ص لا — Continue
- ∴ — Stop at one only. Either the 1st or 2nd but not both
- ص — Suggested Pause
- وقفة سكتة — Stop Sound Not Breath
- أو — Preceding Rule

Initiation & Stopping

- If there appear ـَ ـُ ـِ on the last letter of a word before a stop, then that letter will be recited with a ـْ
- If there appear ـً ـٌ on the last letter of a word before a stop, then that letter will be recited with a ١
- If the letter is a ـٍ the same rules as above apply, it will be prolonged between 1½ and 2 of itself
- If the last letter is a Taa Marbuta ة when stopping, it is recited as a ه

Makhaarij

- **جَوْف** — Pronounced from the empty space inside the mouth: ا و ي
- **أقْصَى الحَلْق** — Lowest portion of the throat closest to the chest: ء ه
- **أدْنَى الحَلْق** — Uppermost portion of the throat: غ خ
- **وَسَط الحَلْق** — Middle portion of the throat: ع ح
- **أقْصَى اللِّسَان** — When the extreme back of the tongue touches the soft palate: ق
- **أقْصَى اللِّسَان** — When the corner of the tongue touches the recess of the upper palate: ك
- **وَسَط اللِّسَان** — When the back of the tongue touches the roots of the top molars and gums: ج ش ي
- **حَافَّة اللِّسَان** — When the front edge of the tongue touches the gum of the six top teeth (right to left canines): ض
- **وَسَط اللِّسَان** — When the front edge of the tongue moves to the region of the top replicas teeth (right to left premolars): ل
- **وَسَط اللِّسَان** — When the tip of the tongue touches the roots of the two top front teeth: ن
- **وَسَط اللِّسَان** — When the tip of the tongue moves to the gums of the top two front teeth: ر
- **وَسَط اللِّسَان** — When the tip of the tongue touches the edge of the two top front teeth: ت د ط
- **وَسَط اللِّسَان** — When the tip of the tongue touches the edge of the two top front teeth: ذ ث ظ
- **وَسَط اللِّسَان** — When the tip of the tongue touches the edge of the two top front teeth: ز س ص
- **خَيْشُوم** — Pronounced from the Nasal Cavity: غُنَّة
- **شَفَتَان** — ب م — The lips close completely; و — The lips close at the side rounding the lips; ف — The bottom lip touches the two top front teeth

THE RULES OF LAAM

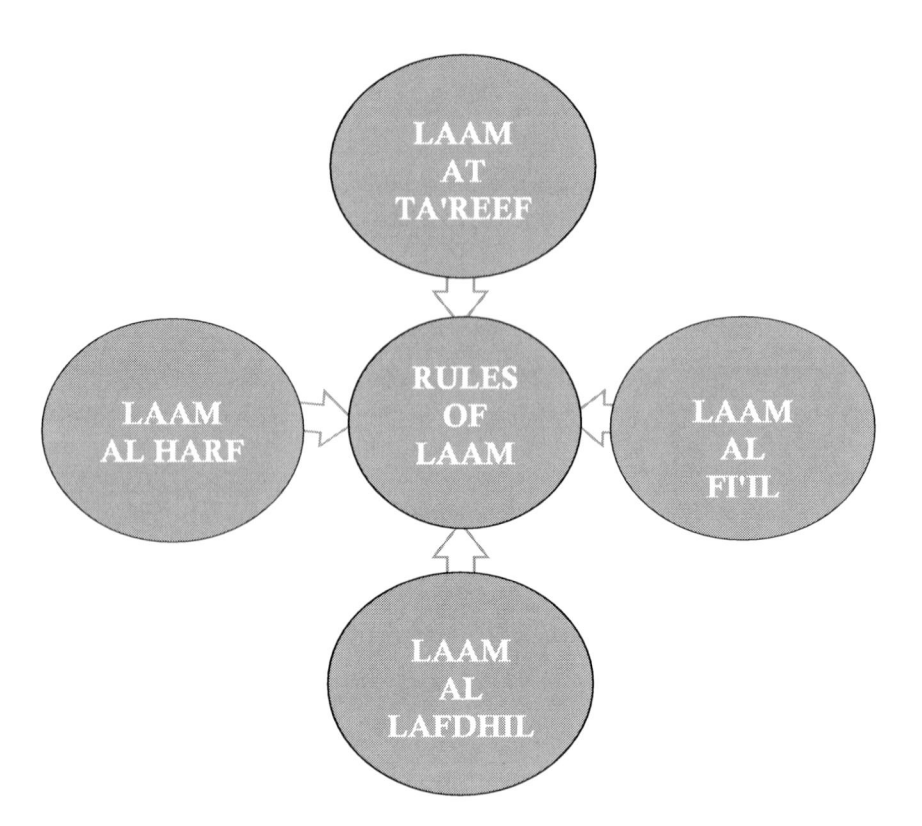

- LAAM AT TA'REEF
- LAAM AL HARF
- RULES OF LAAM
- LAAM AL FI'IL
- LAAM AL LAFDHIL

AHKAM AL HUROOF: 1) RULES OF LAAM

LaamSakin appears in the Holy Qur'an, in many ways, as in a Noun, or a Verb or as a Definite Article. How and where the LaamSakin appears, determines the way in which it will be pronounced. The 4 types of Laam are further Sub-divided into 2 sections each. There are those that are Idh'haar (where the LaamSakin appears and is pronounced clearly) and Idh'ghaam (where the LaamSakin is written but merged or joined into the letter)

4 TYPES OF LAAM SAAKIN

LAAM AT TA'REEF — When the ل appears in the beginning of a Noun
When a Noun (names of places, things, people) begins with a LaamSakin, then it becomes a specific noun and is known as Laam At-Ta'reef or in some places as Laam Al-Ma'arifa

LAAM AL FI'IL — When the ل appears at the end of a Verb
When the LaamSakin appears at the end of a Verb (action word), then the pronounciation of this Verb will be determined by the word that follows this Verb.

LAAM AL HARF — When a word ends with ل. Only 2 words: لهَلْ
• Also known as Laam of the Participle (a word that points out meaning of another word). There are only Two words that end with LaamSakin in the Arabic Alphabet.
They are Hal (هَلْ) and Bal (بَلْ). Their pronounciation is also determined by the word that follows the HAL or BAL

LAAM AL LAFDHIL JALALI — When the ل appears in the name of Allah (swt)
• Depending on the Vowel before the Laam in the name of Allah, the word Allah will be pronounced heavily or lightly

4 TYPES OF LAAM SAKIN – FURTHER DIVIDED

LAAM AT TA'REEF	IDH'HAAR (Where the Laam is clearly pronounced) in the 14 Moon letters **(Qamariyyah)**
	IDH'GHAAM (Where the Laam is merged and not pronounced) in the 14 Sun letters **(Shamsiyyah)**
LAAM AL FI'IL	When the Verb ends with LaamSakin and the word that follows it, begins with any alphabet of the Arabic language Except Ra and Laam, then it is IDH'HAAR (The LaamSakin is pronounced clearly)
	When the Verbs ends with LaamSakin and the word that follows it, begins with Ra or Laam, then it becomes IDH'GHAAM (The LaamSakin is merged and not pronounced)
LAAM AL HARF	If the word following Hal or Bal begins with any of the Arabic Alphabet except Ra or Laam, then IDH'HAAR applies (The LaamSakin is pronounced clearly)
	If the word following Hal or Bal begins with Ra or Laam, then IDH'GHAAM applies (The LaamSakin is merged and not pronounced)
LAAM AL LAFDHIL JALALI	If the letter before the name of Allāh bears a Fat-ha or a Dhamma, then the word Allāh is recited heavily with a full mouth
	If the letter before the name of Allāh bears a Kasra, then the word Allāh is recited lightly with an empty mouth

LAAM SAKIN: 1) LAAM AT TA'REEF (SUN & MOON LAAM)

The 28 Arabic alphabet are divided into 14 Sun letters (Al Huroof Al Shamsiyyah) and 14 Moon letters (Al Huroof Al Qamariyyah). The Sun and Moon letters follow different pronounciation ways when they come directly after the Definite Article 'AL'.

- In English, when we mention the words 'an Apple' or 'a Pear', this means any Apple or Pear. When we say 'the Apple' or 'the Pear', it means that particular Apple or Pear. In Arabic the word 'the' is used as AL (a combination of Alif and Laam). AL is therefore known as the 'Definite Article' as it refers to a particular thing. Nouns beginning with Sun and Moon letters have different pronounciations when they appear directly after the AL.

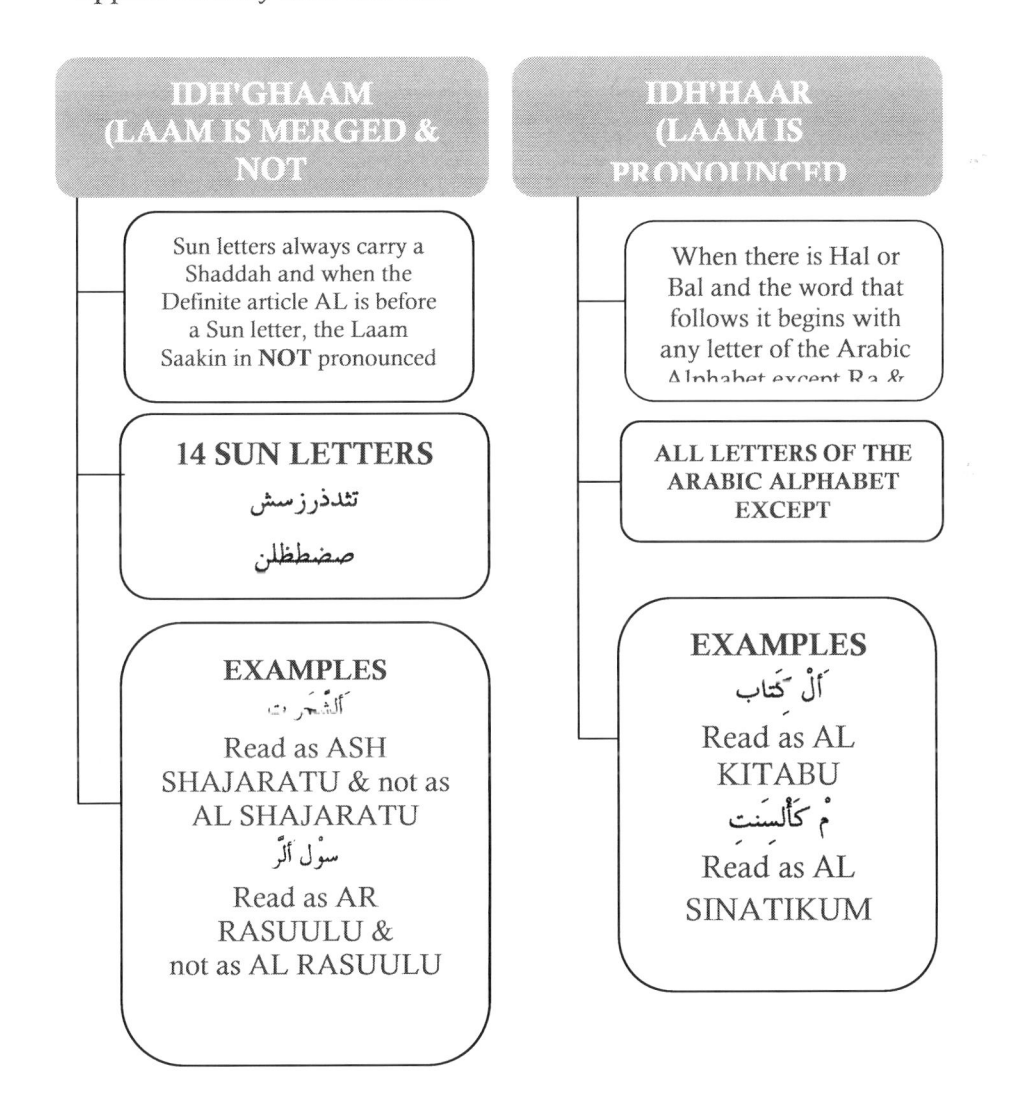

IDH'GHAAM (LAAM IS MERGED & NOT PRONOUNCED)

Sun letters always carry a Shaddah and when the Definite article AL is before a Sun letter, the Laam Saakin in **NOT** pronounced

14 SUN LETTERS

ت ث د ذ ر ز س ش

ص ض ط ظ ل ن

EXAMPLES

اَلشَّجَرَتُ

Read as ASH SHAJARATU & not as AL SHAJARATU

اَلرَّسُولُ

Read as AR RASUULU & not as AL RASUULU

IDH'HAAR (LAAM IS PRONOUNCED)

When there is Hal or Bal and the word that follows it begins with any letter of the Arabic Alphabet except Ra &

ALL LETTERS OF THE ARABIC ALPHABET EXCEPT

EXAMPLES

اَلْكِتَابُ

Read as AL KITABU

كَالْسِنَتِكُم

Read as AL SINATIKUM

LAAM SAKIN: 1) LAAM AT TA'REEF (EXAMPLES OF EACH LETTER)

NOTE: All Sun letters following the 'AL' always have a **shaddah**(The sound therefore doubles and pronounciation of the word is easier). The **laam** before the Sun letter does
Not have a Sakin sign. The **ALIF** in the 'AL' is always a **FAT-HA**.

Word after AL' bignining with Sun letter	Sun letter	Word after AL' bignining with Moon letter	Moon letter
التين	ت	الْحَمْدُ	أ
الثواب	ث	البيت	ب
الدين	د	الجمل	ج
الذكر	ذ	الحجُّ	ح
الرسول	ر	الخالقون	خ
الزكوة	ز	العذاب	ع
السماء	س	الغرق	غ
الشيطان	ش	الفتنة	ف
الصمد	ص	القوم	ق
الضّعفآء	ض	الكهف	ك
الطير	ط	المغضوب	م
الظالم	ظ	الواقعة	و
الليل	ت	الهيم	هـ
النفس	ن	اليقين	ي

LAAM SAKIN: 2) LAAM AL FI'IL

IDH'GHAAM (LAAM IS MERGED & NOT PRONOUNCED)

- When there is Hal or Bal and the word that follows it begins with Ra or Laam

- ONLY 2 LETTERS RA or LAAM
  ل or ر

- **EXAMPLES**

  هَلَّكُمْ

  Read as HALLAKUM and not as HAL LAKUM

  اَللّٰهُ رَّفَعَهُ بَلْ

  Read as BAR RAFA AHULLAHU and not as BAL RAFA AHULLAHU

- This rule of Idh'ghaam applies to all the Ra or Laam that follow either Hal or Bal, **EXCEPT**, the word **BAL RAANA**, because the compulsory pause (sakt) prevents assimilation

  بل ران

  (SURAH MUTAFFIFEEN 83:14)

IDH'HAAR (LAAM IS PRONOUNCED)

- When there is Hal or Bal and the word that follows it begins with any letter of the Arabic Alphabet except Ra & Laam

- ALL LETTERS OF THE ARABIC ALPHABET EXCEPT RA & LAAM

- **EXAMPLES**

  هَلْ أَتَاكَ

  Read as HAL ATAAKA

  بَلْ كَانَ

  Read as BAL KAANA

UNDERSTANDING HEAVY AND LIGHT LETTERS THE ARABIC ALPHABET

TAFKHEEM (THICKENING/TO MAKE HEAVY)
In recitation of the Holy Qur'an it means giving the letter a quality of heaviness by elevation of the tongue to the roof of the mouth (filling the space of the mouth with the sound of the letter)

TARQEEQ (THINNING/TO MAKE LIGHT)
In recitation of the Holy Qur'an it means giving the letter a quality of lightness by lowering the tongue away from the roof of the mouth.

LETTERS THAT ARE: SOMETIMES HEAVY & SOMETIMES LIGHT
(The letters RA & LAAM – these will be discussed in the other chapters)

The letters that have a Heavy quality are the 7 letters of Huruful Halqiyya (Throat letters)

خ ص ض ط ظ غ ق

The letters that have a Light quality are the rest of the Alphabet apart from the Throat letters (19 Letters)

THE RULE OF LAAM: 4) LAAM AL LAFDHIL JALALI

The letter LAAM is normally recited lightly with a thin sound. However, when it appears in the name of اللّٰه (LafdhilJalalah), or in اَللّٰهُمَّ, it's pronounciation depends on the following 2 rules:

RULE 1: Read with a Full mouth (TAGHLEEDTH)

When a FAT-HA or a DHAMMA appears on the letter before the word Allah, the LAAM
in the word Allah is pronounced heavily with a full mouth.

حُدُودُاللّٰه	رَسُولُاللّٰه	مِنَ اللّٰه	اِنَّ اللّٰه
Full mouth if a letter with a DHAMMA is before the word Allah		Full mouth if a letter with a FAT-HA is before the word Allah	

RULE 2: Read with an Empty mouth (TARQEEQ)

When a KASRA appears on the letter before the word Allah, the LAAM in the word Allah,
is pronounced lightly with an empty mouth.

بِاذنِ اللّٰه	بَلِ اللّٰه	اللّٰهُ يُوَفِّقُ	بِسْمِ اللّٰه
Empty mouth if KASRA before the word Allah			

NOTE: This rule applies only when ﻝّ is in the word Allah. The rule does not apply when the لّ is NOT in the word Allah. Example: هُوَ الَّذِيْنَ (Has a Fat-ha, but recited lightly)

THE RULE OF LAAM: 4) LAAM AL LAFDHIL JALALI

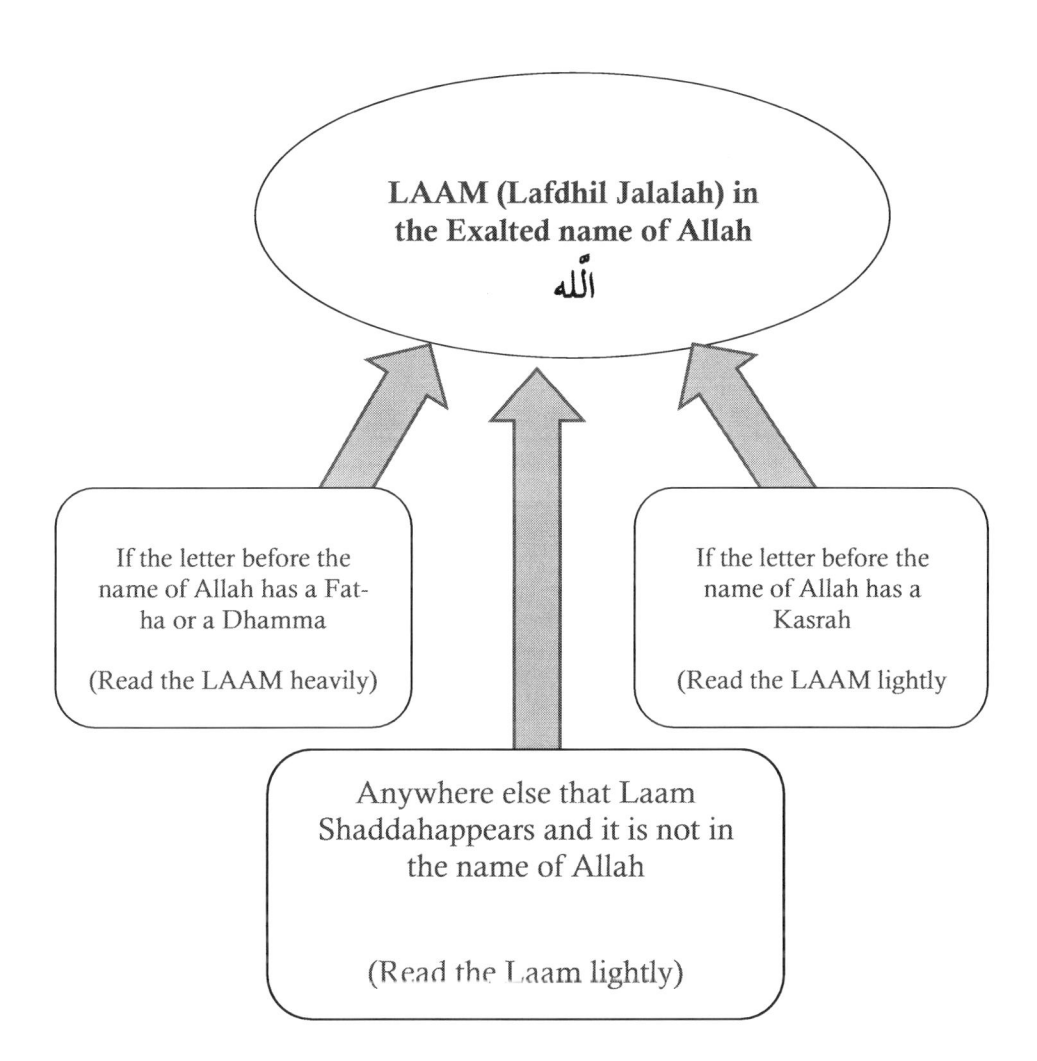

LAAM (Lafdhil Jalalah) in the Exalted name of Allah

اللّه

If the letter before the name of Allah has a Fatha or a Dhamma

(Read the LAAM heavily)

If the letter before the name of Allah has a Kasrah

(Read the LAAM lightly)

Anywhere else that Laam Shaddah appears and it is not in the name of Allah

(Read the Laam lightly)

THE RULES OF NUN SAKIN ن and TANWEEN

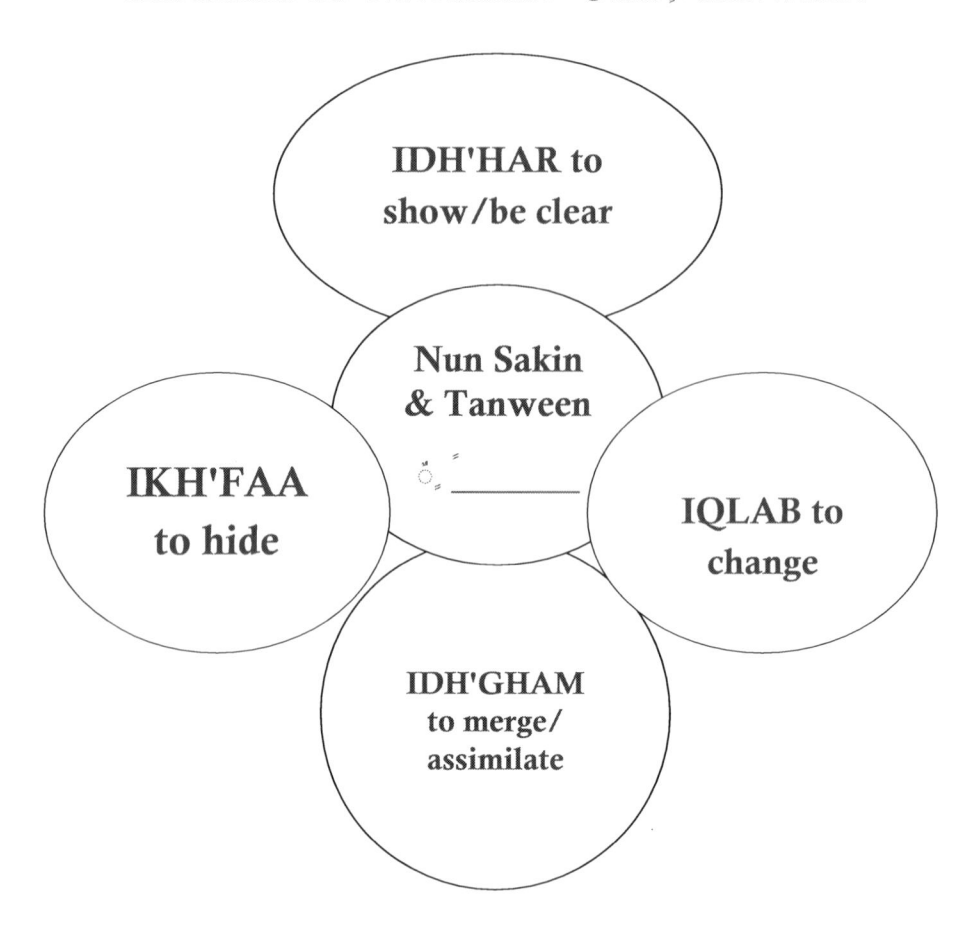

- **IDH'HAR** to show/be clear
- **IKH'FAA** to hide
- **Nun Sakin & Tanween**
- **IQLAB** to change
- **IDH'GHAM** to merge/assimilate

RULES OF NUN SAKIN AND TANWEEN

When letters of the Arabic Alphabet appear after a Nun Sakin or Tanween letter, then there are 4 rules which affect their pronounciation. All the Arabic letters are divided into these 4 rules.

The Nun Sakin and letters with Tanween both have the same sound at the end, the Nunation sound, as in An, In and Un.

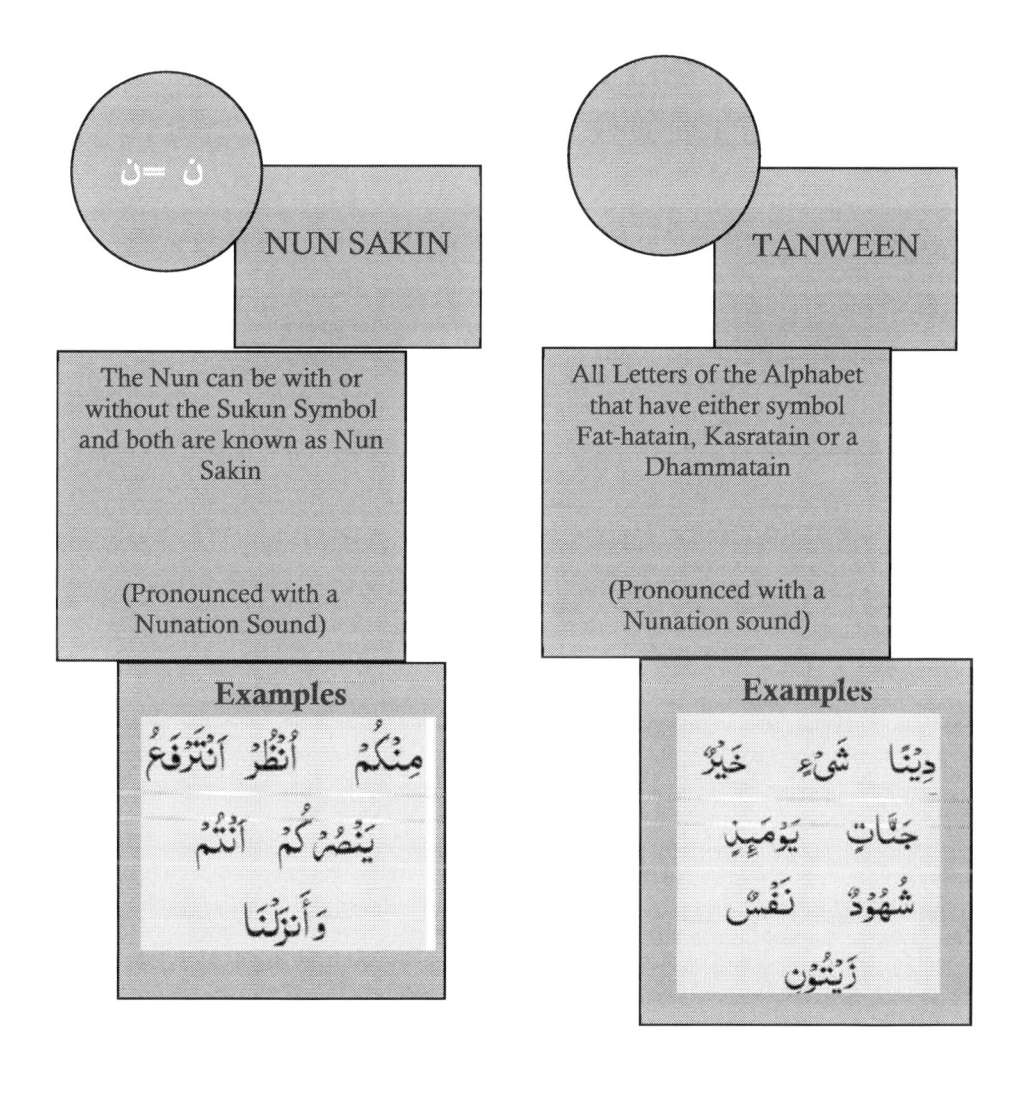

NUN SAKIN

ن = نْ

The Nun can be with or without the Sukun Symbol and both are known as Nun Sakin

(Pronounced with a Nunation Sound)

Examples

مِنْكُمْ   أُنْظُرْ   اِنْتَرَفَعَ

يَنْصُرُكُمْ   اَنْتُمْ

وَأَنْزَلْنَا

TANWEEN

All Letters of the Alphabet that have either symbol Fat-hatain, Kasratain or a Dhammatain

(Pronounced with a Nunation sound)

Examples

دِينًا   شَىْءٍ   خَيْرٌ

جَنَّاتٍ   يَوْمَئِذٍ

شُهُودٌ   نَفْسٌ

زَيْتُونٌ

RULES OF NUN SAKIN AND TANWEEN

Nun Sakin is the Nun with or without the Sukun whereas, Tanween is basically Nun Sakin added to the end of the word. Nun Sakin is a Nun free from any vowel (Fat-ha, Kasra or Dhamma). Tanween is written as a double Fat-ha, Kasra or Dhamma. In Tajweed, Nun Sakin and Tanween are the same. So whatever applies to Nun Sakin, also applies to Tanween.

In continuous recitation of the Holy Qur'an, it is pronounced.

How it is pronounce of pausing or stopping	How it is pronounced in continuous recitation	The Word
كبيرا	كبيرنْ	كبيرًا
فئهْ	فئتنْ	فئةً
حكيمْ	حكيمنْ	حكيمٌ

However, when pausing or stopping, the Nun Sakin is omitted and not pronounced.

نْ

- This is the Nun with or without a Sakin sign
- It's pronounciation depends on the letter which follows it.
- It can be found in continuous reading as well as when one stops
- It is present in all parts of speech of the Arabic language(Noun, Verb and Particle)

- The Tanween appears in connected speech. It is thepronounciation of an additional non-vowelled Nun at the end of a word.
- It is not pronounced when a stop is made at the end of a word
- The Nun is not written, It's sign is either two Fat-ha, two Kasrah or two Dhamma.

THE FOUR RULES OF NUN SAKIN AND TANWEEN

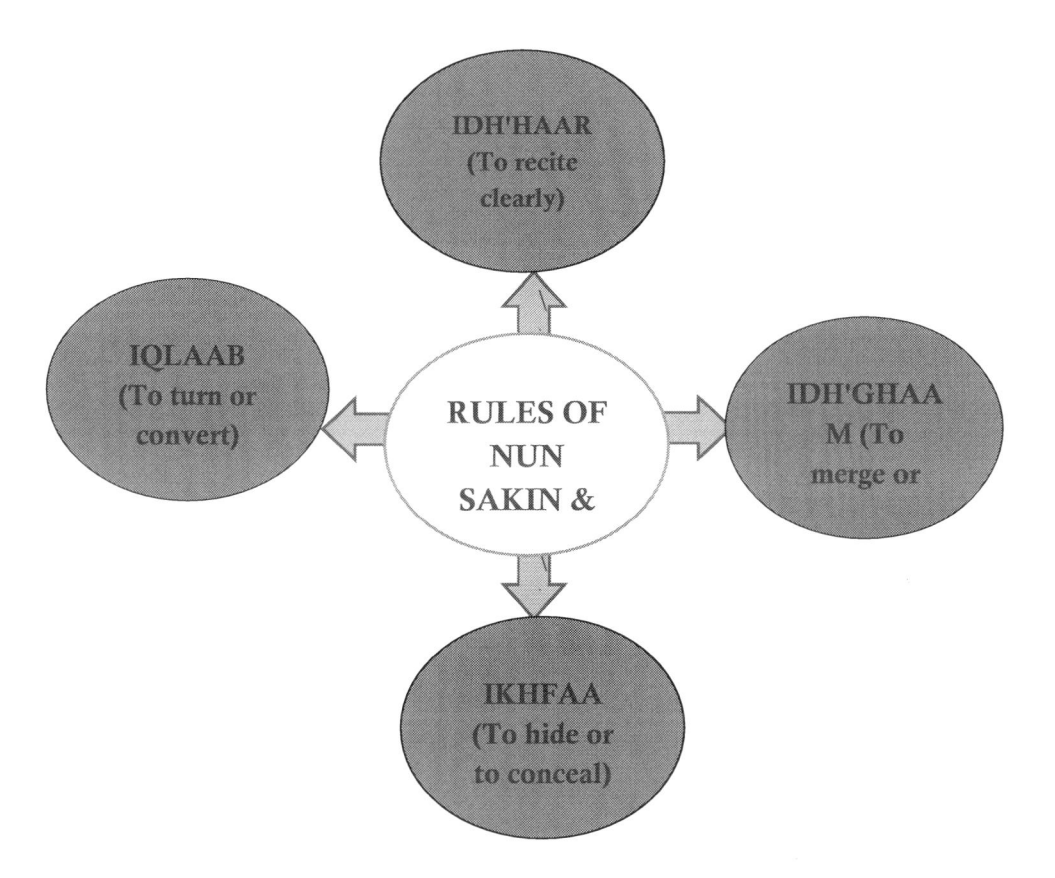

- **RULES OF NUN SAKIN &**
  - **IDH'HAAR** (To recite clearly)
  - **IDH'GHAAM** (To merge or
  - **IKHFAA** (To hide or to conceal)
  - **IQLAAB** (To turn or convert)

THE LETTERS RELATED TO THE NUN SAKIN AND TANWEEN RULES

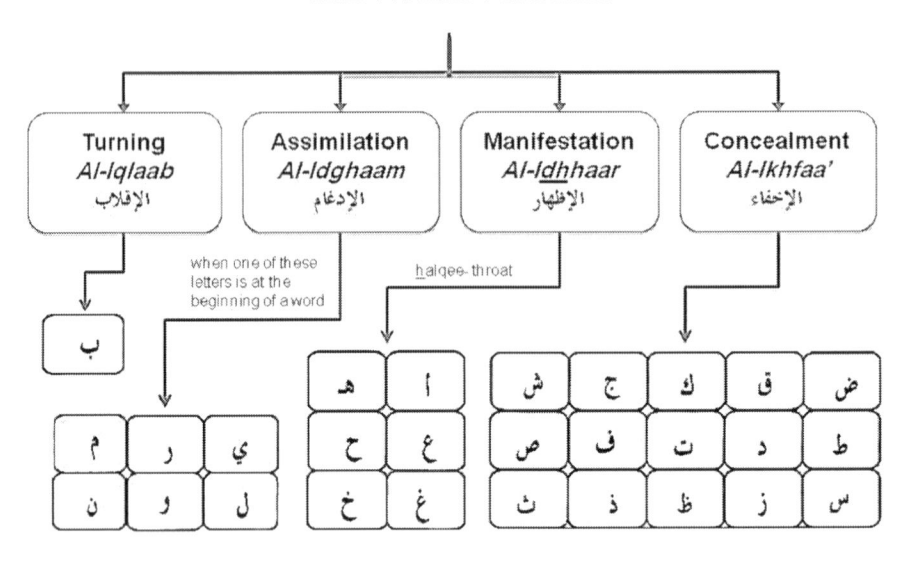

```
                    |
    ┌───────────┬───────────┬───────────┐
Turning    Assimilation  Manifestation  Concealment
Al-Iqlaab   Al-Idghaam    Al-Idhhaar    Al-Ikhfaa'
  الإقلاب    الإدغام       الإظهار        الإخفاء
```

- Turning (Al-Iqlaab): ب — when one of these letters is at the beginning of a word
- Assimilation (Al-Idghaam): م ر ي / ن و ل
- Manifestation (Al-Idhhaar) — halqee-throat: ه ا / ح ع / خ غ
- Concealment (Al-Ikhfaa'): ش ج ك ق ض / ص ف ت د ط / ث ذ ظ ز س

Name	Letters that follow	Ruling
Idh'haar	ءهعحغخ	Nun Sakin or Tanween will be pronounced clearly (NO hiding or merging)
Idh'gaam	ونمي / لر	Nun Sakin will be merged into the following letter and be pronounced with Ghunnah Nun Sakin will be merged into the following letter but no Ghunnah will take place
Ikhfaa	ششسذدجصزتثفظططضكق	Nun Sakin or Tanween will be pronounced with a Ghunnah of 2 harakah. The Ghunnah must be strong because it is hidden.
Iqlab	ب	Nun Sakin or Tanween will be changed to the letter 'meem' and pronounced with Ghunnah of 2 harakah.

NUN SAKIN AND TANWEEN

RULE 1: IDH'HAAR (to say CLEARLY)

NUN SAKIN AND TANWEEN: RULE 1 IDH'HAAR (to say CLEARLY)

a) **WHAT IS THE MEANING OF IDH'HAAR** – To recite the Nun Sakin or Tanween **Clearly**. The Nun sound has to be touched and let go with a slight ghunnah, it should not be extended. The letter following the Nun Sakin or Tanween should also be pronounced clearly with NO change.

Note: Slight Ghunnah to be applied due to the Nun

Nun Sakin example	Tanween example
يَنْحِتُونَ	رَغَداً حَيْثُ

b) **THE DIFFERENT STEPS IN APPLYING IDH'HAAR**
Step 1: Find Nun Sakin or Tanween or Tanween
Step 2: Look at the letter immediately after Nun Sakin or Tanween
Step 3: The letter after must be a Huroof ul Halqi letter (Throat letter)
Step 4: Recite the Nun Sakin or Tanween clearly.

c) **THE LETTERS OF IDH'HAAR** – These are the 6 Throat letters (Huruful Halqiyyah) also known as the Idh'haar letters.

ح	خ	ع	غ	ء	ه

d) **IDENTIFYING & APPLYING IDH'HAAR** – The Nun should NOT be pronounced as if it is carrying a vowel, it should be a quick passing and clear with slight ghunnah, otherwise it will sound as if it is carrying a Shaddah.

أنعمت	وانحر	منغضب	عليم خبير
شيء عليم	نوحاً هدينا	قوما غيرا	عنه
طيرا أبابيل	من أرضكم	من آمن	قوما هاد

NUN SAKIN AND TANWEEN: RULE 1 IDH'HAAR (to say CLEARLY)

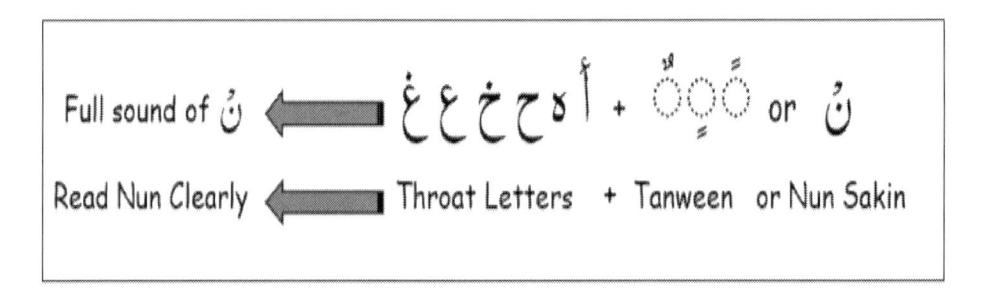

Full sound of نْ ⬅ غ ع خ ح ه أ + ـًـٍـٌ or نْ

Read Nun Clearly ⬅ Throat Letters + Tanween or Nun Sakin

PRACTICING RULE OF IDH'HAAR – Nun is an original Ghunnah letter. Therefore even if it is in Idh'haar, a slight Ghunnah must be applied. The Ghunnah of Idh'haar Nun Sakina is 1 haraka (pause or gap)

<u>READING IDH'HAAR WITH EACH OF THE THROAT LETTERS</u>

كُفُوًا أَحَنٌ	عَذَابٌ أَلِيمٌ	مِنْ أَهْلِ	أ
تَحْتِهَا الْأَنْهَارُ	سَلَامٌ هِيَ	مِنْهُمْ	ه
رِزْقًا حَسَنًا	مِنْ حَوْلِهِمْ	يَنْحِتُونَ	ح
مِنْ خِزْيِ	إِنْ خِفْتُمْ	مُنْخَيْرٌ	خ
وَاسِعٌ عَلِيمٌ	مِنْ عَيْنٍ	أَنْعَمْتَ	ع
عَزِيزٌ غَفُورٌ	قَوْمًا غَيْرَكُمْ	مِنْ غِلٍّ	غ

REMEMBER: An Alif with any of the vowels is also known as a Hamza. Hamza is the King of Letters provided with a seat. Hamza Alif is just a seat of Hamza, therefore we pronounce the Hamza sound because Alif is a silent letter or Maddiya letter. In the Arabic script, when Alif appears without the Hamza, it is a vowel and when it appears with a Hamza, it is a consonant.

NUN SAKIN AND TANWEEN: RULE 2 IDH'GHAAM (To Merge or Join)

IDH'GHAAM LETTERS (Merge or join) يرملون

IDH'GHAAM BILA GHUNNAH (Join without Ghunnah) لر

IDH'GHAAM MA'AL GHUNNAH (Join with Ghunnah) يمون

a) **WHAT IS THE MEANING OF IDH'GHAAM** - To merge or join one letter into the other. We join the letter of Nun Sakin or Tanween with the letter of the following word. In this rule, when pronouncing the letters, you have to hide the sound of Nun Sakin and Tanween, by adding a Nasal sound (Ghunnah)

NOTE: Care must be taken when adding the nasal sound to avoid pulling too much. Idh'ghaam cannot be applied in a single word but must be the joining of 2 separate words, thus making them into one emphasized word. Example:

Nun Sakin example	Tanween example
أمن يُجِيبُ	توابٌ رحيمٌ
Ammayyyujeebu	Tawwa Bur Raheemun
Notice the sound of Nun Sakin and Tanween is hidden and is not pronounced	

b) **THE LETTERS OF IDH'GHAAM** are: نولمري These letters can be remembered by memorising the acronym YARMALUN

c) THE DIFFERENT STEPS IN APPLYING IDH'GHAAM

Step 1: Find Nun Sakin or Tanween

Step 2: Look at the letter immediately after Nun Sakin or Tanween

Step 3: The letter after must be a YARMALUN letter (نولمري)

- ❖ With Ghunnah ونمي
- ❖ Without Ghunnah رل

Step 4: Join or merge the letter of the Nun Sakin or Tanween with the Yarmalun letter of the following word.

d) THE DIFFERENT TYPES OF IDH'GHAAM – There are two types of Idh'gham. The type of Idh'ghaam pronounced depends, on which letter from the letters of Yarmalun, follows the Nun Sakin and Tanween.

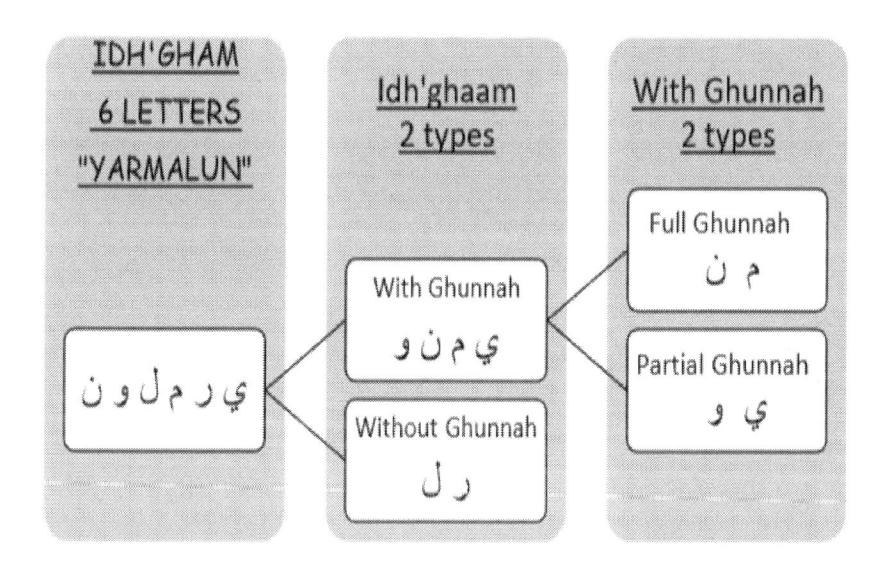

IDH'GHAM 6 LETTERS "YARMALUN" ي ر م ل و ن	Idh'ghaam 2 types	With Ghunnah 2 types
	With Ghunnah ي م ن و	Full Ghunnah م ن
	Without Ghunnah ر ل	Partial Ghunnah ي و

TYPE 1 – IDH'GHAAM MA'AL GHUNNAH – Merging with Nasal Sound – LETTERS يمنو also known in acronym as YAMNU letters

Whenever a word ends with Nun Sakin or Tanween, and the next word starts with the letters Ya, Nun, Meem or Waw, then these letters are pronounced in one of the following two manners:

❖ Full Ghunnah - Letters –من Complete Merging letters which when they appear, will have a Shaddah and are pronounced from the nose (with Ghunnah – 2 counts)

| جزاء من | من نطفة |

❖ Partial Ghunnah – Letters وي – Incomplete Merging letters which are literally hummed. Sometimes these appear with NO Shaddah sign

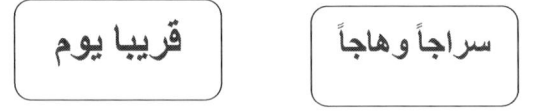

| قريبا يوم | سراجاً وهاجاً |

NUN SAKIN AND TANWEEN: RULE 2 IDH'GHAAM (To Merge or Join)

TYPE 1 – IDH'GHAAM MA'AL GHUNNAH – Merging with Ghunnah of 2 harakah

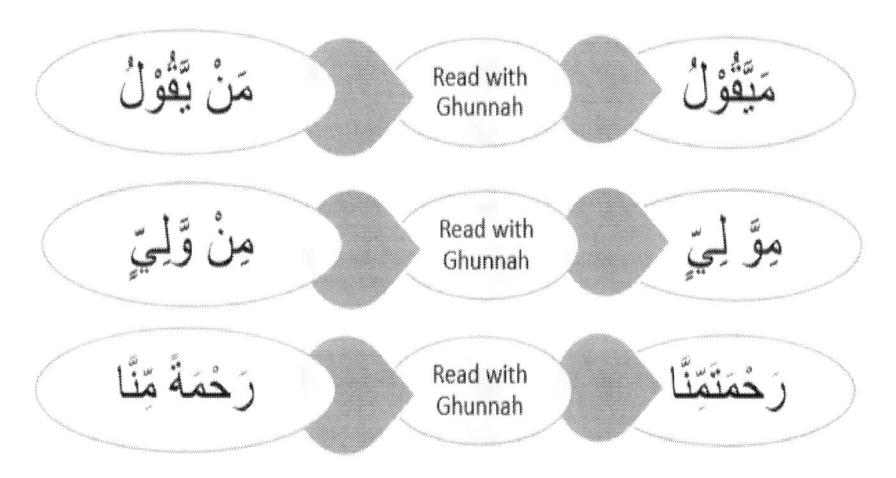

مَنْ يَقُوْلُ	Read with Ghunnah	مَيَّقُوْلُ
مِنْ وَلِيٍّ	Read with Ghunnah	مِوَّلِيٍّ
رَحْمَةً مِّنَّا	Read with Ghunnah	رَحْمَتَمِّنَّا

TYPE 2 – IDH'GHAAM BILA GHUNNAH – Merging without Nasal Sound - LETTERS

ل ر - Whenever a word ends with Nun Sakin or Tanween, and the next word starts with the letters Laam and Ra, then the letters Laam and Ra are pronounced with a Shaddah and both the Nun Sakin and Tanween are dropped completely. **The Nun is hidden.** There is no trace of Nun in the recitation and there is NO Ghunnah (Nasal sound)

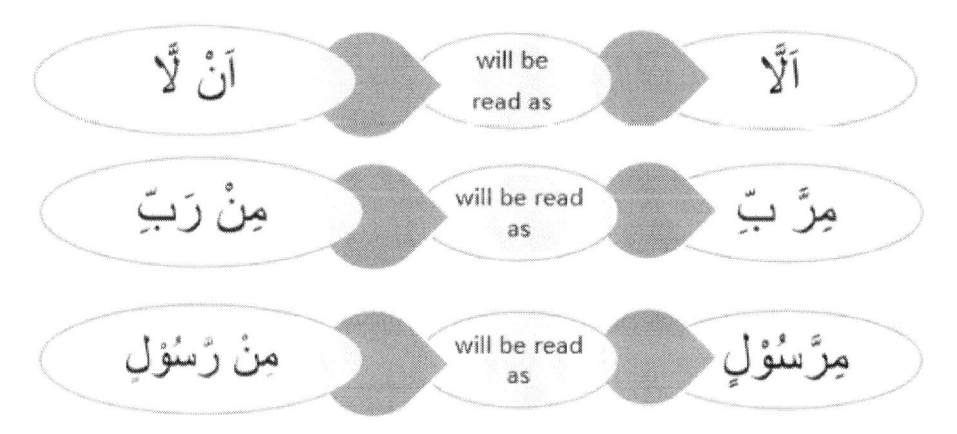

اَنْ لَّا	will be read as	اَلَّا
مِنْ رَبٍّ	will be read as	مِرَّبٍّ
مِنْ رَسُوْلٍ	will be read as	مِرَّسُوْلٍ

e) IDENTIFYING & APPLYING IDH'GHAAM

Idh'ghaam Ma'al Ghunnah – Merging with Nasal Sound (Ghunnah)

بعض يتسآءلون	فمن يعمل	ي
من مارج	من مثله	م
سدًا ومن خلفهم	لهب وتبّ	و
إن نحن	من نشاء	ن

Idh'ghaam Bila Ghunnah – Merging without Nasal Sound (Ghunnah)

غفوراً رحيما	من ربك	ر
لم يكن له	كل لمّا	ل

f) EXCEPTIONS TO THE IDH'GHAAM RULE

In these words, rule of Idh'ghaam is not applied as the Yarmalun letter appears after the Nun Sakin and Tanween in one word and not in two separate words. This is known as IZHAAR MUTLAQ. Ghunnah of harakah is applied.

قنوانٌ	صنوانٌ	بنيانٌ	الدنيا
Qinnwaanun	Sinnwaanun	Bunnyaanun	Dunnya

NUN SAKIN AND TANWEEN

RULE 3: IKHFAA (to Hide or to Conceal)

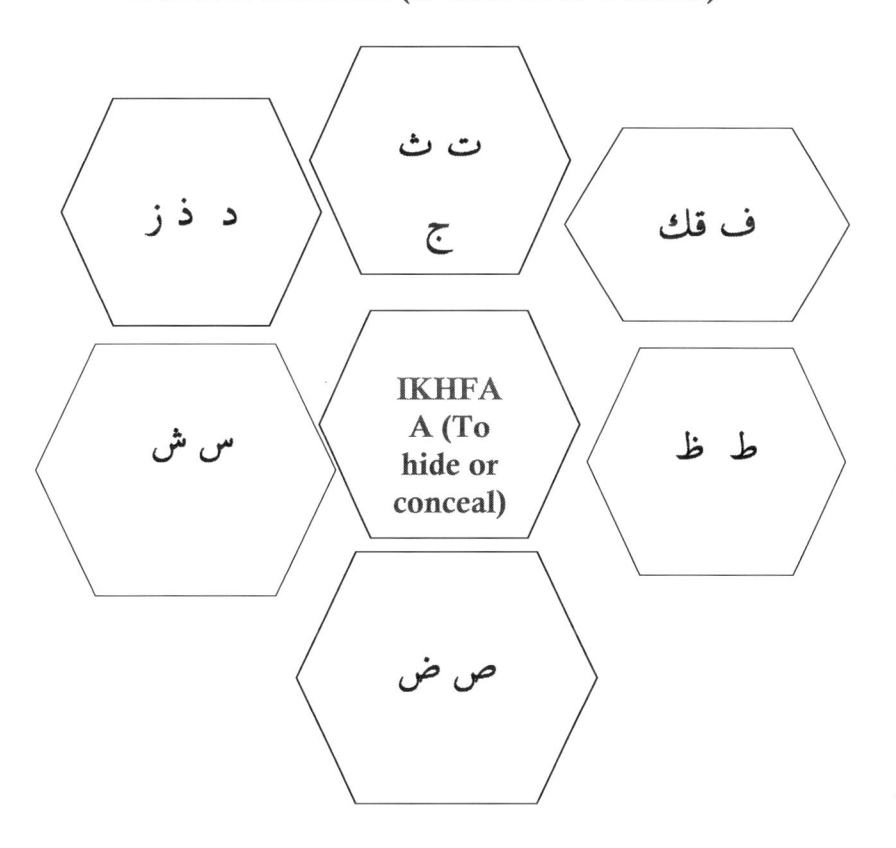

- ت ث ج
- د ذ ز
- ف ق ك
- **IKHFAA (To hide or conceal)**
- ط ظ
- س ش
- ص ض

NUN SAKIN AND TANWEEN: RULE 3 IKHFAA (To Hide or Conceal)

a) **WHAT IS THE MEANING OF IKHFAA** - Whenever Nun Sakin and Tanween precede one of the fifteen Ikhfaa letters, then the actual sound of Nun is concealed or covered to a point where only its nasal sound is evident and is stressed for the count of two.

Question: What is hiding or concealed in Ikhfaa

Both Nun Sakin and the Tanween end with the Nun Sound. In Ikhfaa, the full Nun sound is NOT pronounced. We partly hide the makharij of the Nun sound and hold it (do Ghunnah for two counts), then it continues, behind the makharij of the Ikhfaa letter that is coming up. **Example**:

Notice when you read as Antum, the tip of the tongue touches the upper palate, but when you hide the full Nun and do Ghunnah, the tongue is floating, as it prepares to say the letter Ta, which is the next letter	أَنْتُمْ Read as Annn Tum And not Antum

b) **THE LETTERS OF IKHFAA** - 15 Letters - The letters that are in shaded boxes are heavy letters

ك	ق	ف	ظ	ط	ض	ص	ش	س	ز	ذ	د	ج	ث	ت

An easy way to remember the Ikhfaa letters. All the 28 letters of the Arabic alphabet are divided into the 4 rules of Nun Sakin and Tanween, therefore we remove all the letters of Idh'haar, Idh'ghaam and Iqlab, the rest are all Ikhfaa letters

هءغععخح	IDH'HAAR – 6 Throat Letters (HurufulHalqiyya)
نوملري	IDH'GHAAM – 6 Yarmalun letters
ب	IQLAB – 1 Qalb letter

كقفظططصضشسزذجثت	IKHFAA – All the rest of the Arabic Alphabet – 15 letters

NUN SAKIN AND TANWEEN: RULE 3 IKHFAA (To Hide or Conceal)

c) The Different Steps In Applying Ikhfaa

Step 1: Find Nun Sakin or Tanween
Step 2: Look at the letter immediately after Nun Sakin or Tanween
Step 3: The letter after must be an Ikhfaa letter (from the 15 letters)

- heavy letters, read with heavy Ikhfaa صضططظق
- 10 light letters, read with light Ikhfaa تثجدذزسشفك

Step 4: The full sound of Nun is hidden and we partially pronounce it and hold for 2 counts (ghunnah), then join it with the Ikhfaa letter that follows it.

d) THE DIFFERENT TYPES OF IKHFAA - 2 Types

- Heavy Ikhfaa – If the letter after Nun Sakin and Tanween, is a letter of Ikhfaa and a heavy letter, recite the Ikhfaa heavily
- Light Ikhfaa – The rest of the Ikhfaa letters are read lightly.

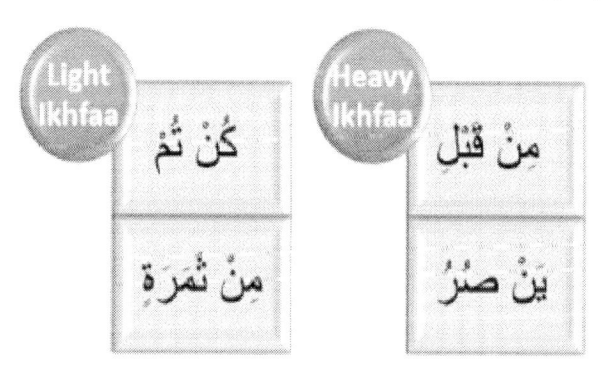

Light Ikhfaa	Heavy Ikhfaa
كُنْ ثُمَّ	مِنْ قَبْلِ
مِنْ ثَمَرَةٍ	يَنْ صُرُ

e) **IDENTIFYING & APPLYING IKHFAA**

Light Ikhfaa		Heavy Ikhfaa	
أَنْذَرْنَاكُمْ	فَمَنْ شَآءَ	مَنْ طَغَىٰ	يَنْظُرُ
يَوْمَئِذٍ شَأْنٌ	وَكَأْسًا دِهَاقًا	كُتُبٌ قَيِّمَةٌ	عَذَابًا قَرِيبًا
تَنْزِيلَ	أَنْفُسِهِمْ	عَنْ ضَيْفِ	شَيْءٍ قَدِيرٌ

NUN SAKIN AND TANWEEN: RULE 4 IQLAB (To Change or Convert)

a) **WHAT IS THE MEANING OF IQLAB** – To change or convert. The Nun Sakin or Tanween is converted into a Meem. Therefore, one letter changes into another.

NOTE: The 'MEEM' here refers to the small 'MEEM' between or on top of a word. It is always very small and shaded. In most copies of the Qur'an, a small 'MEEM' is written above Nun or Tanween, as a reminder of the rule.
Example:

NUN SAKIN	TANWEEN
من بعد	سميعا بصيرا
MimmmBa'di	SamiiAmmBaseeraa

b) **THE DIFFERENT STEPS IN APPLYING IQLAB** Step 1: Find Nun Sakin or Tanween

Step 2: Look at the letter immediately after Nun Sakin or Tanween

Step 3: The letter after must be the letter baa ب

Step 4: Convert the Nun Sakin or Tanween into a Meem. Pronounce the Meem with a
Nasal sound and hold the Meem sound for 2 counts.

c) **THE LETTER OF IQLAB** is the letter baa ب when it appears after the Nun Sakin or Tanween.

d) **IDENTIFYING & APPLYING IQLAB IN THE QUR'AN** – In the rule of Iqlab, the letter Meem (م) hides in the letter Be (ب) in such a way, that the lips do not meet, they get near each other and a very narrow space will be left, sufficient for a very thin paper to pass through.

أن تبسل نفس بما كسبت	AnToobsalaNafsummbimaaKasabat

NUN SAKIN AND TANWEEN: RULE 4 IQLAB (To Change or Convert)

In the rule of Al Qalb, the lips should not entirely be pressed together, this will allow the Meem sound to come through the nasal passage. The mouth should be prepared to say the Baa after sounding the Meem for two counts.

IMPORTANT TO NOTE: Do not mix up the two types of Meem that appear on top of the letters. The full shaped Meem (م) indicates Iqlab or change and the cut Meem (مـ) indicates a compulsory stop.

EXAMPLES:

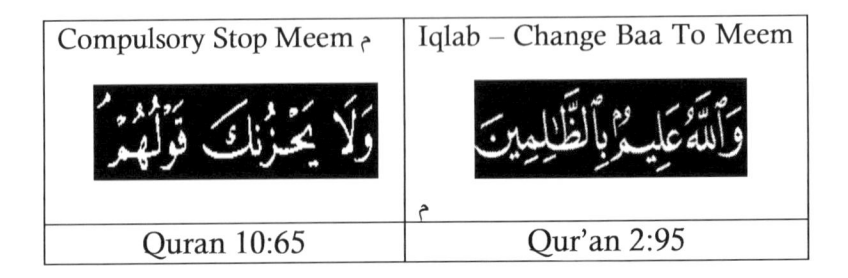

Compulsory Stop Meem مـ	Iqlab – Change Baa To Meem
وَلَا يَحْزُنْكَ قَوْلُهُمْ	وَاللَّهُ عَلِيمٌ بِالظَّالِمِينَ
Quran 10:65	Qur'an 2:95

مِنْ بَعْدُ	مِنْ بُيُوتِهِنَّ	مَنْ بَخِلَ
مِنْ بَنِي إِسْرَائِيلَ		مِنْ بَقْلِهَا
لَنَسْفَعًا بِالنَّاصِيَةِ	أَبَدًا بِمَا	نَفْسٍ بِمَا
مُطْمَئِنٌّ بِالْإِيمَانِ		مُنْفَطِرٌ بِهِ
آيَاتٌ بَيِّنَاتٌ		لَيًّا بِأَلْسِنَتِهِمْ
قَرْيَةٍ بَطِرَتْ		عَلَىٰ بَيِّنَةٍ

NUN SAKIN AND TANWEEN SUMMARY

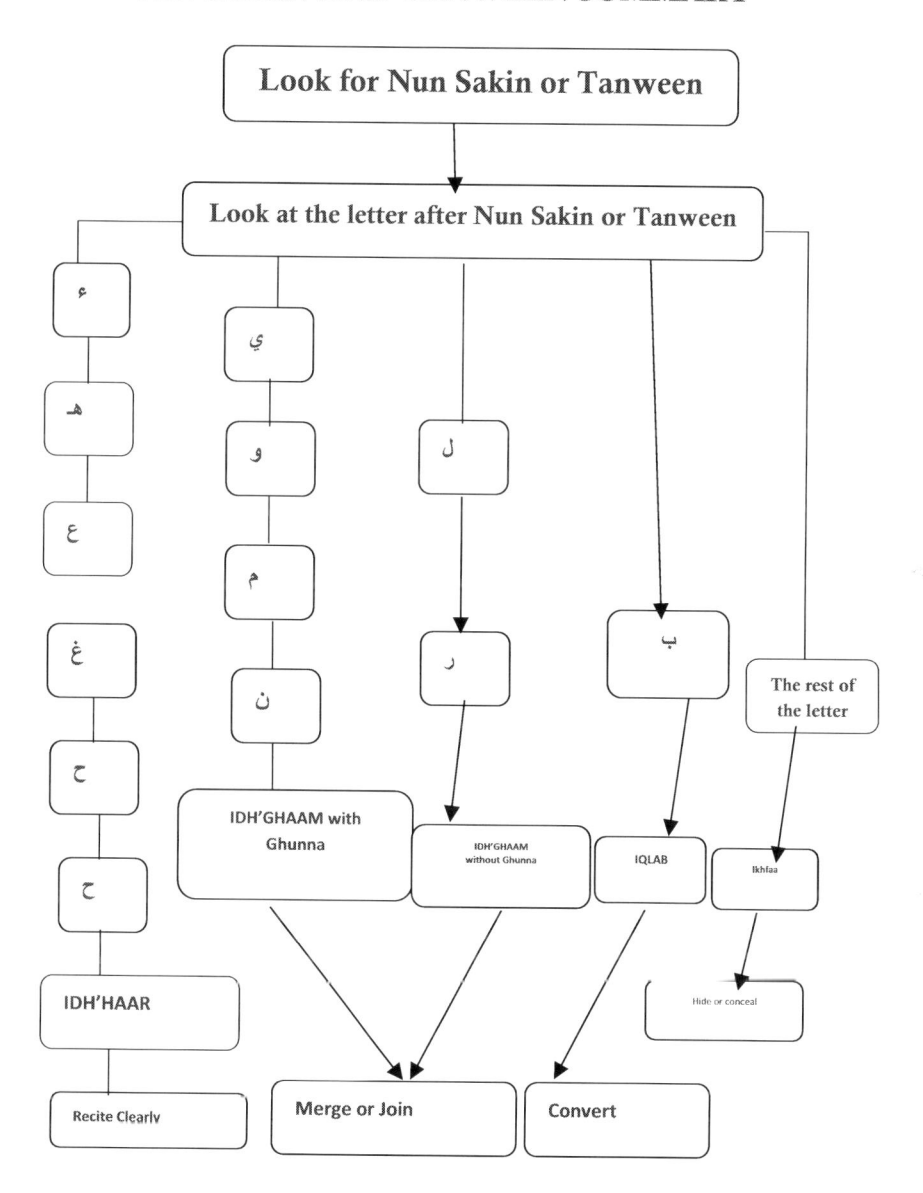

```
                    Look for Nun Sakin or Tanween
                                │
                                ▼
              Look at the letter after Nun Sakin or Tanween
```

Letters branching:

- ء ، هـ ، ع ، غ ، ح ، خ → **IDH'HAAR** → Recite Clearly
- ي ، و ، م ، ن → **IDH'GHAAM with Ghunna** → Merge or Join
- ل ، ر → **IDH'GHAAM without Ghunna** → Merge or Join
- ب → **IQLAB** → Convert
- The rest of the letters → **Ikhfaa** → Hide or conceal

RULES OF NUN SHADDAH AND MEEM SHADDAH

Nun Shaddah and Meem Shaddah are also known as Nun and Meem Mushaddadah (meaning a doubled letter or letters bearing a Shaddah)

When these two letters appear with a Shaddah sign in any word, a Ghunnah has to be applied for a period of 2 counts. This is because the Shaddah is already a double letter + the Ghunnah (2 counts).

The Ghunnah is applied to Nun and Meem Mushaddadah, whether they occur in the middle or the end of a word, in continuous reading or when stopping and in all parts of speech.

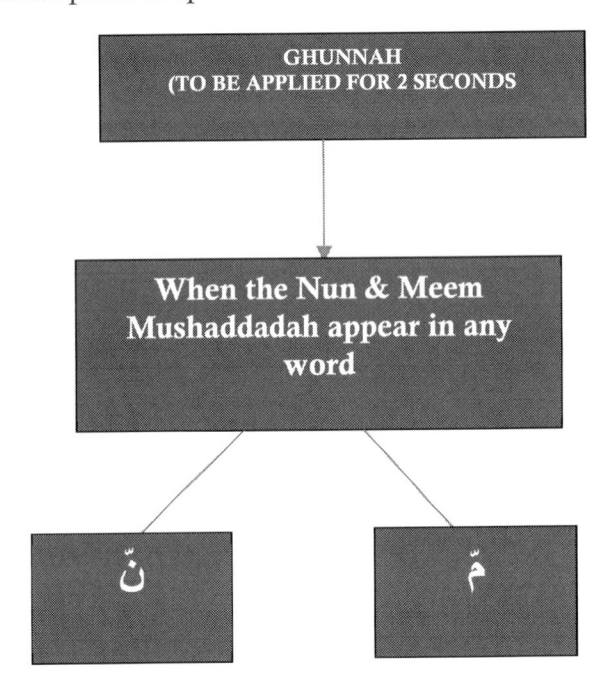

```
           ┌─────────────────────────────┐
           │        GHUNNAH              │
           │ (TO BE APPLIED FOR 2 SECONDS│
           └──────────────┬──────────────┘
                          │
                          ▼
           ┌─────────────────────────────┐
           │   When the Nun & Meem       │
           │   Mushaddadah appear in any │
           │           word              │
           └──────┬───────────────┬──────┘
                  │               │
            ┌─────┴────┐     ┌────┴─────┐
            │    نّ    │     │    مّ    │
            └──────────┘     └──────────┘
```

WHAT IS GHUNNAH?

a) Ghunnah is applied when Nun and Meem have a Shaddah.
b) Ghunnah is a sound emitted from the Nasal Passage, without any function of the tongue.
c) This is when a certain sound is held in the nasal cavity (Nasalisation) for a length that is longer than the short harakah (about 2 beats)
d) Professional Qur'an reciters pay much attention to these sounds.
e) Application of Ghunnah by the reciter, adds beauty to the recitation.

NOTE: Ghunnah is divided into 4 parts:

- In م and ن, the Ghunnah is applied for 2 counts (2 Harakah)
- In م and ن, in Idh'haar the Ghunnah is applied for 1 count (1 Harakah)
- In م and ن, in Idh'ghaam the Ghunnah is applied for 2 counts (2 Harakah)
- In م and ن, with Short vowels, the Ghunnah is applied for ½ count (1/2 Harakah)

RULES OF NUN SHADDAH AND MEEM SHADDAH

EXAMPLES: The letters Nun and Meem have original Nasal sounds. Notice the Meem Shaddah and Noon Shaddah are stretched through the Nasal cavity and not the tongue.

إِنَّ — Read as In....na (Not Inna)

ثُمَّ — Read as Thum....ma (Not Thumma)

Meem with Tashdeed		Nun with Tashdeed	
قَوْمًا مَّا	فَلَمَّ	مِنَّ	إِنَّكَ
Qaw-mammmm-maa	Fa-lammmm-ma	Minnnna	Innnn-na-ka
نَفْسٌ مَّا	عَبْدًا مِّنْ	إِنَّ الَّذِينَ	جَهَنَّمَ
Naf-summmm-maa	Ab-dammmm-min	Innnn-nal-ladhii-na	Ja-hannnn-nama
بَيِّنَةٌ مِّنْ	سِحْرٌ مُّبِينٌ	أَعْيُنِ النَّاسِ	كَأَنَّكَ
Bay-yinatummmm-min	Sih-rummmm-mubeen	A'a-yuninnnn-naasi	Ka-annnn-naka
وَهُم مُّسْتَكْبِرُونَ	فَأَمَّهُ	وَلَيَمَسَّنَّكُم	مَسَّ
فِي الْأُمِّيِّينَ	إِمَامٍ مُّبِينٍ	وَالنَّجْمُ	لَنَرْجُمَنَّكُم
ضَلَالٍ مُّبِينٍ	دَمَّرَ	عَنِ النَّعِيمِ	يَكُونُ النَّاسُ

THE RULES OF MEEM SAKIN مْ

Rule	Meaning	Formula
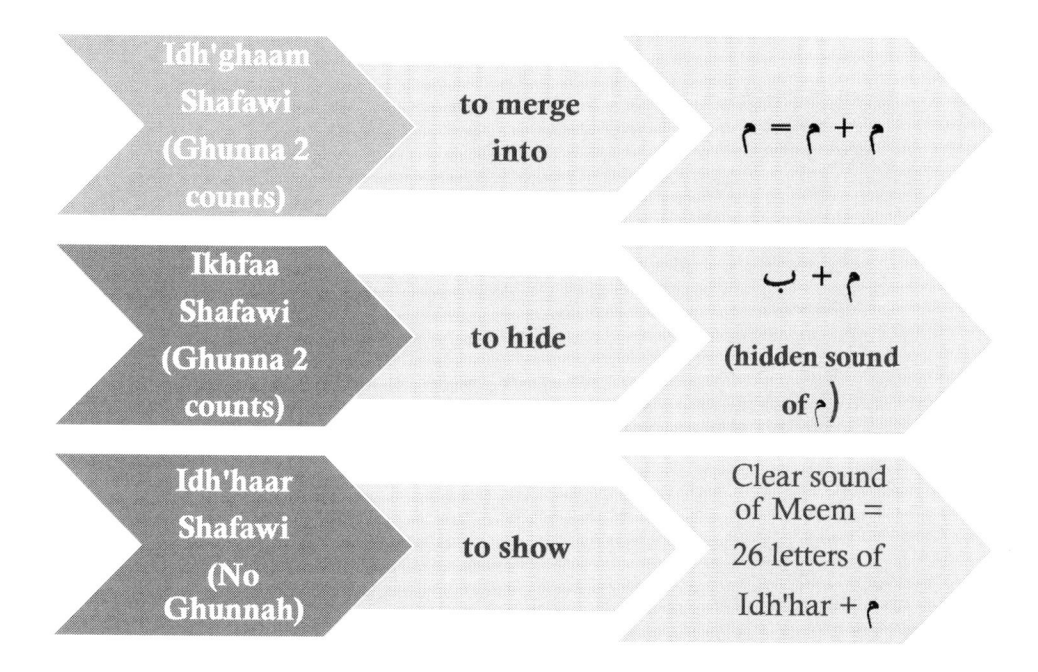 Idh'ghaam Shafawi (Ghunna 2 counts)	to merge into	م + م = م
Ikhfaa Shafawi (Ghunna 2 counts)	to hide	م + ب (hidden sound of م)
Idh'haar Shafawi (No Ghunnah)	to show	Clear sound of Meem = 26 letters of Idh'har + م

THE RULES OF MEEM SAKIN م

Meem Sakin is simply a Meem with a Sukun sign. The Meem Sakin can appear with or without a Sukun symbol.

Example:

Meem Sakin with a sukun	الحمدُ	ALHAMDU
Meem Sakin without a sukun	ترميهم بحجارة	TARMEEHIMMM BIHIJARATIN

The pronounciation of the Meem Sakin depends on the letter which follows it. There are 3 rules that take place when certain letters appear after the Meem Sakin.

a) Idghamshafawi
b) Ikhfaashafawi **shafawi** means articulated from
c) Idh'har shafawi   the two lips

THE 3 RULES OF MEEM SAKIN

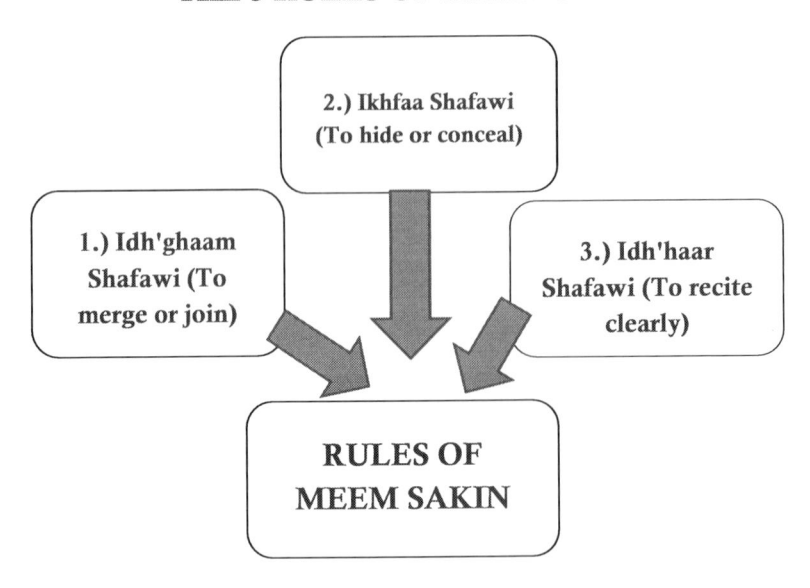

- 1.) Idh'ghaam Shafawi (To merge or join)
- 2.) Ikhfaa Shafawi (To hide or conceal)
- 3.) Idh'haar Shafawi (To recite clearly)

→ RULES OF MEEM SAKIN

MEEM SAKIN: RULE 1 - IDH'GHAAM SHAFAWI (To merge or join)

f) **WHAT IS THE MEANING OF IDH'GHAAM SHAFAWI** – Idh'ghaam means to merge or join. When Meem Sakin is followed by another Meem carrying a vowel, instead of reading 2 meems, they merge into each other and the sound of meem is held in a ghunnah. There is a difference between Idh'ghaam and Idh'ghaamShafawi. **Example**:

IDH'GHAAM SHAFAWI Meem Sakin followed another Meem	IDH'GHAAM Nun Sakin followed by the letter Meem
ولكم ماكسبتم	ما ماء
Ghunnah is applied to both the above for 2 harakah, Meem Shaddah + Meem Sakin = 2 counts of ghunnah	

g) **THE DIFFERENT STEPS IN APPLYING IDH'GHAAM SHAFAWI**
Step 1: Find Meem Sakin

Step 2: Look at the letter immediately after Meem Sakin

Step 3: The letter after must be the letter Meem: م

Step 4: The first Meem is assimilated (or disappears) into the second Meem. The second Meem takes on a Shaddah during pronounciation, indicating Idh'ghaam. Nasal sound (Ghunnah) is applied with the lips closed for 2 counts.

h) **IDENTIFYING & APPLYING IDH'GHAAM SHAFAWI –**

كم من	كمن
لكم ما	لكم ما
إليكم مرسلون	إليكم مرسلون
إنهم معكم	إنهم معكم

MEEM SAKIN: RULE 2 - IKHFAA SHAFAWI (To hide or conceal)

a) **WHAT IS THE MEANING OF IKHFAA SHAFAWI** – Ikhfaa means to hide or conceal – to partly hide or conceal the sound of Meem Sakin in the nose. When Meem Sakin مْ is followed by the letter Ba, the letter Meem مْ is concealed by it and a nasal sound is retained. The Meem is hidden with Ghunnah (Nasal Sound) to a count of two. The lips should not be completely closed to avoid making the evident. There is a difference between Ikhfaa and Ikhfaa Shafawi.

Example:

IKHFAA SHAFAWI Meem Sakin followed by the letter Ba	IKHFAA Ikhfaa in the rules of Nun Sakin
ترميهم بحجارة	منفكين

b) **THE DIFFERENT STEPS IN APPLYING IKHFAA SHAFAWI**
Step 1: Find Meem Sakin
Step 2: Look at the letter immediately after Meem Sakin
Step 3: The letter after must be the letter Ba: ب
Step 4: The Meem is concealed or hidden by the Ba and the word is pronounced with a nasal sound (Ghunnah) held for 2 counts, with a paper thin gap between the lips.

c) **IDENTIFYING & APPLYING IKHFAA SHAFAWI** – The rule applied for all the words below is the same and Ghunnah of 2 counts will be applied as we partly hide the sound of Meem Sakin in our nose (flattening the lips).

أنتم به	إهم بادون	رهم هم
أمدا بعيدا Read		من بعد Read as
أمدم بعيدا		مم بعد

IMPORTANT NOTE: - Do not confuse the small Meem of Iqlab مْ with the Baa and Meem Sakin of Ikhfaa Shafawi.

MEEM SAKIN: RULE 3 – IDH'HAAR SHAFAWI (To recite clearly)

a) **WHAT IS THE MEANING OF IDH'HAAR SHAFAWI** – Idh'haar means to recite clearly – to show. When Meem Sakin is followed by any of the 26 letters (apart from Ba and Meem), then the Meem Sakin is pronounced clearly and distinctly from its makharij, without the nasal sound (ghunnah) There is a difference between Idh'haar and Idh'haarShafawi. Example:

IDH'HAAR SHAFAWI Meem Sakin followed by any of the 26 letters (apart from Ba & Meem)	IDH'HAAR Idh'haar in the rules of Nun Sakin
فجعلهم كعصف	منحا

b) **THE DIFFERENT STEPS IN APPLYING IDH'HAAR SHAFAWI**
Step 1: Find Meem Sakin
Step 2: Look at the letter immediately after Meem Sakin
Step 3: The letter after must be any of the 26 letters of the alphabet, except for the letter Ba: ب (which falls under the rule of IkhfaaShafawi) and the letter Meem: م (which falls under the rule of Idh'ghaamShafawi)
Step 4: The Meem is recited clearly, without a nasal sound (no ghunnah)

c) **IDENTIFYING & APPLYING IDH'HAAR SHAFAWI:** When pronouncing the letter Meem Sakin with Idh'har note the following:
1. It should not be given a sound as if it is carrying a vowel. A clear pronounciation and a quick passing of the letter Meem Sakin should be observed, otherwise it will sound as if it is carrying a Shaddah.
2. If the letter Meem is followed by either Fa or Waw extra effort should be made to retain Idh'har, because the letter Meem easily becomes hidden next to the letter Fa and is easily merged in the letter Waw.

ألم تر	الحمد	لكمجزاء	سلهمأيهم	وهم سالمون

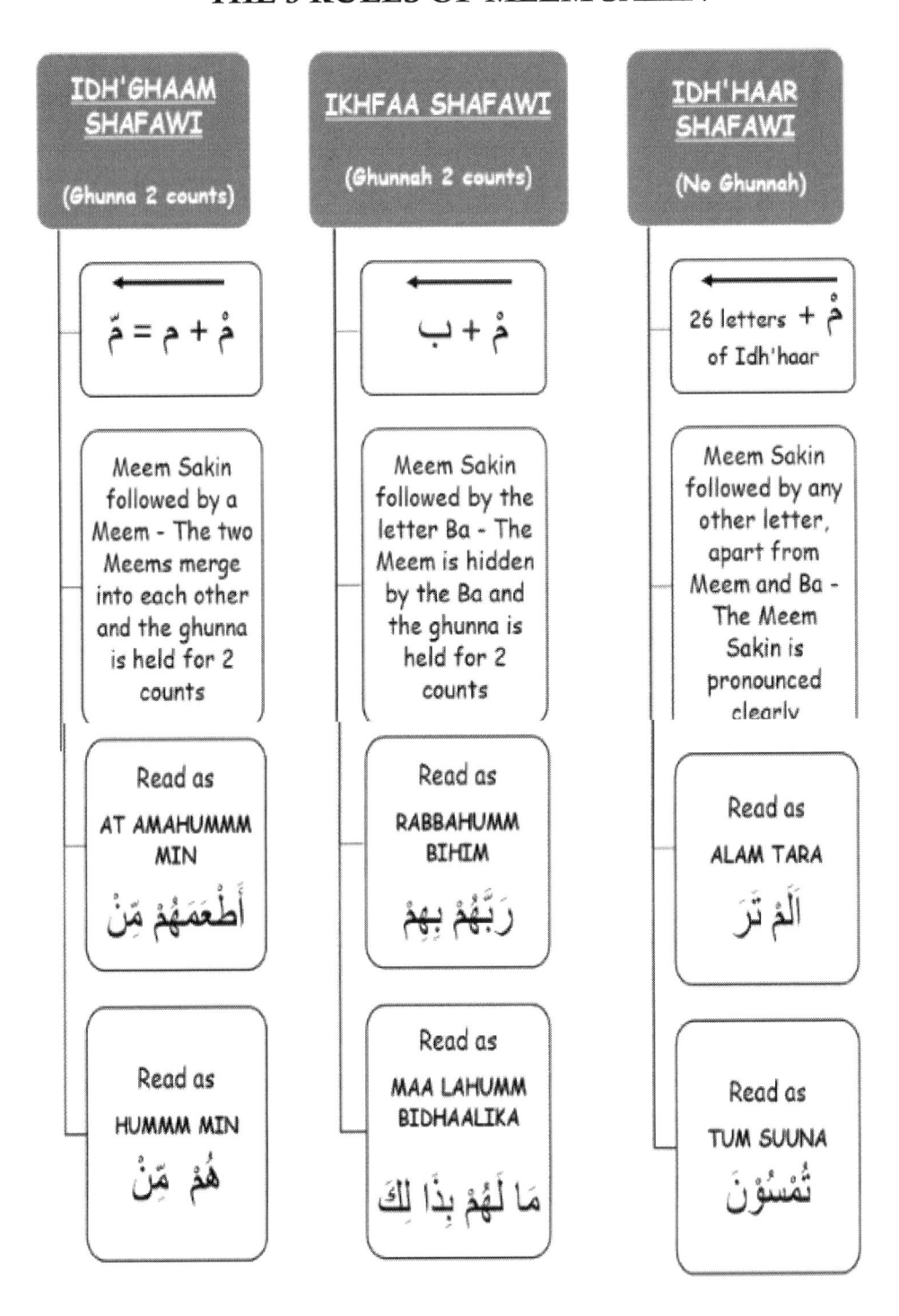

THE 3 RULES OF MEEM SAKIN

IDH'GHAAM SHAFAWI
(Ghunna 2 counts)

مْ + م = مّ

Meem Sakin followed by a Meem - The two Meems merge into each other and the ghunna is held for 2 counts

Read as
AT AMAHUMMM MIN

أَطْعَمَهُمْ مِنْ

Read as
HUMMM MIN

هُمْ مِنْ

IKHFAA SHAFAWI
(Ghunnah 2 counts)

مْ + ب

Meem Sakin followed by the letter Ba - The Meem is hidden by the Ba and the ghunna is held for 2 counts

Read as
RABBAHUMM BIHIM

رَبَّهُمْ بِهِمْ

Read as
MAA LAHUMM BIDHAALIKA

مَا لَهُمْ بِذَا لِكَ

IDH'HAAR SHAFAWI
(No Ghunnah)

مْ + 26 letters of Idh'haar

Meem Sakin followed by any other letter, apart from Meem and Ba - The Meem Sakin is pronounced clearly

Read as
ALAM TARA

أَلَمْ تَرَ

Read as
TUM SUUNA

تُمْسُوْنَ

THE RULES OF MEEM SAKIN IN BRIEF

1. **IDH'GHAM of Meem Sakin–** If after Meem Sakin, comes a Meem, there will be Idh'gham of the lips (Idh'gham Ash Shafawi - Both Meems will Assimilate into each other) with a nasal sound.

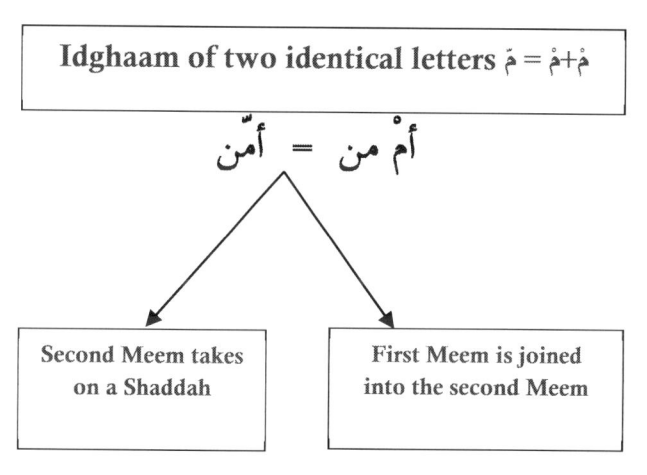

Idghaam of two identical letters مْ = مْ+مْ

أمْ من = أمّن

- Second Meem takes on a Shaddah
- First Meem is joined into the second Meem

2. **IKHFAA of Meem Sakin–** If after Meem Sakin, comes a Ba, there will be Ikhfaa of the lips (Ikhfaa Ash Shafawi). Ikhfaa literally means to hide, the qualities of Meem are concealed and instead a nasal sound is produced.

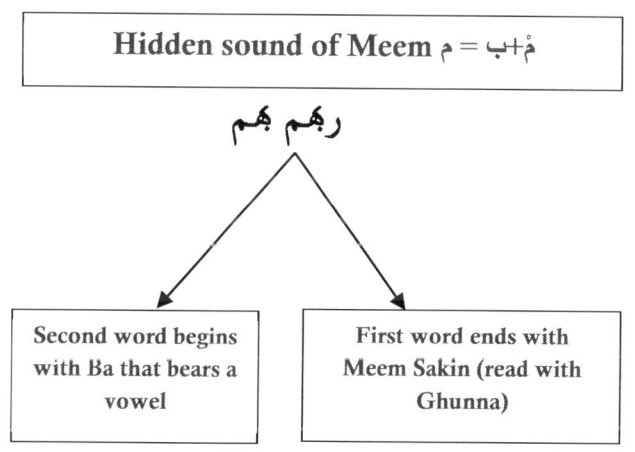

Hidden sound of Meem م = مْ+ب

ربّهم بهم

- Second word begins with Ba that bears a vowel
- First word ends with Meem Sakin (read with Ghunna)

3. **IDH'HAR of Meem Sakin–** If after Meem Sakin, comes any letter besides Ba or Meem, there will be Idh'har of the lips (Idh'har Ash Shafawi - to make clear) and the Meem Sakin will be pronounced normally, without a nasal sound (no ghunnah)

Clear sound of Meem 26 letters of Idh'har مْ

THE RULES OF OTHER IDH'GHAM

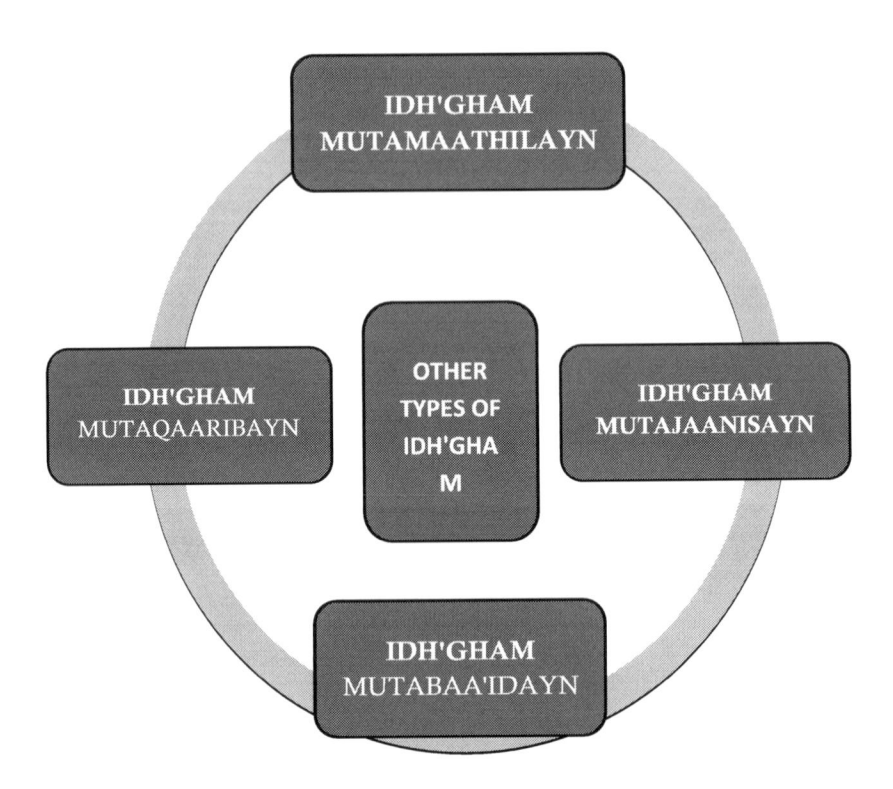

- IDH'GHAM MUTAMAATHILAYN
- IDH'GHAM MUTAQAARIBAYN
- OTHER TYPES OF IDH'GHAM
- IDH'GHAM MUTAJAANISAYN
- IDH'GHAM MUTABAA'IDAYN

THE RULES OF OTHER IDH'GHAM

Idh'gham means to merge, blend, assimilate or absorb. It is the merging of a letter carrying a Sukun into the following letter, which carries a vowel, so that they become one. The letter accompanied by a Sukun is omitted and the following letter is then pronounced with a Shaddah. This merging can be either complete or incomplete:

> **Complete merging or Idh'gham al-Kaamil** implies a complete blending of a letter into the letter it follows, to a point where there is no trace of the first letter in pronounciation.
> **Incomplete merging or Idh'gham an-Naaqis** implies a partial blending of a letter into the letter it follows.

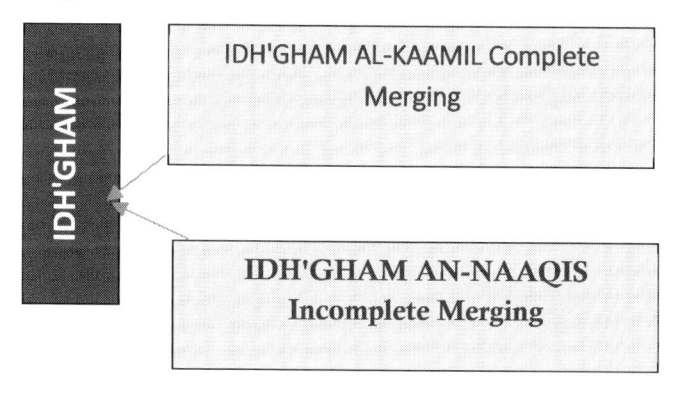

IDH'GHAM
- IDH'GHAM AL-KAAMIL Complete Merging
- IDH'GHAM AN-NAAQIS Incomplete Merging

WHY IDH'GHAM

Idh'gham is designed for easy pronunciation. It is difficult to pronounce two similar letters, one after the other. Idh'gham is applied to remove this difficulty. There are different types of Idh'gham

TYPES OF OTHER IDH'GHAM

1. Idh'ghamMutamaathilayn – Merging of same letters, with the same Makharij andsame Sifat.
2. Idh'ghamMutajaanisayn – Merging of related letters, with the same Makharij butdifferent Sifat.
3. Idh'ghamMutaqaaribayn – Merging of similar letters, that are close to each other inMakharij and Sifat.
4. Idh'ghamMutabaa'idayn – Merging of distant letters, whose Makharij is far fromeach other. There is NO Idh'gham between distant letters.

IDH'GHAM MUTABAA'IDAIN – Letters whose Makharij is far from each other. There is NO Idh'gham between two distant letters

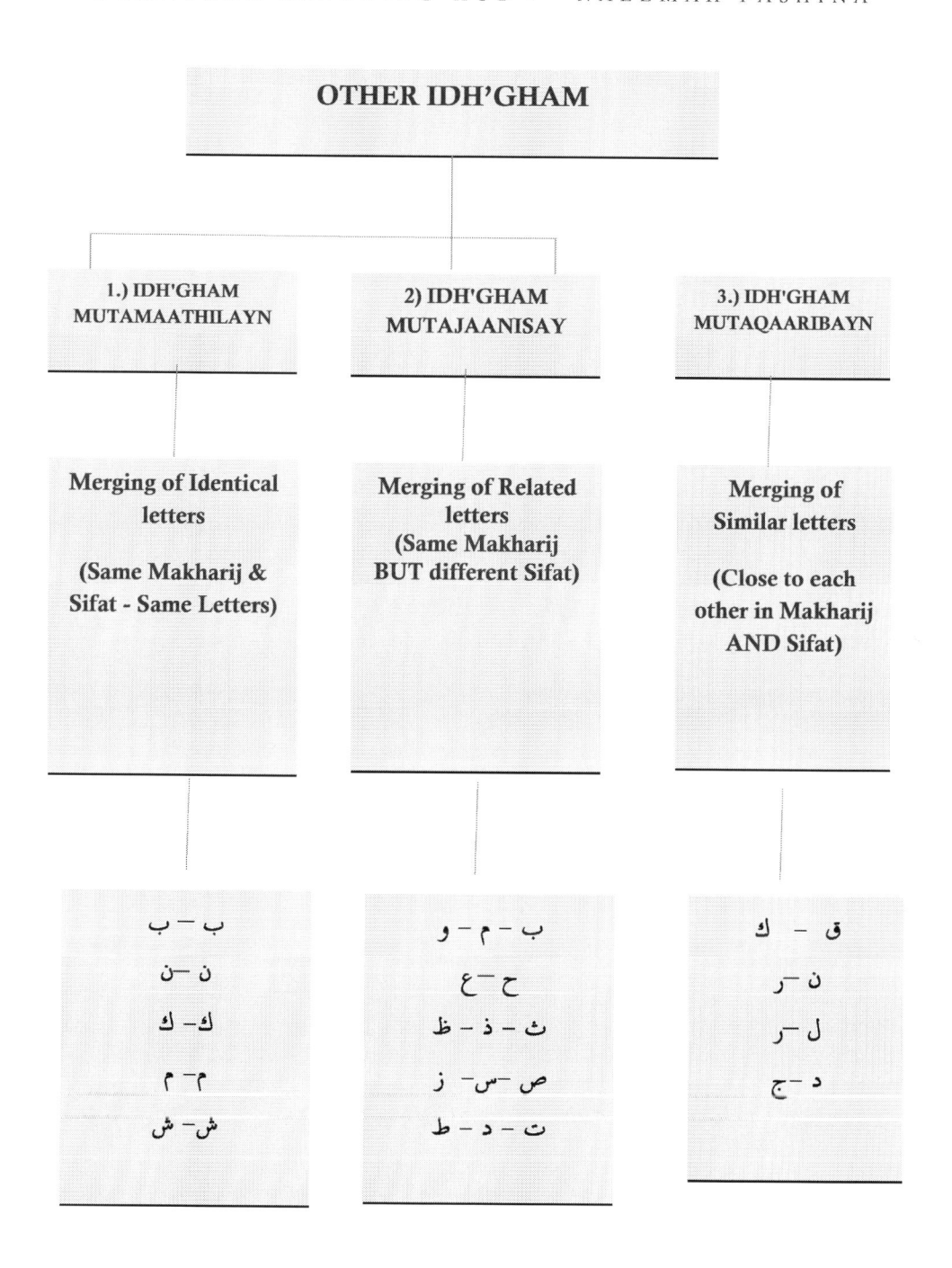

OTHER IDH'GHAM

1.) IDH'GHAM MUTAMAATHILAYN

Merging of Identical letters

(Same Makharij & Sifat - Same Letters)

ب – ب
ن – ن
ك – ك
م – م
ش – ش

2) IDH'GHAM MUTAJAANISAY

Merging of Related letters
(Same Makharij BUT different Sifat)

ب – م – و
ح – ع
ث – ذ – ظ
ص – س – ز
ت – د – ط

3.) IDH'GHAM MUTAQAARIBAYN

Merging of Similar letters

(Close to each other in Makharij AND Sifat)

ق – ك
ن – ر
ل – ر
د – ج

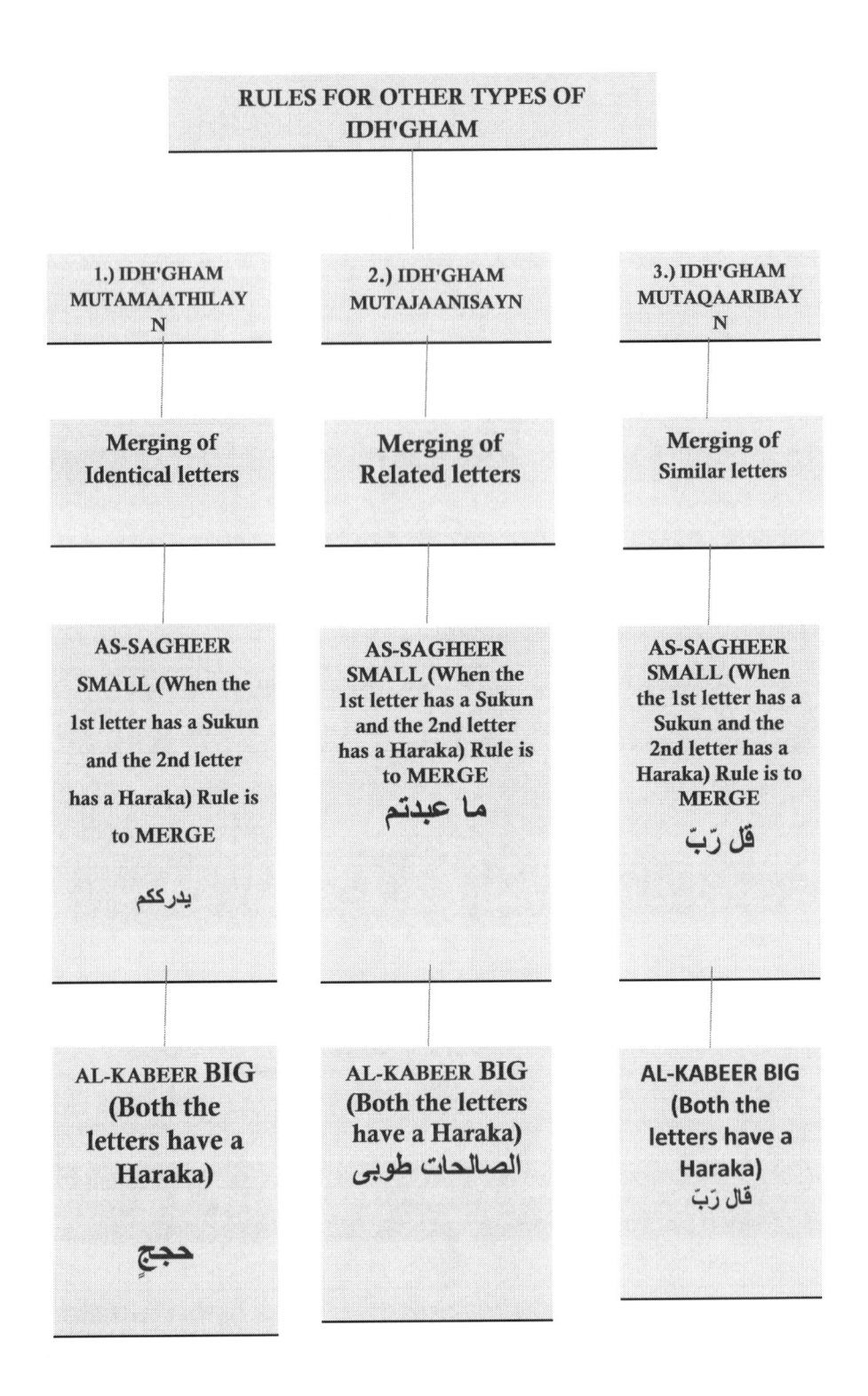

RULES FOR OTHER TYPES OF IDH'GHAM

1.) IDH'GHAM MUTAMAATHILAYN

Merging of Identical letters

AS-SAGHEER SMALL (When the 1st letter has a Sukun and the 2nd letter has a Haraka) Rule is to MERGE

يدرككم

AL-KABEER BIG (Both the letters have a Haraka)

حججٍ

2.) IDH'GHAM MUTAJAANISAYN

Merging of Related letters

AS-SAGHEER SMALL (When the 1st letter has a Sukun and the 2nd letter has a Haraka) Rule is to MERGE

ما عبدتم

AL-KABEER BIG (Both the letters have a Haraka)

الصالحات طوبى

3.) IDH'GHAM MUTAQAARIBAYN

Merging of Similar letters

AS-SAGHEER SMALL (When the 1st letter has a Sukun and the 2nd letter has a Haraka) Rule is to MERGE

قل رّبّ

AL-KABEER BIG (Both the letters have a Haraka)

قال رّبّ

RULES OF OTHER IDH'GHAM – 1.) IDH'GHAM MUTAMAATHILAYN

The assimilation of same letters. This rule is applied when two identical letters follow each other in either the same word or in between two words, where the first one is Sakin and the Second one has a vowel, the Sakin letter is assimilated (merged) into the one with the vowel and the vowelled letter is pronounced as if it has a Shaddah.

Examples of Identical Letters: (مم) (نن)(دد)(طط)

Example: Merging of Identical Letters.

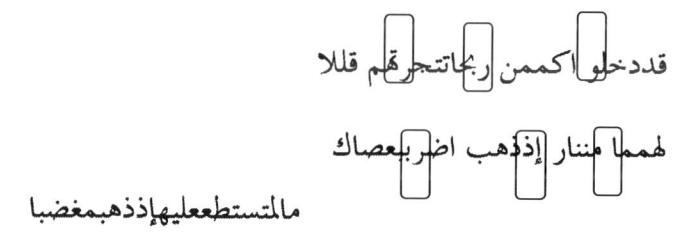

قددخلوا اكممن ربحاتتجر قهم قللا

لهمما مننار إذذهب اضربعصاك

مالمتستطععليها إذذهبمغضبا

قددخلوا	قدّخلوا
يدرركم	يدرّكم
أقللك	أقلّك

NOTE: Ghunnah is applied, whenever two Nuns or two Meems are assimilated into one.

CAUTION: If a Sakin letter is a letter of Maddah (Alif, Waw and Ya), then it will not be assimilated. Below is an example of two identical letters of which, one letter is a letter of Maddah

Note: Two similar letters 'YA' are next to each other. In this example the Ya Sakin or Waw Sakin, will not be assimilated (merged), as they are acting as a Maddah		
ءامنواوعملوا	فييوم	الذييوسوس

RULES OF OTHER IDH'GHAM – 2.) IDH'GHAM MUTAJAANISAYN

The assimilation of related letters. The term related letters used here refers to the letters that are from the same Makharij (point of origin) but having different Sifat (qualities, characteristics).

When two letters from the same Makharij but having different qualities, follow each other, in either, the same word or in between two words, where the first letter has a Sakin and the second letter has a vowel, the Sakin letter is assimilated into the letter with the vowel and the vowelled letter is pronounced as if it has a Shaddah.

Examples of Related Letters:

ث – ذ – ظ ص – س – ز ت – د – ط ح – ع ب – م – و

بسطتإلىيد كأجيبتدعوتكإنهمإذظلموا وقالتالطائفة

NOTE: Ghunnah is applied on the Meem Mushaddadah.

OBSERVE: With the exception of the letter Ta (ط), all the Sakin letters of Idh'ghamMutajaanisayn undergo a complete assimilation and are not pronounced. The letter (ط) involves a partial merging, where it will have a trace of its characteristics in pronounciation.

MUTAJANISAYN EXCEPTION: One exception of two related letters which occurs only in the case of letters Ba (ب) and Meem (م) appears only in **Surah Hood, Ayah 42**

Read as:	Written as:
اركمّعنا	اركبمعنا

Examples of Idh'ghamMutajaanisayn – Related letters

Related letters	Written as:	Read as:
تد	أثقلتدعواالله	أثقلدعواالله
دت	قدتبين	قتّبين
تط	ودتطائفة	ودّطائفة
طت	بسطت	بستّ
ثذ	يلهثذالك	يلهذّالك
ذظ	إذذهب	اظّلموا

Common mistakes of 2 words that are merged, where they should NOT be merged.

فقدضلّ	بسطتَّ
The Makharij for د is different from theMakharij of ض ض is from the edge of the tongue, whereas د is from the tip of the tongue. Therefore both د and ض are read with their characteristics and not merged.	And ت have the same Makhraj point but different Sifaat. ط is from the heavy letters. We have to be careful to pronounce the heaviness of the ط Therefore both ط and ت are read with their characteristics and not merged.

135

RULES OF OTHER IDH'GHAM – 3.) IDH'GHAM MUTAQAARIBAYN

The assimilation of similar letters or letters that are next to each other. Similar letters refer to the letters that:

> - Their Makharij (articulation point or place of origin) and Sifat (attributes, characteristics) are very similar to each other
> - Their Makharij is the same and their Sifaat is different
> - Their Makharij is different and their Sifaat is the same When similar letters follow each other in either the same word or in between two words, where the first one is Sakin and the second letter has a vowel. The Sakin letter is completely merged into the vowelled letter, to a point where there is no trace of the Sakin letter and the vowelled letter is pronounced as if it has a Shaddah.

Similar Letters are: قك

Near in Makharij   (لر) (رل)

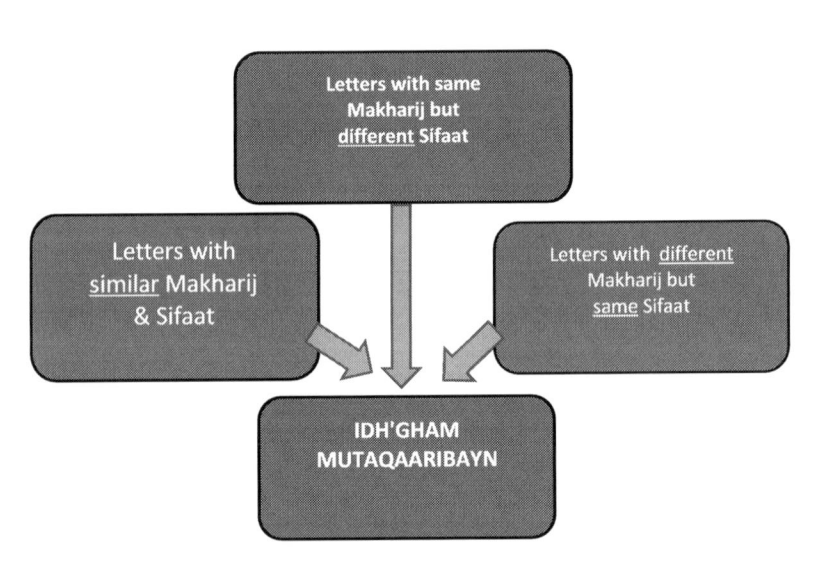

```
              ┌────────────────────┐
              │ Letters with same  │
              │     Makharij but   │
              │   different Sifaat │
              └─────────┬──────────┘
                        │
┌──────────────────┐    │    ┌──────────────────────┐
│   Letters with   │    │    │ Letters with different│
│  similar Makharij│    │    │     Makharij but      │
│     & Sifaat     │    │    │      same Sifaat      │
└────────┬─────────┘    │    └───────────┬──────────┘
         └──────────┐   │   ┌────────────┘
                    ▼   ▼   ▼
                ┌──────────────────┐
                │    IDH'GHAM      │
                │  MUTAQAARIBAYN   │
                └──────────────────┘
```

THE 4 RULES OF IDH'GHAM MUTAQAARIBAYN

meets the Idh'gham letters	ق + ك	ال+Shams letter	ر+ل
When the Nun Sakin meets any of the Idh'gham letters	When the Qaf meets the Kaf. Appears only once in the Holy Qur'an	When Laam At-Tareef (The AL' where we make something specific meets any of the 14 Shams (Sun) letters, the Laam is not pronounced	When the Laam Sakin meets the Raa. The Laam is not pronounced and it merges into the Raa
Rule: To Merge	**Rule:** To Merge	**Rule:** To Merge	**Rule:** To Merge
منوليّ Read as MIW WALLIY YIN	ألمنخلقكم Can be read in 2 ways ALAM NAKH LUK KUM Or ALAM NAKH LUQ KUM (Notice here we pronounce the heaviness of the Qaf)	لساعة Read as AS SAA AH	وقلرب Read as WA KUR RABBI
يكنله Read as YA KUL LAHU		والشمس Read as WASH SHAMS	بلرفعهالله Read as BAR RAFA AHULLAAHU

Surah Al-Qiyamah 75 Ayah 27
The above verse is **an exception to the rules of Idh'gham**. When reciting the above verse, the Holy Prophet (saw) stopped between the Nun Sakin and Raa (He did a SAKT*) and he did not merge them. This Ayah is therefore read as 'WA QIILA MAN RAAQ'

How The Rules Of Idh'gham Mutaqaribayn Are Read

Similar letters	Written as	Read as
كق	اَلَمْنَخْلُقْكُمْ	اَلَمْنَخْلُكُمْ
لر	قلربي	قربي
نل	من لدنك	ملدنك
نر	من رسول	مرسول

RULES OF OTHER IDH'GHAM – 4.) IDH'GHAM MUTABAA'IDAIN

Distant Letters are two letters whose Makharij is far from each other. They are articulated from two different areas. For example: (ح), (ح - ي) is articulated from the throat and (ي) is articulated from the tongue. And if the letters are articulated from one area they must be separate by at least one Makharij or more. For example: (,(خ-هر)) is articulated from the deepest part of the throat and (خ) is articulated from the part of the throat nearest to the mouth. The Makhraj of the mid-throat separates them.

NOTE: There is NO Idh'gham between two distant letters

THE RULES OF NUN QUTNI

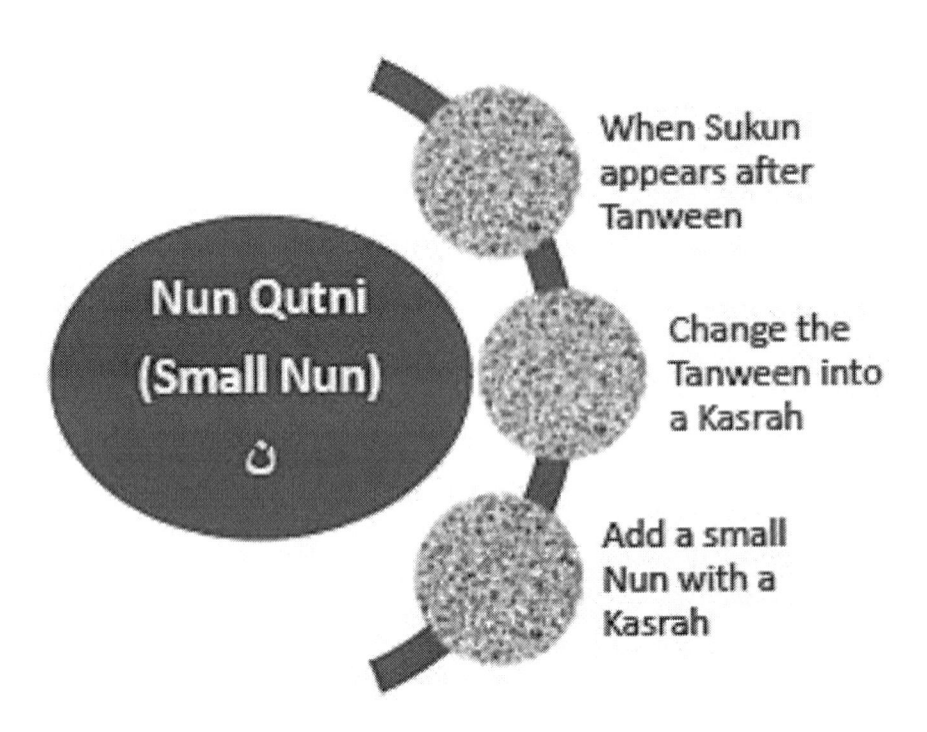

Nun Qutni (Small Nun) ڻ

- When Sukun appears after Tanween
- Change the Tanween into a Kasrah
- Add a small Nun with a Kasrah

NUN QUTNI (THE SMALL ن)

RULE: Two Sukun letters cannot be read in the Qur'an. Example:

يَوْمَئِذٍ السَّلْمِ
ن + ذ = ذ (as it appears) ل
ذ = ن + ذ (changed to) ل
Here the 2 Sakin meet each other or the Tanween is followed by the Sakin. Therefore, the Nun Sakin of the Tanween letter is converted into a Nun with a Kasrah. In Arabic 2 Sukun cannot be pronounced, therefore نِ is added. When reading Qur'an with an Uthmani script, one is expected to know this and do the conversion themselves, whereas in the Majeedi script, a small Nun with a Kasrah is indicated. This small Nun is known as NUN QUTNI

QUR'AN WITH MAJEEDI SCRIPT	QUR'AN WITH UTHMANI SCRIPT
Preferred by those from Indo/Pak, South Africa & other countries	Used by those familiar with the Arabic Language
يَوْمَئِذٍنِ السَّلْمِ	يَوْمَئِذٍ السَّلْمِ
Nun in the Tanween is always converted into a Nun Kasrah. The small Nun Kasrah indicates this	The Tanween is followed by LaamSakin and you have to convert the Nun in the Tanween into Nun Kasrah There is no indication and the reader has to be aware of the rules
Both the above are pronounced as yawmaidhinissalama	
NOTE: The Uthmani and Majeedi script Qur'an both produce the same results in terms of final pronounciation. The difference is in their fonts and some indications which are different.	

NUN QUTNI (SMALL NUN ن)

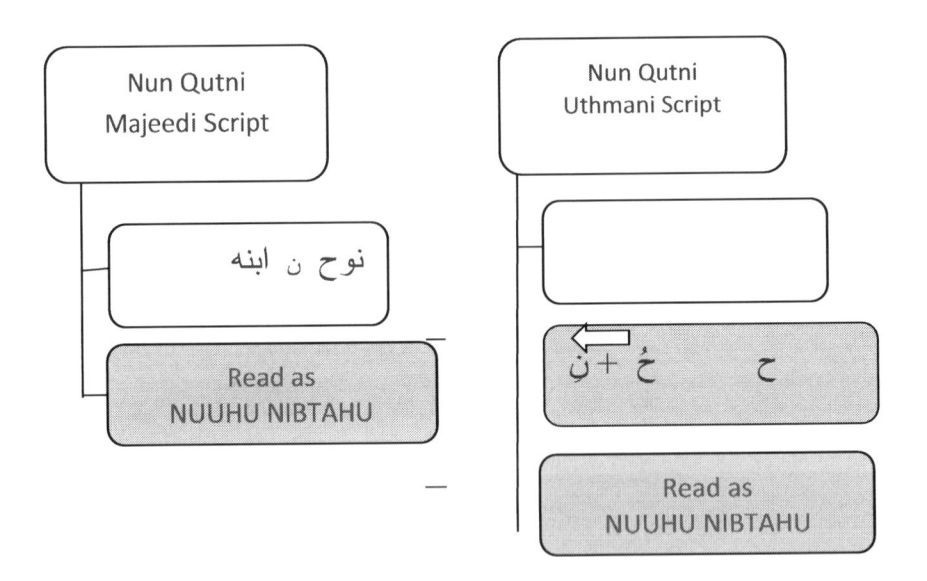

Nun Qutni Majeedi Script

نوح ن ابنه

Read as
NUUHU NIBTAHU

Nun Qutni Uthmani Script

ح + نُ   ح

Read as
NUUHU NIBTAHU

PRACTICE READING NUN QUTNI

لُوطٍ ۨالْمُرْسَلِين	طُوًى ۨاذْهَبْ
فَخُورًا ۨالَّذِين	خَبِيثَةٍ ۨاجْتُثَّتْ
بِزِينَةٍ ۨانْقَلَبَ أَحَدٌ ۨاللهُ	نُوحٌ ۨابْنَهُ
زُجَاجَةٍ ۨالزُّجَاجَةُ	نُوحٍ ۨالْمُرْسَلِين
جَزَاءٌ ۨالْحُسْنَى	نُفُورًا ۨاسْتِكْبَارًا

NUN QUTNI (SMALL NUN ن)

When the Nun Qutni appears after a full stop, there are 2 options:
- ❖ The reciter can stop at the full stop and then start the new sentence with the Nun Sakin of the Nun Qutni OR
- ❖ The reciter can choose not to stop and just ontinue

Example

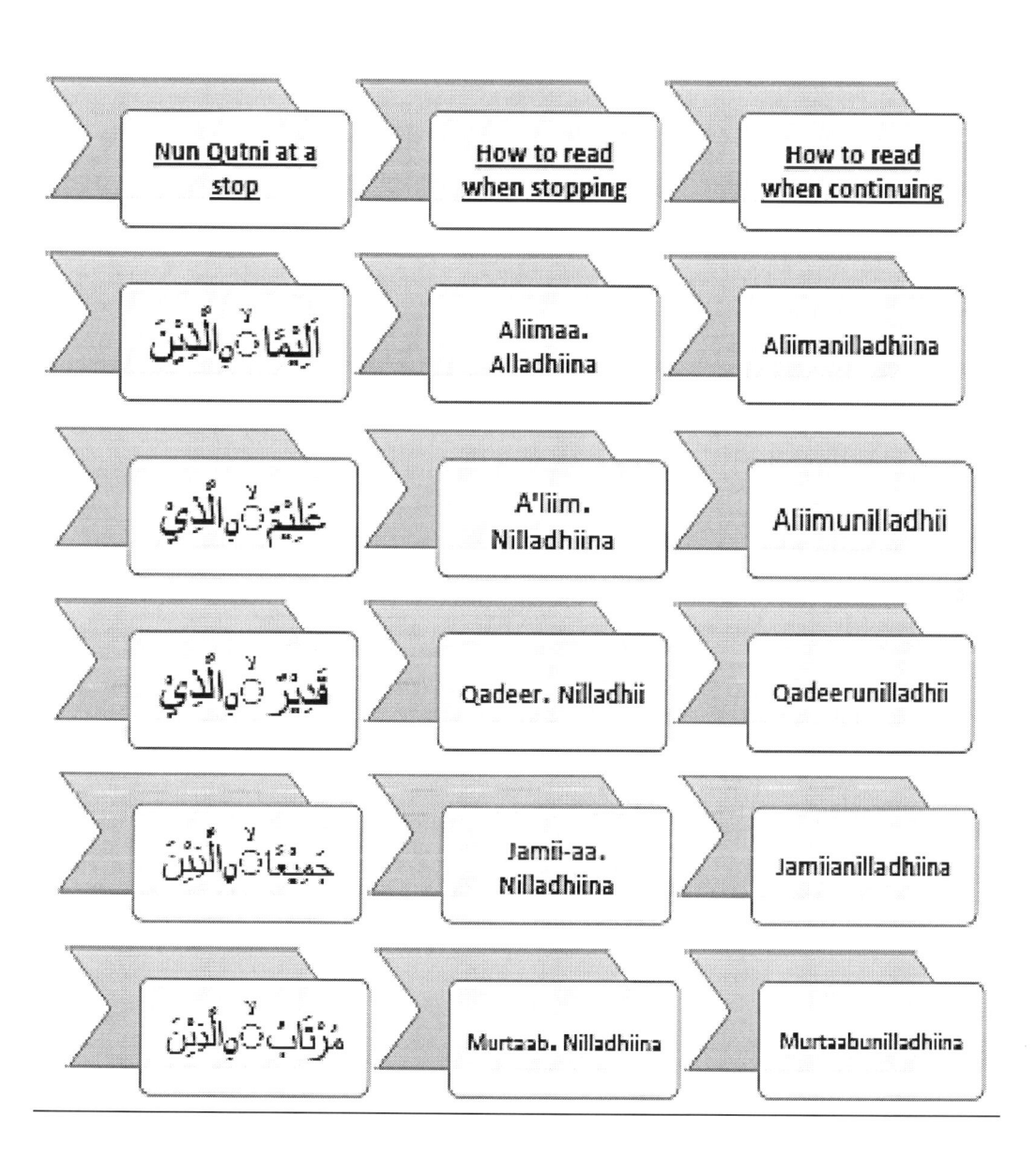

Nun Qutni at a stop	How to read when stopping	How to read when continuing
اَلْيَمَاٌ وَالَّذِينَ	Aliimaa. Alladhiina	Aliimanilladhiina
عَلِيْمٌ وَالَّذِي	A'liim. Nilladhiina	Aliimunilladhii
قَدِيْرٌ وَالَّذِي	Qadeer. Nilladhii	Qadeerunilladhii
جَمِيْعاً وَالَّذِينَ	Jamii-aa. Nilladhiina	Jamiianilladhiina
مُرْتَابٌ وَالَّذِينَ	Murtaab. Nilladhiina	Murtaabunilladhiina

THE RULES OF RAA

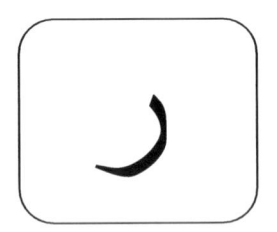

ر

THE RULES OF RAA ر

The letter Raa(ر) is sometimes pronounced with Tafkheem (heavy, with a full mouth), and sometimes pronounced with Tarqeeq (light, with an empty mouth). When Raa(ر) is pronounced with Tafkheem (heavy, with a full mouth), the tip of the tongue moves upward towards the roof of the mouth and the lips are rounded. When Raa(ر) is pronounced with Tarqeeq (light, with an empty mouth), the tip of the tongue moves towards the gum of theNtop incisors and the lips stretched to form a smile

15 RULES OF RAA

- 8 rules to Fat-ha Dhamma, always read as Tafkheem (Heavy, with a full mouth)
- 4 rules related to Kasrah, always read as Tarqeeq (Light, with an empty mouth)
- 2 exception rules for Kasra, always read as Tafkheem (Heavy, with a full mouth)
- Certain words where both Tafkheem and Tarqeeq are allowed

THE 8 RULES OF RAA TAFKHEEM RELATED TO FAT-HA & DHAMMA

Raa is pronounced with **Tafkheem (full mouth)** when it is bearing a Fat-ha or a Dhamma or a Fat-hatain or a Dhammatain, or the last sound before the Raa (when it is bearing a Sakin or when it appears at the end of the sentence – at stops) is the letter with a Fat-ha or a Dhamma.

8 RULES OF RAA TAFKHEEM WITH EXAMPLES

1) When Raa is bearing a Fat-ha **(Rule 1)** OR a Dhamma **(Rule 2)** or the Tanween of Fat-ha or Dhamma. Even when there is a Shaddah sign with the Fat-ha or Dhamma, it will still be pronounced with a full mouth – Tafkheem

فَرَضْ   رُزِقُ   قُدِرَ   رَحِمَ   رَّحْمَاءُ   لَيْسَ الْبِرُّ

2) When Raa is bearing a Sukun, preceded by a letter carrying a Fat-ha **(Rule 3)** OR a Dhamma **(Rule 4)**

قُرْءَانَ   فُرْقَانَ   مَرْيَمَ   دُسُرْ   الْقَمَرْ

3) When Raa is bearing a Sukun, preceded by a letter with a Sukun, preceded by a letter carrying a Fat-ha **(Rule 5)** OR a Dhamma **(Rule 6)**. This rule is used at stops and difficult to pronounce. To practice this, listen to a Qari.

وَالْفَجْرْ   الْيُسْرْ   مِعْشَارْ   فَخُورْ   نُورْ

4) When Raa is bearing a Sukun, preceded by Alif – the long vowel **(Rule 7)** OR Waw – the long vowel **(Rule 8)**. This is a rule used at stops.

اَلنَّهَارْ   غَفُورْ   مِعْشَارْ   فَخُورْ   نُورْ

THE RULES OF RAA TAFKHEEM

(Heavy – Full mouth pronounciation)

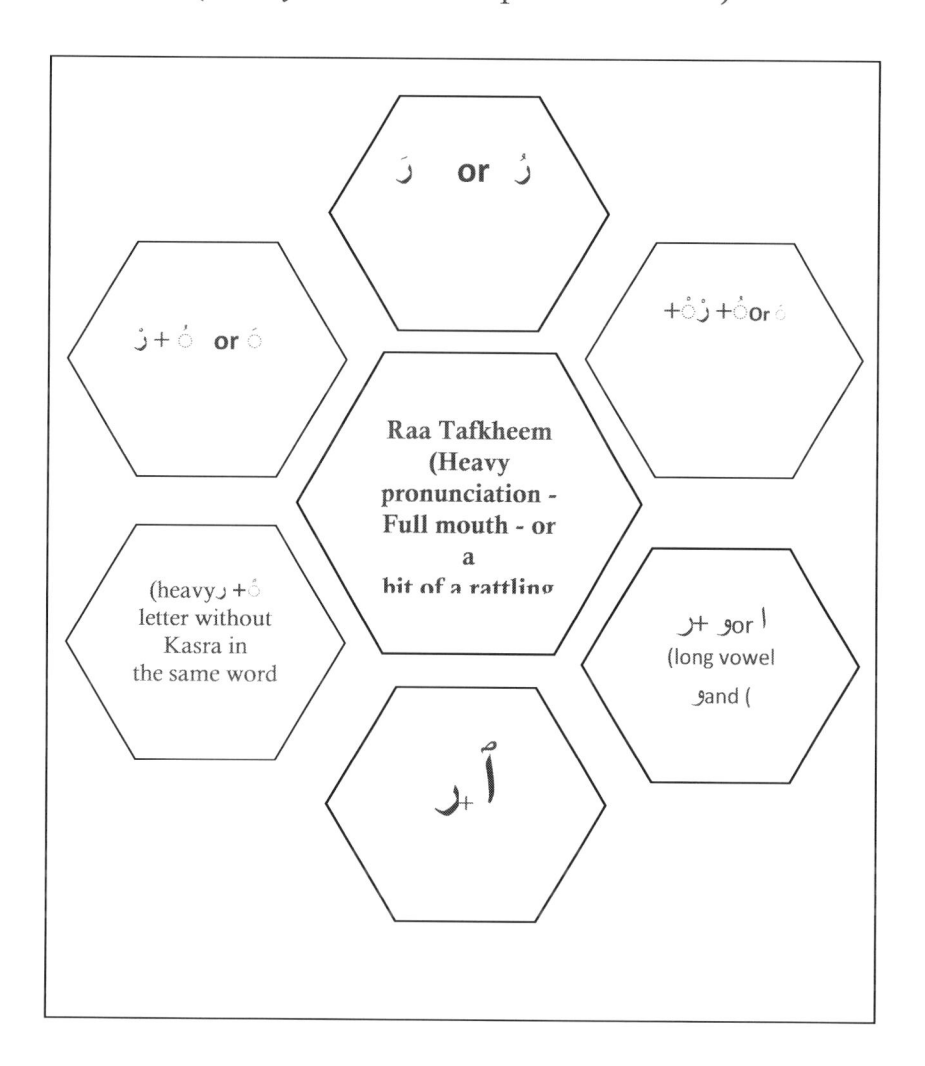

- رَ or رُ
- رْ + ـَ or ـَ
- ـُ + رْ + ـُ or ـُ
- Raa Tafkheem (Heavy pronunciation - Full mouth - or a bit of a rattling
- ـُ + ر (heavy letter without Kasra in the same word)
- ر+ ا or ر+ و (long vowel ا and و)
- اَ + ر

THE 4 RULES OF RAA TARQEEQ RELATED TO KASRA

Raa is pronounced Tarqeeq (Lightly with an Empty mouth) when it is bearing a Kasrah, OR the last sound before the Raa (when it is bearing a Sakin or when it appears at the end of the sentence – at stops) is Kasra

1) When Raa is bearing a Kasra or the Tanween of Kasra. Even when there is a Shaddah sign with a Kasra, it will be pronounced with an empty mouth – Tarqeeq.

    أرِنَ   أَخْرِجْنَا   مِن شرماً   خلق   حرمت   نحرٍ

2) When Raa is bearing a Sukun and preceded by a letter carrying a Kasra

    مرية   ويجركم   يغفرلكم   يوم عسر   فرعون

3) When Raa is bearing a Sukun, preceded by a letter carrying a Sukoon, preceded by a letter carrying a Kasra. This rule is used at stops and difficult to pronounce. To practice this, listen to a Qari.

    أهل الذكر   لذي حجر   في سدر   به السحر

4) When Raa is bearing a Sukun, preceded by Yaa – the long vowel or Yaa Sakin – Yaa bearing Sukun). This rule is used at stops.

    يسير   خبير   نصير   بشير   نذير   قدير

    لا ضير   بأ خير   غير   الطير   السير

THE RULES OF RAA TARQEEQ
(Light – Empty Mouth Pronounciation)

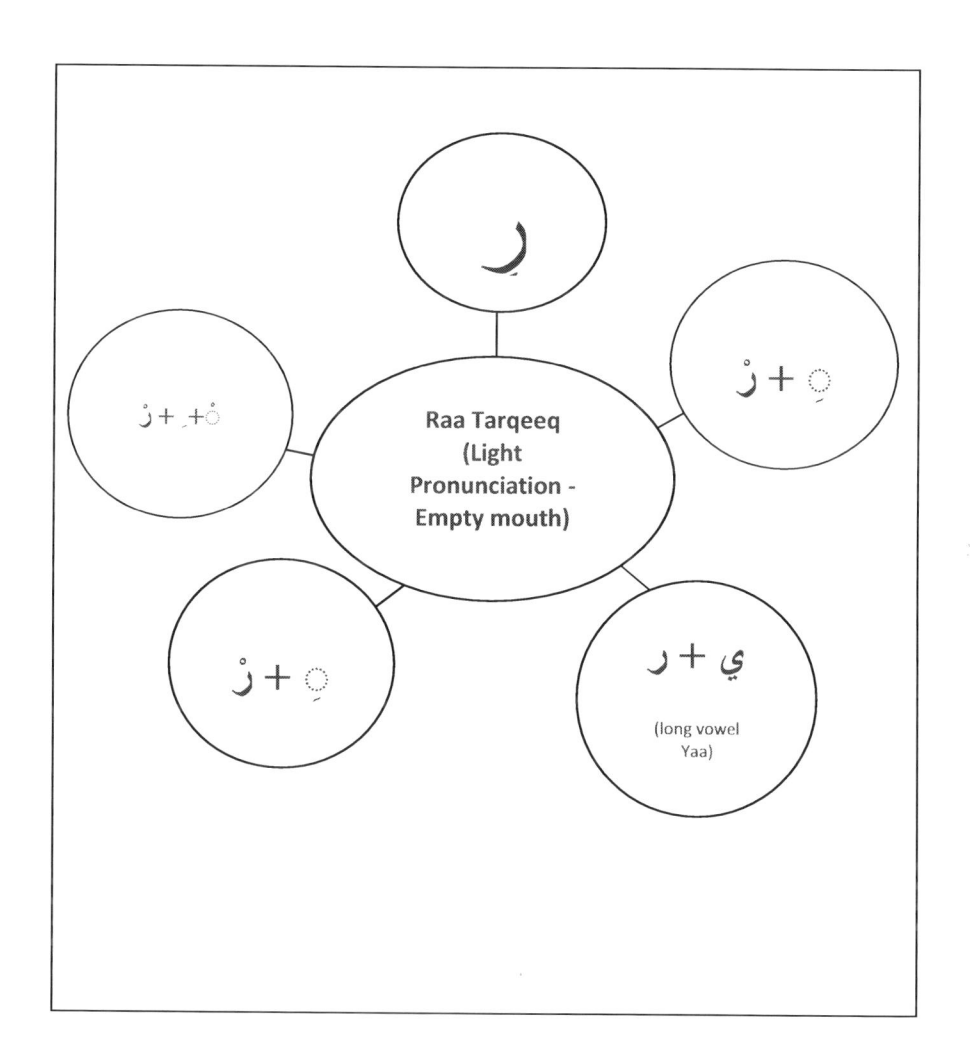

- ر
- رْ + ِ ْ
- رْ + ِ
- ي + ر (long vowel Yaa)
- رْ + ِ

Raa Tarqeeq (Light Pronunciation - Empty mouth)

THE 2 EXCEPTION RULES OF RAA TAFKHEEM RELATED TO KASRA

When RaaSakin (Raa bearing a Sukun) is followed by a Tafkheem letter (Heavy letter), OR preceded by HamzatulWasl, the Raa is pronounced with Tafkheem (full mouth).

2 EXCEPTION RULES WITH EXAMPLES

1. When the Raa is bearing a Sukun and is preceded by the connecting Hamza (HamzatulWasl) in any circumstance.

| رب ارجعون | ان ارتبتم | رب ارحم |

When RaaSukun is preceded with HamzatulWasl, with whatever sound the HamzatulWasl is to be pronounced (even if it is a Kasra – even if the letter before the Hamzatul Wasl is a Kasra), the letter (ر) will be pronounced with Tafkheem)

2. When Raa is bearing a Sukun and although preceded by a letter carrying a Kasra, it is **followed by a heavy elevation letter** of Iste'laa, then it is pronounced with Tafkheem (heavy). The Heavy letters are:

ص ض ط ظ غ خ ف

| فرقه | قرطاس | ارصادا | لبالمرصاد |

For the above rule to be followed correctly, the following conditions have to take place:
a) There has to be a heavy letter. i.e. A Kasra letter, then RaaSakin, followed by a heavy letter.
b) The Heavy letter should NOT be having a Kasra
c) The heavy letter has to be in the same word, i.e. A Kasra letter, then RaaSakin, then followed by the heavy letter, all in one word.

Any Kasra letter ⇐ Raa Sakin ⇐ Heavy letter, without a kasra, in the same word

If the above 3 conditions are not met, then the Raa is to be pronounced lightly

CERTAIN WORDS WHERE BOTH TAFKHEEM AND TARQEEQ IS ALLOWED

There are some words in the Holy Qur'an which can be pronounced heavily or lightly.

Both Tafkheem and Tarqeeq can be **applied if reading continues and there is no stopping**.	كل فرق كالطود العظيم Surah Shuara, Verse 63
Both Tafkheem and Tarqeeq can be **applied if stopping**. Other words are in: يسر In Surah Wal-Fajr: verse 4 نذر In Surah Wal-Qamar: verse 16 أسر In Surah Hud: verse 81, Surah Al-Hijr: verse 65, Surah Duhaa: verse 77, Surah Ash-Shu'a'raa: verse 52, and Surah Ad-Dukhan: verse 23	لقومكما بمصر بيوتا Surah Yunus, Verse 87 وقال الذى اشتريه مصر لامر اته Surah Yusuf, Verse 21 وقال ادخلوا مصر ان شاء الله امنين Surah Yusuf, Verse 99 اليس لئ ملك مصر وهذه الاهار Surah Zukhruf, Verse 51 واسلنا له القطر ومن الجن Surah Sabaa, Verse 12

NOTES to remember:

1. The general rule in the pronunciation of the letter Raa ر is that the short vowels Fat-ha and Dhamma are the cause of heavy pronunciation.
2. The short vowel Kasra is the cause for light pronunciation of letter Raa ر

3. The vowels Fat-hateen and Dhammateen, and the long vowel Alif ا and Waw و are similar as the short vowels of Fat-ha and Dhamma, and they all are the cause of heavy pronunciation of the letter Raa ر

4. The vowel Kasrateen, and the long vowel Yaa ي are similar as the short vowel Kasra, they are the cause of light pronunciation of the letter Raa ر

5. ر RaaSukun can sometimes be pronounced as both Tafkheem (Heavy) and Tarqeeq (Light) eg the word فِرْقٍ (Surah Ash-Shu'araa, Ayah 63), Tafkheem because it is followed by a letter of elevation and Tarqeeq because it is accompanied by Sukun and is situated between two letters that are accompanied by Kasra.

6. وقال اركبوا فيها بسم الله مجريها ومرسها ان ربي لغفور رحيم

The letter Raa in the word MAJRIIHA in Surah Hud: verse 41 is pronounced with **Tarqeeq** because the long vowel of (ا) has the rule of the big lean.

RULES OF RAA

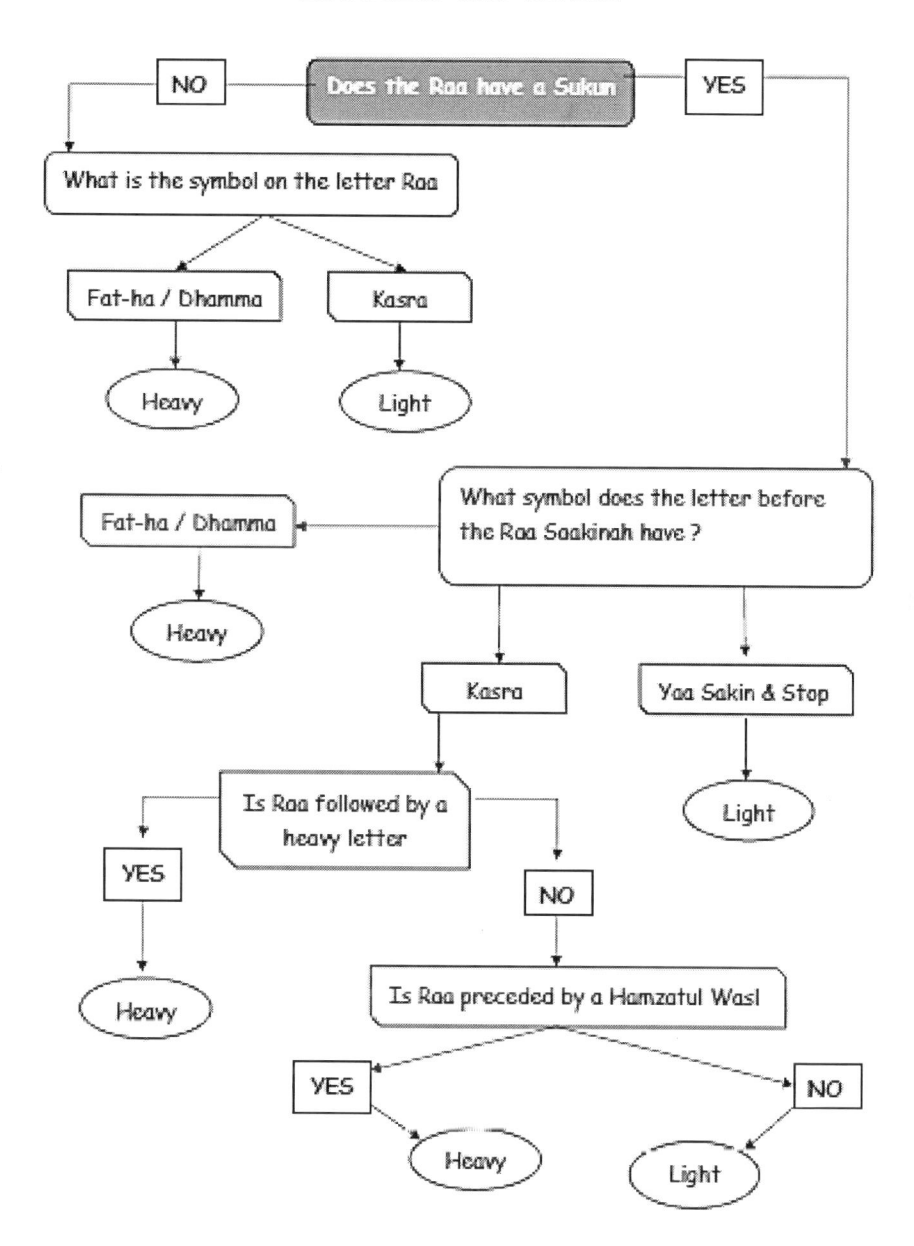

- **Does the Raa have a Sukun?**
  - **NO** → What is the symbol on the letter Raa?
    - Fat-ha / Dhamma → Heavy
    - Kasra → Light
  - **YES** → What symbol does the letter before the Raa Saakinah have?
    - Fat-ha / Dhamma → Heavy
    - Kasra → Is Raa followed by a heavy letter?
      - YES → Heavy
      - NO → Is Raa preceded by a Hamzatul Wasl?
        - YES → Heavy
        - NO → Light
    - Yaa Sakin & Stop → Light

AHKAM AL MUDOOD (THE RULES OF MADDAH)

المد
Al Madd
means to stretch the letters of madd

المد الفرعي
Al Madd Al Fari
When there is a hamza or or sukoon after any letter of Madd
Length: more than one alif

المد الأصلي
Al Madd Al Asli
When there is no hamza or sukoon after any letter of Madd
Length: one alif

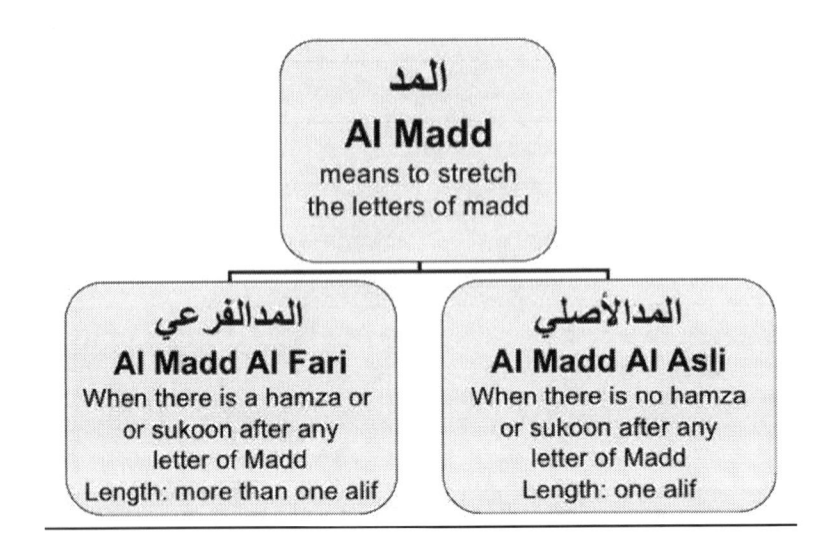

AHKAM AL MUDOOD - THE RULES OF MADDAH

The linguistic meaning of Madd is to prolong or to do something extra. Maddah simply means Elongation of Sounds.

- ❖ Madd means the elongation of the letters (another meaning is to stretch or to lengthen the letters)
- ❖ The letters of Maddah are three: اوي
- ❖ The duration of the elongation is measured in terms of the length of the vowels (Harakah)
- ❖ There are **Three kinds of duration of the elongation** for different syllables that are regulated by certain principles.

   i. **QASR (Shortness)** – the duration of the elongation should not be more than 2 harakah long.
   ii. **TAWASSUT (Intermediate)** – the duration of the elongation is between 3 – 5 harakah long
   iii. **TUUL (Lengthy)** – The duration of the elongation is between 4 – 6 harakah long.

Individual single Maddah are called **Maddah** (Singular), whereas, many Maddah are referred to as **Mudood** (Plural).

DURATION OF ELONGATION OF MADDAH
THE 9 TYPES OF MUDOOD

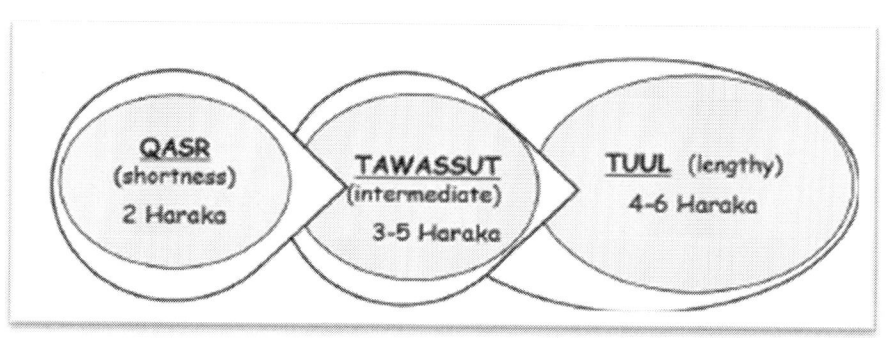

QASR (shortness) 2 Haraka

TAWASSUT (intermediate) 3-5 Haraka

TUUL (lengthy) 4-6 Haraka

The Maddah letters of Alif, Waw and Ya, have rules which determine how the Maddiya letters are pronounced. These rules are known as the **'Rules of Maddah'**. They are divided into 2 groups, Maddul Asli or Tabee (Original/Natural Madd) and MaddulFar'i (Secondary/Derived Madd).

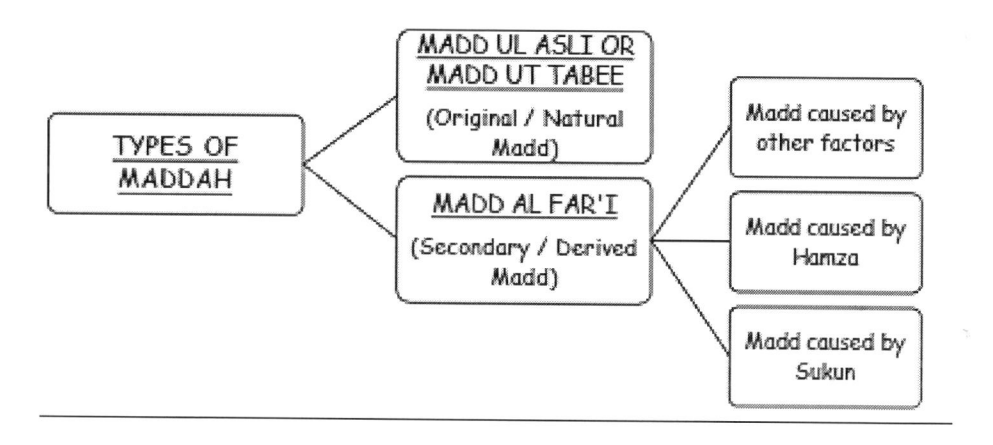

TYPES OF MADDAH
- **MADD UL ASLI OR MADD UT TABEE** (Original / Natural Madd)
- **MADD AL FAR'I** (Secondary / Derived Madd)
  - Madd caused by other factors
  - Madd caused by Hamza
  - Madd caused by Sukun

BREAKDOWN OF THE 9 TYPES OF MUDOOD

1) MADD UL ASLIYYA also known as MADD UT TABEE is the Original Madd

The rest of the Madd come under **MADD UL FAR'I** which is the Secondary Madd.

CAUSED BY OTHER FACTORS

2) MADD UL-BADAL – The Substitute Madd
3) MADD UL-SILAH – The Connecting Madd
4) MADD UL-EWAD – The Replacement Madd

CAUSED BY HAMZA

5) MADD UL-MUTTASIL – The Connected Madd
6) MADD UL-MUNFASIL – The Detached Madd

CAUSED BY SUKUN

7) MADD UL-LAAZIM – The Compulsory Madd
8) MADD UL-LIN – The Gentle Madd
9) MADD UL-ARID LIS SUKUN – The Abrupt Stop Madd

TYPES OF MADDAH

MADD AL-FARI
(SECONDARY/DERIVED MADD)
8 TYPES

MADD AL ASLIYYA OR AL-TABEE
1.) Original / Natural Madd

CAUSED BY OTHER FACTORS
2.) MADD UL-BADAL – The Substitute Madd
3.) MADD UL-SILAH – The Connecting Madd
4.) MADD UL-EWAD – The Replacement Madd

CAUSED BY HAMZA
5.) MADD UL-MUTTASIL – The Connected Madd
6.) MADD UL-MUNFASIL – The Detached Madd

CAUSED BY SUKUN
7.) MADD UL-LAAZIM – The Compulsory Madd
8.) MADD UL-LIN – The Gentle Madd
9.) MADD UL-ARID LIS SUKUN – The Abrupt Stop Madd

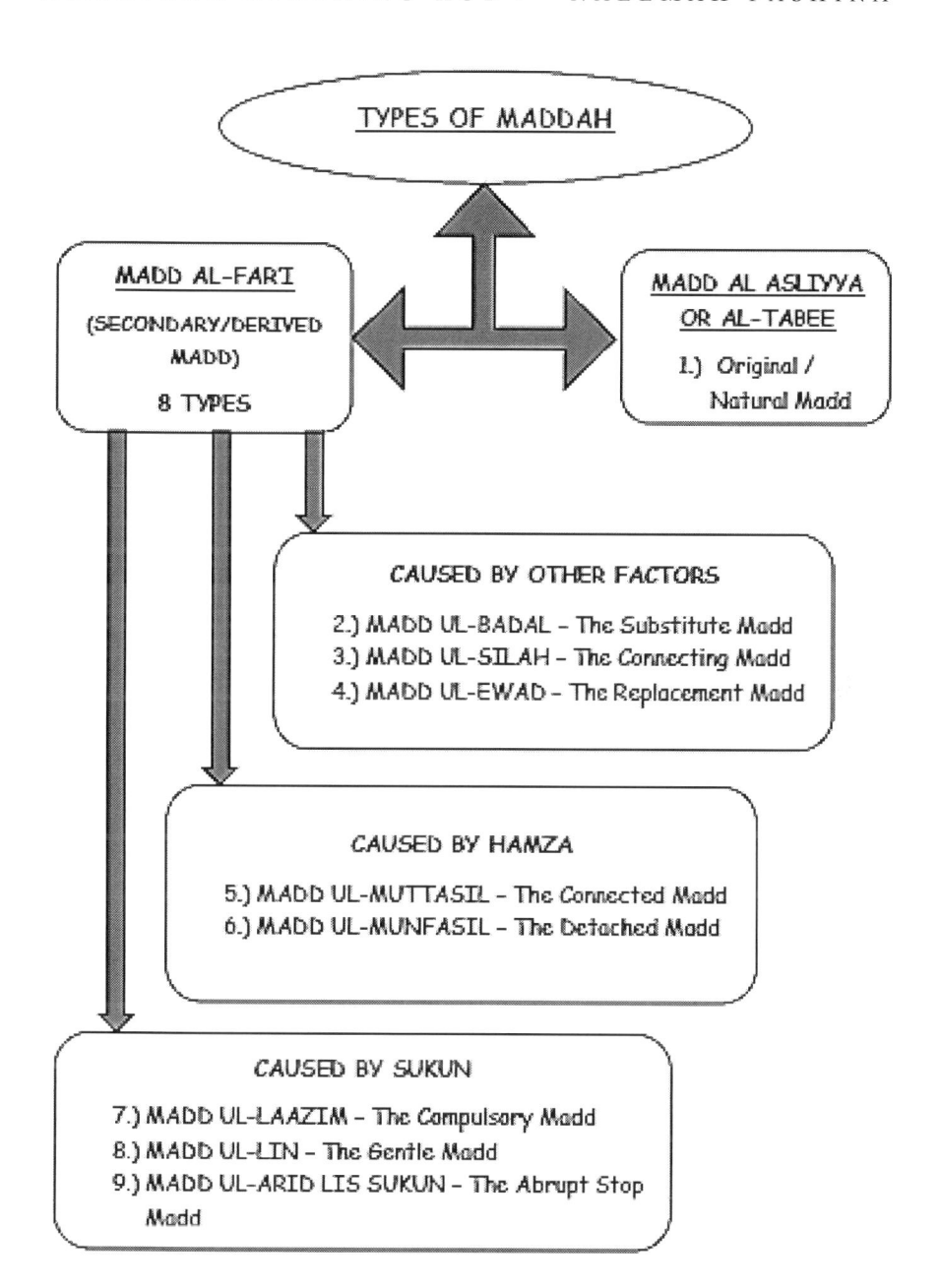

TYPES OF MADD: 1.) MADD AL ASLIYYA OR AT-TABEE NATURAL OR ORIGINAL MADD

It is named Original because it is the origin of all Mudood (lengthening). It is called natural because it follows the sound's normal and natural (Tabee) way of pronounciationwithout any decrease or increase in its timing.

CONDITION OF MADD AT-TABEE– The Madd letter Alif should be preceded by any letter carrying a Fat-ha, the Madd letter Yaa should be preceded by any letter carrying a Kasra and the Madd letter Waw should be preceded by any letter carrying a Dhamma. There should be no Hamza before the word or Hamza or Sukun after the word.

TIMING: It is lengthened for two vowel counts

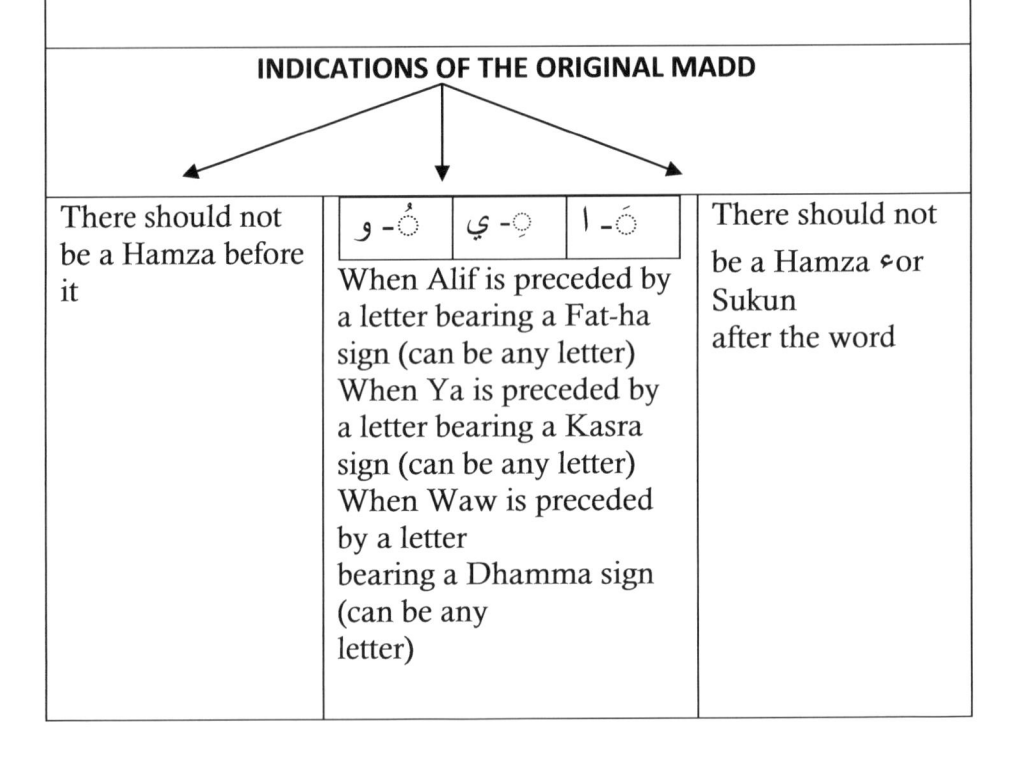

	INDICATIONS OF THE ORIGINAL MADD	
There should not be a Hamza before it	ُو - يْ ِ - اَ ْ - When Alif is preceded by a letter bearing a Fat-ha sign (can be any letter) When Ya is preceded by a letter bearing a Kasra sign (can be any letter) When Waw is preceded by a letter bearing a Dhamma sign (can be any letter)	There should not be a Hamza ءor Sukun after the word

WHAT IS A VOWEL COUNT OR LENGTHENED FOR 2, 4, 6 HARAKA MEAN?

When reading Maddah, we have to extend or lengthen the sound. How does one measure the length of the sound? Some count the fingers on the hand and some use the seconds of the watch. The oldest and preferred method is the time it takes to say a haraka (vowel)

بَبَبَبَبَ	بَبَبَبَ	بَبَبَ	بَبَ	بَ
5 counts ba ba ba ba ba	4 counts ba ba ba ba	3 counts ba ba ba	2 counts ba ba	1 count ba

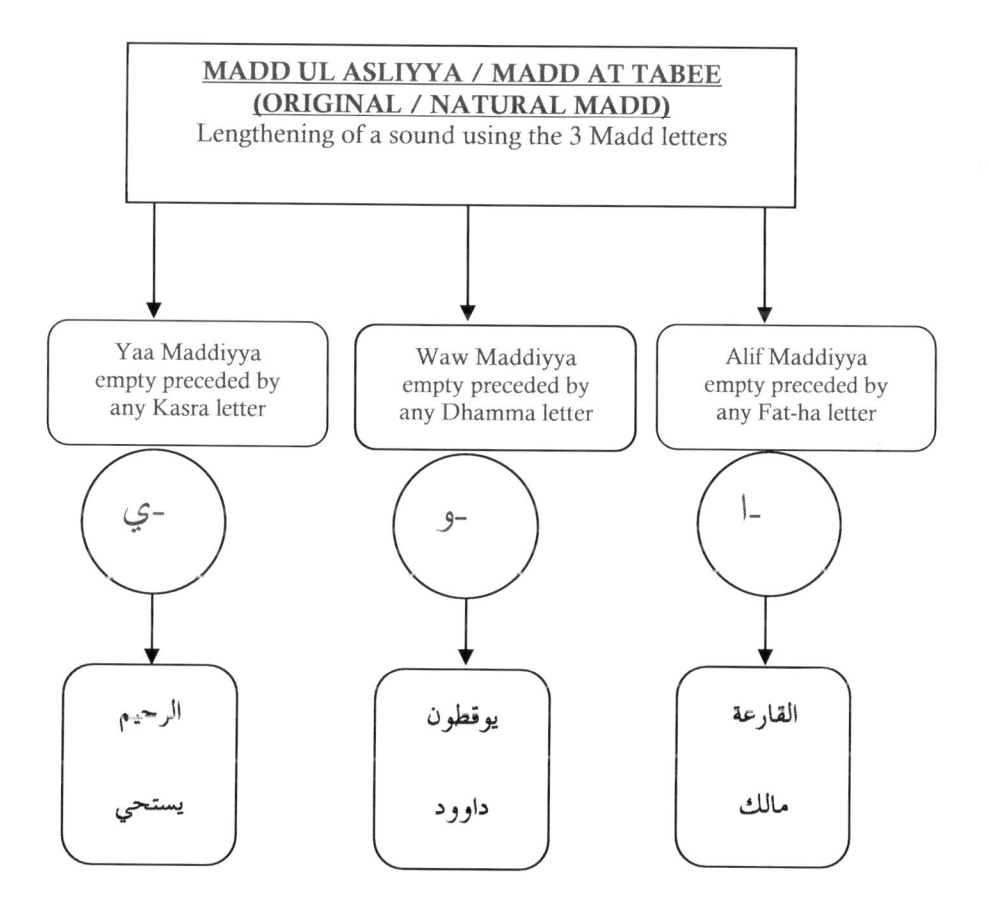

**MADD UL ASLIYYA / MADD AT TABEE
(ORIGINAL / NATURAL MADD)**
Lengthening of a sound using the 3 Madd letters

Yaa Maddiyya empty preceded by any Kasra letter	Waw Maddiyya empty preceded by any Dhamma letter	Alif Maddiyya empty preceded by any Fat-ha letter
ي-	و-	ا-
الرَّحِيم يستحي	يوقطون داوود	القارعة مالك

THE ORIGINAL MADD CONDITIONS

1. The Madd letters of ايو are empty and do not have any haraka (Fat-ha, Kasra or Dhamma)
2. Madd letters must be preceded by its own haraka i.e. Madd letter Alif by Fat-ha, Madd letter Waw by Dhamma and Madd letter Ya by Kasra.
3. There is no Hamza before the word and no Hamza or Sukun after the word.
4. To be extended for Two haraka OR Two counts only

MADD AL FAR'I – 8 TYPES OF MADD

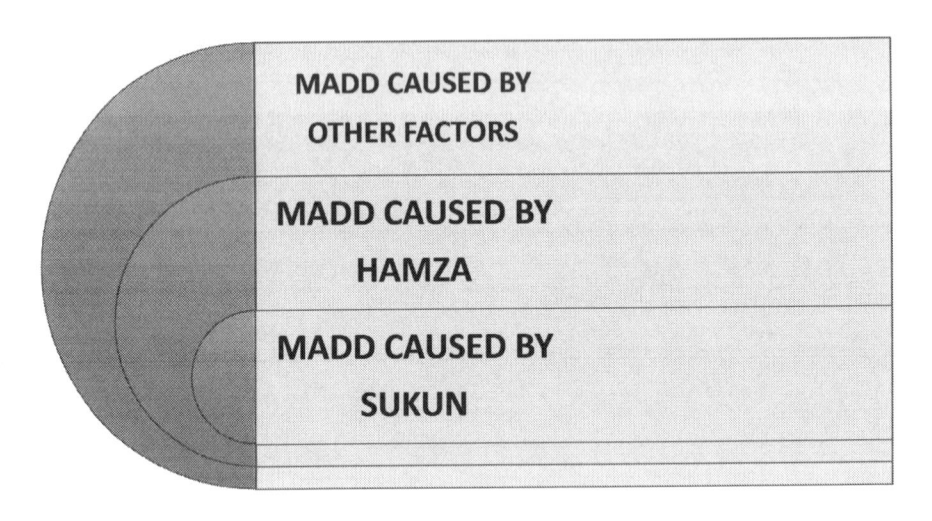

| MADD CAUSED BY OTHER FACTORS |
| MADD CAUSED BY HAMZA |
| MADD CAUSED BY SUKUN |

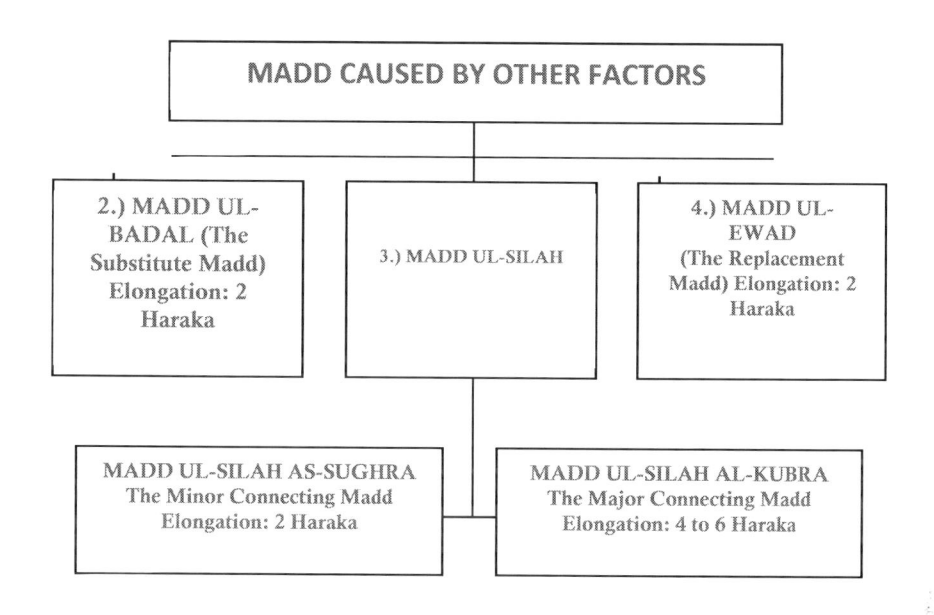

```
                    ┌─────────────────────────────────┐
                    │   MADD CAUSED BY OTHER FACTORS  │
                    └─────────────────────────────────┘
                                    │
         ┌──────────────────────────┼──────────────────────────┐
         │                          │                          │
┌──────────────────┐      ┌──────────────────┐      ┌──────────────────┐
│ 2.) MADD UL-     │      │                  │      │ 4.) MADD UL-     │
│ BADAL (The       │      │ 3.) MADD UL-SILAH│      │ EWAD             │
│ Substitute Madd) │      │                  │      │ (The Replacement │
│ Elongation: 2    │      │                  │      │ Madd) Elongation:│
│ Haraka           │      │                  │      │ 2 Haraka         │
└──────────────────┘      └──────────────────┘      └──────────────────┘
                                    │
                     ┌──────────────┴──────────────┐
                     │                             │
        ┌────────────────────────┐    ┌────────────────────────┐
        │ MADD UL-SILAH AS-SUGHRA│    │ MADD UL-SILAH AL-KUBRA │
        │ The Minor Connecting   │    │ The Major Connecting   │
        │ Madd                   │    │ Madd                   │
        │ Elongation: 2 Haraka   │    │ Elongation: 4 to 6     │
        │                        │    │ Haraka                 │
        └────────────────────────┘    └────────────────────────┘
```

MADD AL FAR'I: MADD CAUSED BY OTHER FACTORS

a) **MADD UL-BADAL** – The Substitute Madd – When any of the Madd letters of اوي are **preceded by a ء,** and not followed by a Hamza or Sukun. This Madd is stretched to 2 Haraka.	
بئاياتنا / رءات / ءامن / أوت ا	
b) **MADD UL-SILAH** – is the prolonging of the Haa(ه) of the pronoun that represents a third party of male gender. ➢ The Haa(ه) has to fall between two voweled letters (neither of them have a Sukun) ➢ You must continue to the next word in order to sound this Madd. eg. If you stop on this Haa, then NO Madd. ➢ The Madd will be with Waw if the Haa has a Dhamma, and by Yaa if the Haa has a Kasra. Eg انه علي رجعه لقادر **NOTE: Letter Haa does not bear a Fat-ha**	
There are 2 types of Madd ul-Silah	
Madd ul-Silah as-Sughra (Lesser)	Madd ul-Silah al-Kubra (Longer)

➢ The two vowels between which the Haa sits, should be a Fat-ha, Kasra or Dhamma and not a Sukun ➢ The Haa **must be** followed by a ➢ Hamza (ا or ء **Haa**to be stretched for 4 – 5counts just like Madd Munfasil ➢ ماله اخلده ➢ Notice the Hamza after the Haa	➢ The two vowels between which the Haa sits, should be a Fat-ha, Kasra or Dhamma and not a Sukun ➢ The Haa is **not** followed by a Hamza ا) or (ء ➢ **Haa**to be stretched for 2 countsjust like Madd Tabee ➢ ماله ومكسب وأمه وابيه ➢ Notice a vowel after the Haa and NOHamza

EXCEPTIONS OF THE MADD UL-SILAH

a) Notice the word يرضه لكم. The Haa in this word fulfils all the conditions of Madd ul-Silah as-Sughra, yet it is not stretched when reciting. There is a vowel before and after the Haa, and no Hamza after the Haa, yet there is no Madd in this word (Surah Zumar Ch. 39 Ayah 7)

b) Notice the word ويخدر فيه مهانا. The Haa in this word does not fulfil all the conditions of Madd ul-Silah, yet it is stretched when reciting. There is a vowel after the Haa, but there is a Sukun before the Haa, and no Hamza after the Haa, yet a stretch of 2 counts is made on this word (Surah Furqaan Ch. 25 Ayah 69)

Note: Copies of the Qur'an printed in Arab countries usually indicate Madd ul-Silah by a small Ya or Waw next to the Haa. These symbols are not present in copies of the Qur'an printed in India, Pakistan and other countries.

Examples of the small Ya or Waw in Madd ul-Silah as-Sughra

كِتَـٰبَهُۥ وَرَآءَ	عِبَادِهِۦ خَبِيرًا	لَهُۥ مَا فِى
Kitaabahuu waraa'a	'ibaadihii khabeeraa	Lahuu maa fee

Examples of the small Ya or Waw in Madd ul-Silah al-Kubra

وَثَاقَهُۥٓ أَحَدٌ	هَـٰذِهِۦٓ إِيمَـٰنًا	مَالَهُۥٓ أَخْلَدَهُ
Wathaaqahuuu ahadun	Haathiheee eemaanan	Maalahooo akhladahu
Notice the small Ya & Waw have a small Madd on them for Silah al-Kubra		

5) **MADD UL-EWAD** – The Replacement Madd – involves replacing the Fat'hatain that occurs at the end of a word with the Alif Madd with Fat-ha, when a reader stops on it. This Madd is stretched to 2 Haraka. This rule is not applicable to Kasratain or Dhammatain.

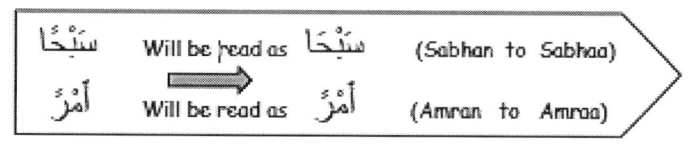

| سَبْحًا | Will be read as | سَبْحًا | (Sabhan to Sabhaa) |
| أَمْرً | Will be read as | أَمْرً | (Amran to Amraa) |

> **NOTE:** This rule applies to all letters including Hamza but not the letter TA MARBUTA . ةTa Marbutah is the exception to this rule as it is pronounced as HA when it occurs at a stop.

Madd Al Far'i: Maddah Caused by Hamza

MADD CAUSED BY HAMZA

- **5.) MADD UL-MUTTASIL** — The Connected Madd — Elongation: 4 to 6 Haraka
- **6.) MADD UL-MUNFASIL** — The Detached Madd — Elongation: 3 to 5 Haraka

1 Madd Al-Wajib Al-Muttasil (Obligatory Prolongation)	Al Madd Al-Jaa'ez Al-Munfasil (Permissible Prolongation)
CONDITIONS: ➤ This Madd is Obligatory as a Hamza follows any Madd letter of Alif, Yaa or Waw in ONE WORD (if it is in two words, then it is Madd al-Munfasil ➤ It is prolonged for either 4 or 6 counts ➤ If you choose to prolong for 4 counts, then this must remain consistent throughout the recitation	**CONDITIONS**: ➤ This Madd is named Munfasil (separated) as it is sounded over TWO WORDS ➤ Occurs when a word ends with a letter of Madd and is followed by a word that begins with Hamza ➤ It is prolonged for either 3 or 5 counts ➤ Al Madd al-Munfasil cannot exceed Al Madd al-Mutasil (Both have to be the same count)
Examples: اذا جاء نصر Ja is to be stretched for 4 to 6 counts	**Examples**: يدا أبي لهب Da is to be stretched for 3 to 5 counts
والسماء Ma is to be stretched for 4 to 6 counts	وفي أنفسهم Fi is to be stretched for 3 to 5 counts

MADD AL FAR'I: MADDAH CAUSED BY SUKUN

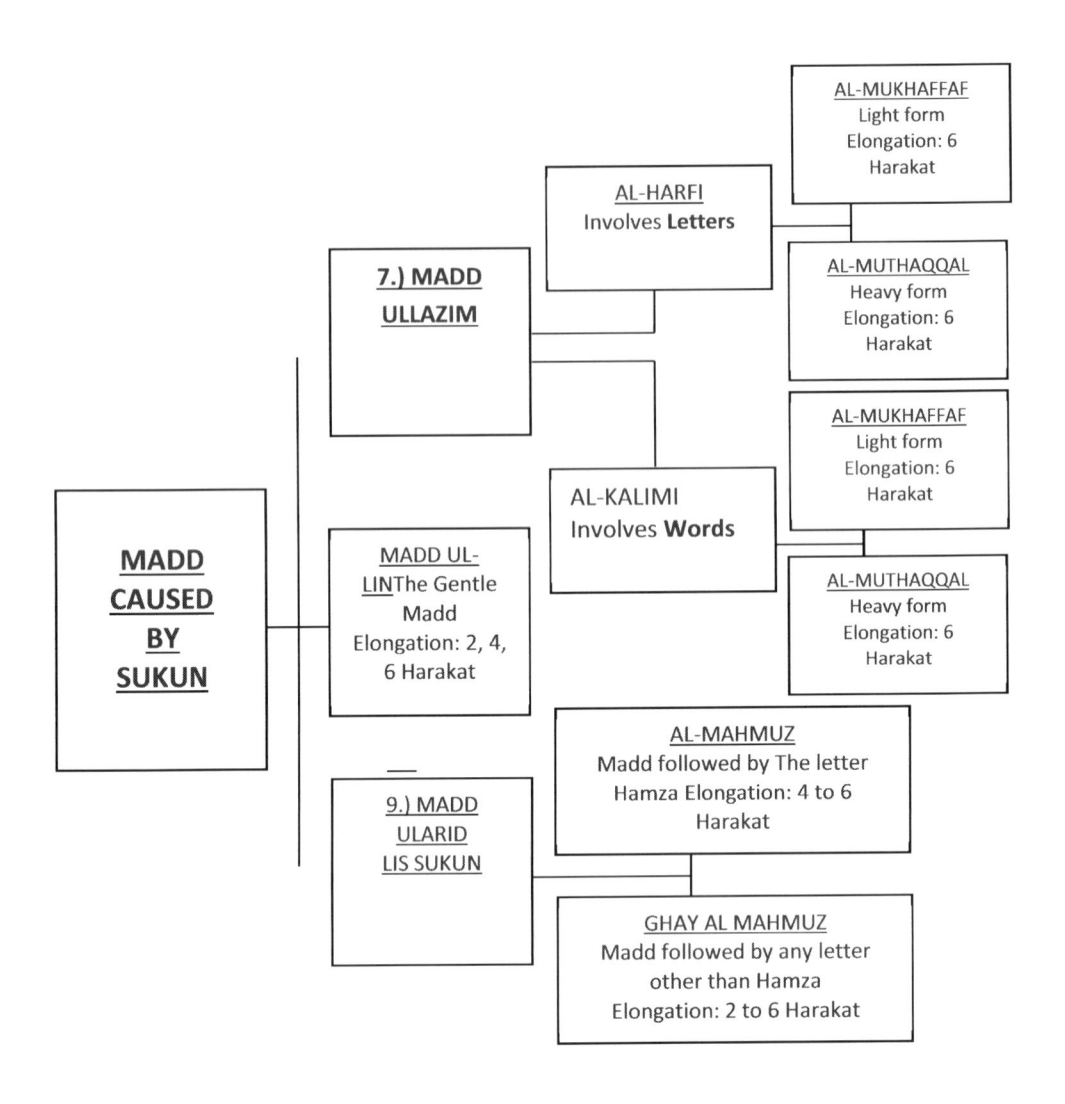

MADD CAUSED BY SUKUN

- **7.) MADD ULLAZIM**
  - **AL-HARFI** Involves **Letters**
    - **AL-MUKHAFFAF** Light form — Elongation: 6 Harakat
    - **AL-MUTHAQQAL** Heavy form — Elongation: 6 Harakat
  - **AL-KALIMI** Involves **Words**
    - **AL-MUKHAFFAF** Light form — Elongation: 6 Harakat
    - **AL-MUTHAQQAL** Heavy form — Elongation: 6 Harakat

- **MADD UL-LIN** The Gentle Madd — Elongation: 2, 4, 6 Harakat

- **9.) MADD ULARID LIS SUKUN**
  - **AL-MAHMUZ** Madd followed by The letter Hamza — Elongation: 4 to 6 Harakat
  - **GHAY AL MAHMUZ** Madd followed by any letter other than Hamza — Elongation: 2 to 6 Harakat

6) **MADD UL-LAAZIM** – The compulsory Madd – Occurs when any of the Huruful Madd is followed by a letter with a Sukun(ْ + ا,و,ي) or a Shaddah(ّ + ا,و,ي). This Madd occurs in either **a word (Kalimi)** or **in a letter (Harfi)**. These are further divided into 2 parts each.

MaddulLazim al Kalimi (Maddah in a word)	MaddulLazim al Harafi (Maddah in a letter)
MaddulLazim al Kalimi al Muthaqqal (Heavy)	MaddulLazim al Harfi al Muthaqqal (Heavy)
MaddulLazim al Kalimi al Mukhaffaf (Light)	MaddulLazim al Harfi al Mukhaffaf (Light)

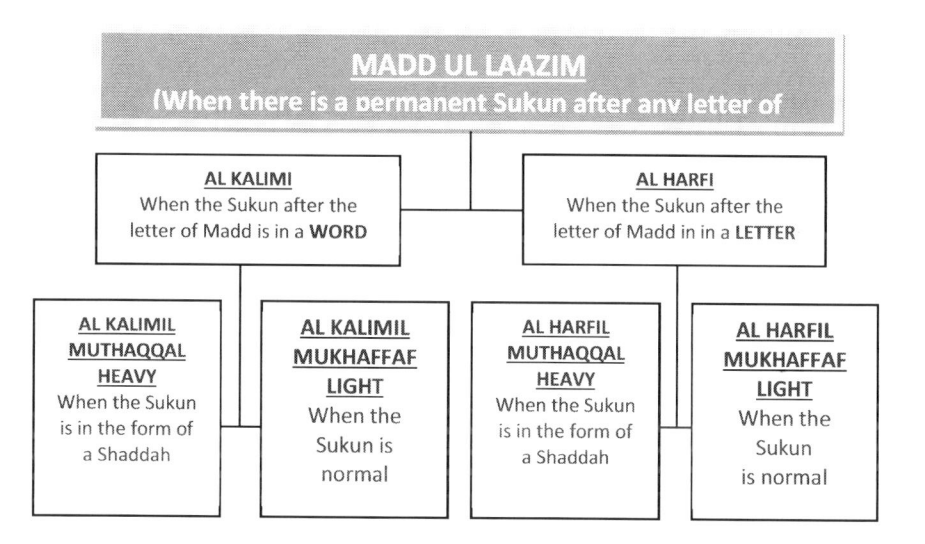

MADD UL LAAZIM
(When there is a permanent Sukun after any letter of

AL KALIMI – When the Sukun after the letter of Madd is in a **WORD**

AL HARFI – When the Sukun after the letter of Madd in in a **LETTER**

- **AL KALIMIL MUTHAQQAL HEAVY** – When the Sukun is in the form of a Shaddah
- **AL KALIMIL MUKHAFFAF LIGHT** – When the Sukun is normal
- **AL HARFIL MUTHAQQAL HEAVY** – When the Sukun is in the form of a Shaddah
- **AL HARFIL MUKHAFFAF LIGHT** – When the Sukun is normal

NOTE: The heavy form of MaddulLazim occurs when a Maddah letter is followed by a letter bearing a Shaddah. The Shaddah indicates that Idhgham has taken place and also represents a doubled letter, the first of which bears a Sukun.

Example: ق = ق+ق   م = م+م   س = س+س

Madd UlLaazim Al Kalimi (Mukhaffaf - Light) When a Sukun ْ follows a Madd letter in a word. It must be prolonged no less than 6 vowel counts only 1 case in the Qur'an ءَآلْـٰٔنَ	**Madd UlLaazim Al Kalimi (Muthaqqal - Heavy)** When a Shaddah follows a Madd letter in a word. It is stretched for 6 vowel counts Examples ٱلطَّآمَّةُ
Madd UlLaazim Al Harfi (Mukhaffaf - Light) If a Madd letter is followed by a Sakin letter, the reader is required to prolong the Madd letter. This Madd must be prolonged to 6 vowel counts.	**Madd UlLaazim Al Harfi (Muthaqqal - Heavy)** If a Madd letter is followed by a Mushaddad letter, the reader is required to prolong the Madd letter. This Madd must be prolonged for 6 vowel counts.

MADD UL LAAZIM (Maddah caused by Sukun)

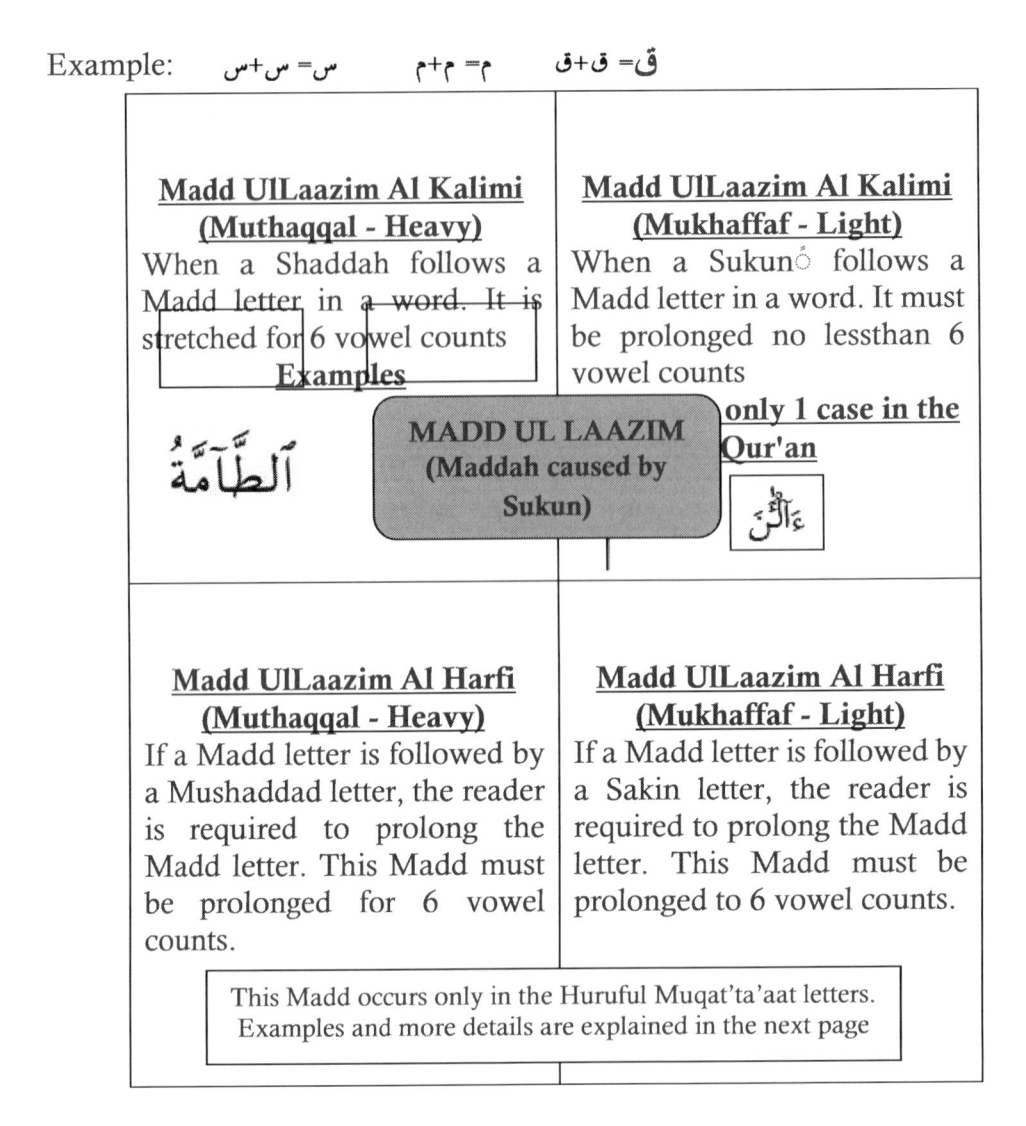

This Madd occurs only in the Huruful Muqat'ta'aat letters. Examples and more details are explained in the next page

DETAILED EXPLANATION & EXAMPLES ON MADD UL-LAAZIM AL-HARFI

The Madd ul-Laazim al-Harfi is the Madd that occurs in **letters** and not words (Madd ul- Laazim al-Kalimi). In this case all the letters are from the HurufulMuqatt'ta'aat (The Mysterious Letters – discussed elsewhere in this book) The letters of HurufulMuqatt'ta'aat are 14 letters (half of the Arabic Alphabets). They appear in 29 chapters in the Holy Qur'an as the opening of the Surah and they appear in 14 different ways, as 1 letter alone, or together as 2, 3 or more letters.

THE 14 HURUFUL MUQATT'TA'AAT

صٓ	قٓ	نٓ	حمٓ
طه	طسٓ	يسٓ	الٓمٓ
الرٓ	طسمٓ	عسقٓ	الٓمٓصٓ
	الٓمٓر	كهيعصٓ	

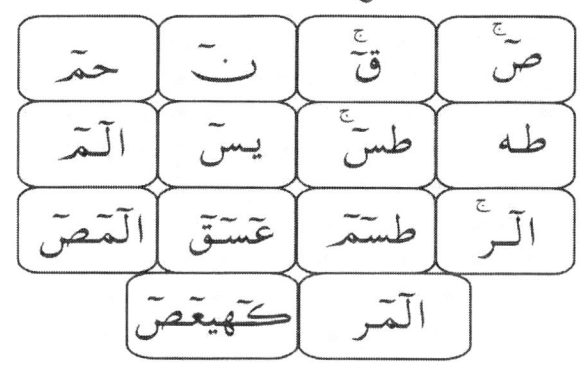

THE 14 HURUFUL MUQATT'TA'AAT IN THE MADD UL-LAAZIM AL-HARFI

1) The individual letters have to be pronounced by reading out their respective names according to their spelling.
2) The length of each letter's prolongation will be determined by the Madd rule inherent within the spelling of it.
3) The difference of the length of its prolongation is determined by the number of letters that are used to spell the name of that particular letter.
4) These Madd can contain one, two, three or more letters.
5) In regards to their lengthening, the HurufulMuqatt'ta'aat are divided into 4 types
6) The divisions into these types is based on how the letters are spelt.

Important Note: When reciting the HurufulMuqatta'at, **"all the letters with a Maddah sign should be read as the letter itself, and all the letters with thestanding Alif, should be read as the sound of that letter"**

DIVISION OF THE 14 HURUFUL MUQATT'TA'AAT ACCORDING TO THEIR PROLONGATION

1.) The letter الف – ا (Alif – when we spell the letter). It does not have a Madd in between it's spelling, therefore we do not stretch it and say it plainly as Alif

2.) The 5 letters of ر ه ط ي ح, are known by the acronym 'HayyTuhr' حي
طهرThese letters are written with their spelling and read out without being followed by a Hamza or Sukun

حا	يا	طا	ها	را
Haa	yaa	taa	haa	Raa

Notice when the above 5 letters are read by their names, they all have the Alif Maddah in-between, this makes it Madd at-Tabee and these letters are stretched for 2 counts

3.) The 7 letters of م ك ل ص ق ن س are known by the acronym SanaqussuLakum, سنقصل كمThese letters are written with their spelling and read out. In these 7 letters, the letter of Madd is within it, when followed by Sukun, it is merged and therefore is has Madd al-Harfi, which is elongated by 6 harakat.

س	ن	ق	ص	ل	ك	م
سين	نون	قاف	صاد	لام	كاف	ميم
seen	noon	qaaf	saad	laam	kaaf	meem

4.) The letter **ARABIC**(Ayn – when we spell the letter). It has the Yaa Madd inbetween, which is the letter of ease. This makes it Madd al-Leen and it iselongated for 2, 4 or 6 Harakat.

DIVISION OF THE 14 HURUFUL MUQATT'TA'AAT ACCORDING TO THEIRPROLONGATION

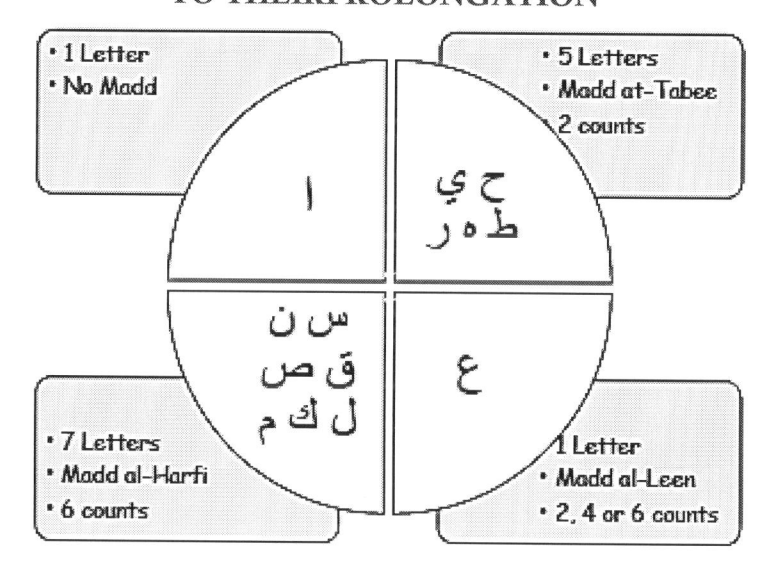

- 1 Letter
- No Madd

ا

- 5 Letters
- Madd at-Tabee
- 2 counts

ح ي
ط ه ر

- 7 Letters
- Madd al-Harfi
- 6 counts

س ن
ق ص
ل ك م

ع

- 1 Letter
- Madd al-Leen
- 2, 4 or 6 counts

ELONGATION OF HURUFUL MUQATT'TA'AAT

حم	يس	طس	طه	Written
حا ميم	يا سين	طا سين	طا ها	Read
6 2	6 2	6 2	2 2	Length of Stretch
ص	طسم	الر	الم	Written
صاد	طا سين ميم	الف لام را	الف لام ميم	Read
6	6 6 2	2 6 1	6 6 1	Length of Stretch
كهيعص		ن	ق	Written
كاف ها يا عين صاد		نون	قاف	Read
6 6 2 2 6		6	6	Length of Stretch

THE MADD AL-HARFI IN THE HURUFUL MUQATT'TA'AAT

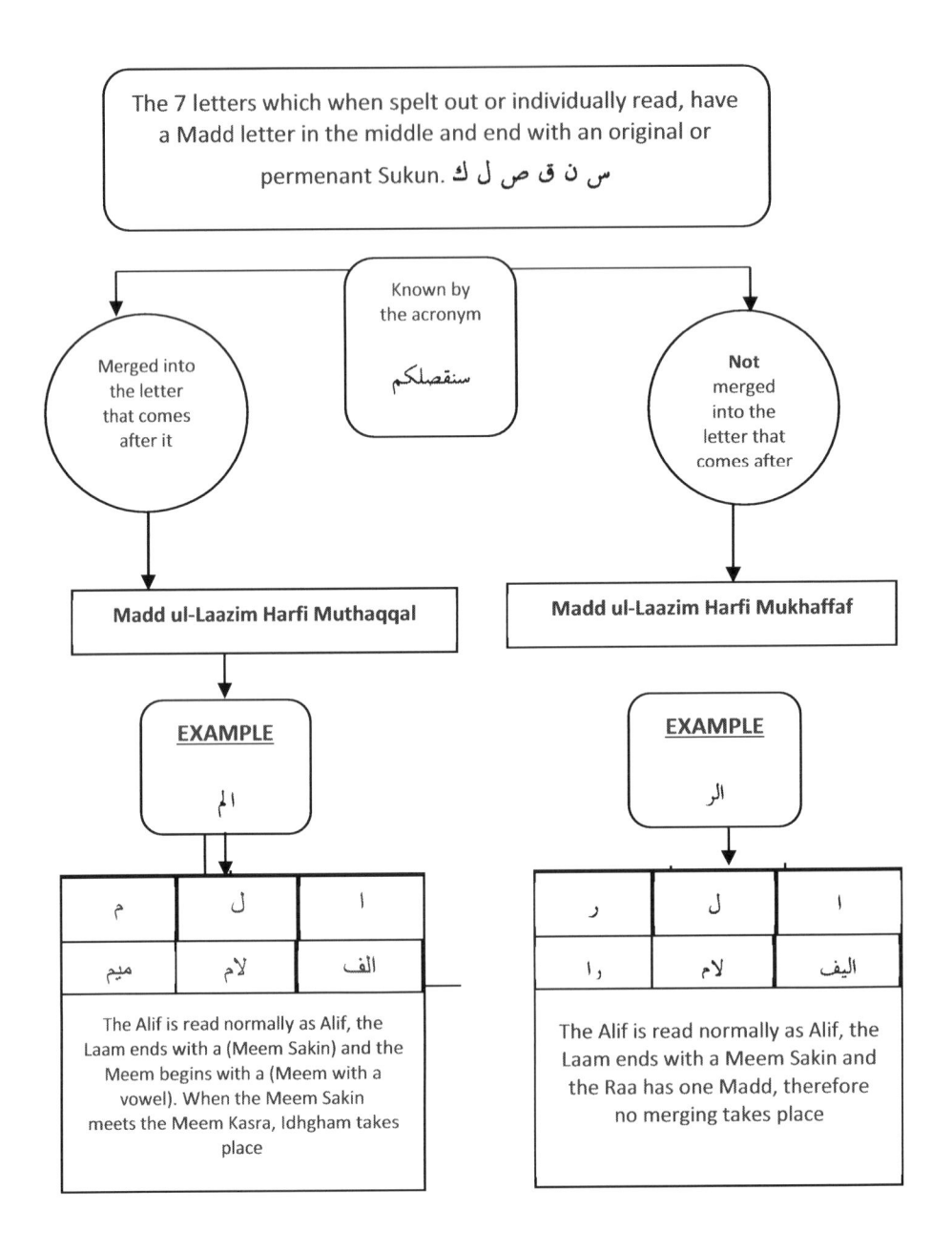

The 7 letters which when spelt out or individually read, have a Madd letter in the middle and end with an original or permenant Sukun. س ن ق ص ل ك

Known by the acronym

سنقصلكم

Merged into the letter that comes after it

Not merged into the letter that comes after

Madd ul-Laazim Harfi Muthaqqal

Madd ul-Laazim Harfi Mukhaffaf

EXAMPLE

الم

ا	ل	م
الف	لام	ميم

The Alif is read normally as Alif, the Laam ends with a (Meem Sakin) and the Meem begins with a (Meem with a vowel). When the Meem Sakin meets the Meem Kasra, Idhgham takes place

EXAMPLE

الر

ا	ل	ر
اليف	لام	را

The Alif is read normally as Alif, the Laam ends with a Meem Sakin and the Raa has one Madd, therefore no merging takes place

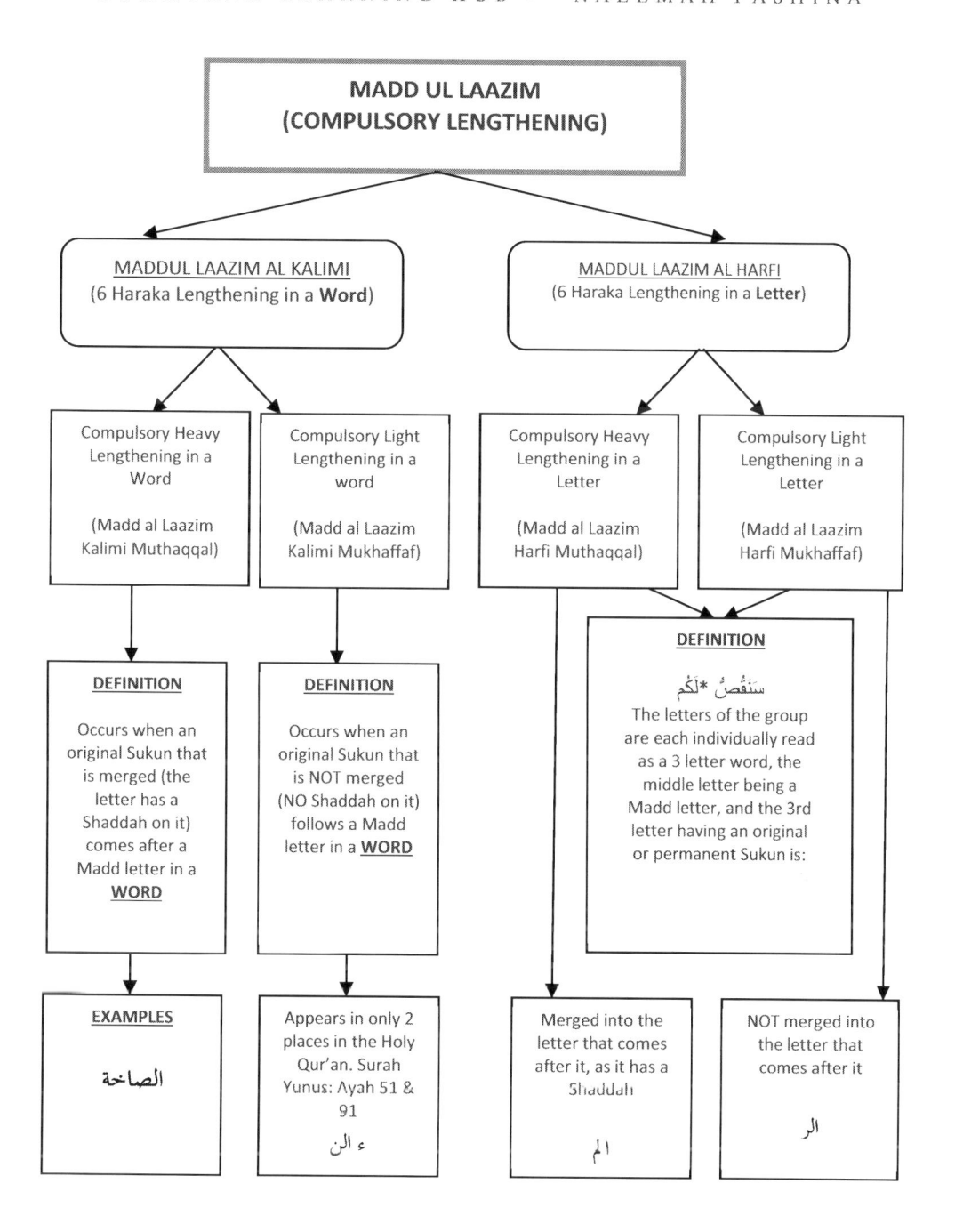

```
                    ┌─────────────────────────────┐
                    │      MADD UL LAAZIM         │
                    │  (COMPULSORY LENGTHENING)   │
                    └─────────────────────────────┘
                           /              \
                          /                \
      ┌──────────────────────────┐   ┌──────────────────────────┐
      │  MADDUL LAAZIM AL KALIMI │   │  MADDUL LAAZIM AL HARFI  │
      │ (6 Haraka Lengthening in │   │ (6 Haraka Lengthening in │
      │        a Word)           │   │       a Letter)          │
      └──────────────────────────┘   └──────────────────────────┘
```

MADDUL LAAZIM AL KALIMI

Compulsory Heavy Lengthening in a Word
(Madd al Laazim Kalimi Muthaqqal)

DEFINITION

Occurs when an original Sukun that is merged (the letter has a Shaddah on it) comes after a Madd letter in a **WORD**

EXAMPLES

الصاخة

Compulsory Light Lengthening in a word
(Madd al Laazim Kalimi Mukhaffaf)

DEFINITION

Occurs when an original Sukun that is NOT merged (NO Shaddah on it) follows a Madd letter in a **WORD**

Appears in only 2 places in the Holy Qur'an. Surah Yunus: Ayah 51 & 91

ء الن

MADDUL LAAZIM AL HARFI

Compulsory Heavy Lengthening in a Letter
(Madd al Laazim Harfi Muthaqqal)

Compulsory Light Lengthening in a Letter
(Madd al Laazim Harfi Mukhaffaf)

DEFINITION

سَنُقَصُّ *لَكُم

The letters of the group are each individually read as a 3 letter word, the middle letter being a Madd letter, and the 3rd letter having an original or permanent Sukun is:

Merged into the letter that comes after it, as it has a Shaddah

الم

NOT merged into the letter that comes after it

الر

EXAMPLES OF MADD UL HARFEE MUTHAQQAL

Pronounced as	Written as
ألف لَام مِّيم صَاد (6 beats)	المص
ألف لَام مِّيم رَا (6 beats)	المر
ألف لَام مِّيم (6 beats)	الم

EXAMPLES OF MADD UL HARFEE MUKHAFFAF

Pronounced as	Written as
كَاف هَا يَا عَيْن صَاد (6 beats)	كهيعص
ألف لَام مِّيم صَاد (6 beats)	المص
ألف لَام مِّيم رَا (6 beats)	الر
ألف لَام مِّيم (6 beats)	الم

MADD AL FAR'I: MADDAH CAUSED BY SUKUN – 8.) MADD UL-LEEN

Leen literally means Softness. Madd al-Leen occurs when certain letters are pronounced softly and with ease. Leen letters are: -

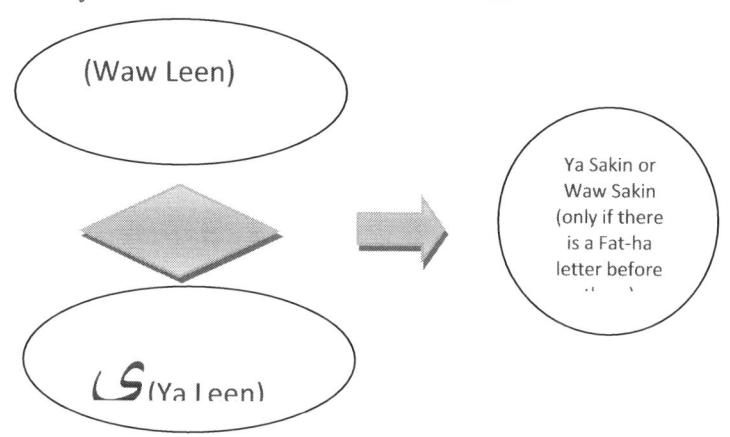

(Waw Leen)

Ya Sakin or Waw Sakin (only if there is a Fat-ha letter before

ﻱ (Ya Leen)

THE RULE OF MADD UL-LEEN: If one of the Leen letters is followed by a letter at the end of a word, which has been Saakin due to stop (If the reader will not stop, no Madd is applied), the reader should prolong the Leen letter. The reader can choose to prolong it 2, 4 or 6 beats.

Examples:

YA LEEN		
طير	عليهم	بالغيب

WAW LEEN		
التوراة	فوقهم	منحوف

Examples of Maddul Leen

(خوف)خوف	(قريش) قريش
If stopping read as: Khawf If continuing read as: Khawfin	If stopping read as: Quraish If continuing read as: Quraishin

MADD AL FAR'I: MADDAH CAUSED BY SUKUN – 9.) MADD UL-ARIDH LISSUKUN

Madd Aridh Lis Sukun means "Temporary Madd for stopping". The reciter must exercise consistency with the length of the applied stretch in the entire recitation.

CONDITIONS OF MADD UL-ARIDH LIS SUKUN

a.) The Madd should be the 2nd last letter in the word
b.) The Sukun is found in stopping on (the sound of) the last letter of the word
c.) The Madd MUST NOT have a Fat-ha, Kasra or Dhamma on it
d.) The letter before the Madd letter, must have a suitable diacritic, i.e. Fat-habefore the Alif, Kasra before the Yaa and Dhamma before the Waw
e.) The reciter must stop after the word being recited in order to sound this Maddfor 2, 4 or 6 counts
f.) The reciter can sound this Madd for 2 counts whether they are stopping or not,but generally, 2 counts are sounded only when the reciter wishes to continue,which should be considered as Madd Tabee (2 counts elongation)

SPECIAL CASE: Where a Fat-ha precedes the Yaa Madd or Waw Madd, it becomes known as Madd al-Leen. Al Madd al-Leen has the same principles as Al Madd al-AridhlilSukun.

In brief MaddulArdhwi– The temporary stop Madd occurs when a letter of Madd is followed by a letter bearing a vowel that becomes Sakin, when the reciter stops or pauses to take a breath, usually at the end of a verse.

Examples of MaddulArdhwi

أطيعون	⟵ أطيعون	الحساب	⟵ الحساب
المرصاد	⟵ المرصاد	يعملون	⟵ يعملون

RULES OF HAA

ۀ ە ﻩ

ALL ARE 'HAA' & CAN BE WRITTEN IN DIFFERENT WAYS

1) Haa Thatee — The Essential Haa

2) Haa Sakt — The Consonant Haa

3) Haa Dhameer — The Pronoun Haa

3 TYPES

RULES OF HAA

The letter Haa(ه) that comes at the end of words in the Holy Qur'an (همه) is one of the three types mentioned below:
1.) HaaThatee, the essential Haa
2.) HaaSakt, the consonant Haa
3.) HaaDhameer, the pronoun Haa

1.) HAA THATEE – THE ESSENTIAL HAA

The essential Haa is the letter (همه) that comes at the end of the word and is part of the word itself, it cannot be separated from it.

Examples:

كره	وجوه	وجه	تنته	ينته	فواقه	نفقة	الله

2.) HAA SAKT – THE CONSONANT HAA

The consonant Haa is the letter (همه) that comes at the end of the word, it is not part of it and does not have any meaning. It is there to confirm the necessity of stopping at the specified word. If you choose to continue with the next word it should be pronounced as a consonant Haa. Examples where the consonant Haa appears in the Holy Qur'an:

لم يتسنه	فبهده اقتده	ماهيه	كتابيه	حسابيه	ماليه	سلطانيه
Surah Al-Baqarah	Surah Al-An'aam	Surah Al-Qaari'ah	Surah Al-Haaqqah	Surah Al-Haaqqah	Surah Al-Haaqqah	Surah Al-Haaqqah
Verse 259	Verse 90	Verse 10	Verse 19 & 25	Verse 20 & 26	Verse 28	Verse 29

3) HAA DHAMEER – THE PRONOUN HAA

The pronoun Haa is the letter (همه) that comes at the end of the word and takes theplace of the name. <u>Example</u>

كتاب	كتابه	من	منه
book	his book	from	from him

The pronoun Haa never carried a Fat-ha, it always carries either a Kasra or a Dhamma. But sometimes the short vowel of the pronoun Haa is pronounced as a long vowel, with Ishbaa, meaning with repletion, and is sometimes pronounced normally as a short vowel, without repletion.

ISHBAA– Means satiate or full. It usually refers to elongation or lengthening. When we mention Ishbaa in Mudood, then it means the longest lengthening of six vowel counts, when we say Ishbaa in Imaalah, it means the grand Imaalah and when we mention Ishbaa invowels, it means lengthening the vowel. In the case of reciting Haa with or without Ishbaa, refers to lengthening the Haa sound with a vowel.

PRONOUN HAA READ WITH ISHBAA

The short vowel of the pronoun Haa is pronounced as a long vowel when both sides of theletter (هـه) are carrying a short vowel. If it carries Dhamma (-ُ) it will be pronouncedas the long vowel (و) and if it carries Kasra (-ِ) it will be pronounced as (ي)

Examples:

رهبكلمات = رهوبكلمات	انه لقول = انهو لقول
به ولا = به ولا	موا ضعه ونسوا = مواا ضعه ونسوا

PRONOUN HAA READ WITHOUT ISHBAA

The short vowel of the pronoun **Haa will be pronounced normally**, with the short vowel it is carrying when:

i. One side or both sides of the pronoun (هـه) are accompanied by a Sukun			
وله الحمد	اليه المصير	منه جما	لديه خبرا
ii. A letter accompanied by Shaddah follows the pronoun (ه مه)			
قيل له اتق الله	به لاذين	يعلمه الله	
iii. The pronoun (همه) is preceded by a long vowel			
فيه هدي	نصروه	انزلناه	

NOTE:
1.) The Haa(ه) at the end of the word (هذه), even though it is an essential Haa, is pronounced with Ishbaa (under the rule of Ishbaa)

179

2.) The pronoun Haa(ﻤﻪ) in these two words is accompanied by Sukun, (ارجه) inSurah Al-A'raaf, Ayah 111 and in Sura Ash-Shu'araa, Ayah 36 and (فالقه) inSurah An-Naml, Ayah 28

3.) The pronoun Haa(ﻤﻪ) in (يرضه لكم) in Surah Az-Zumar, Ayah 7 is readwithout Ishbaa.

4.) The pronoun Haa(ﻤﻪ) in (ويخلد فيه مهانا) in Surah Al-Furqaan, Ayah 69 isread with Ishbaa.

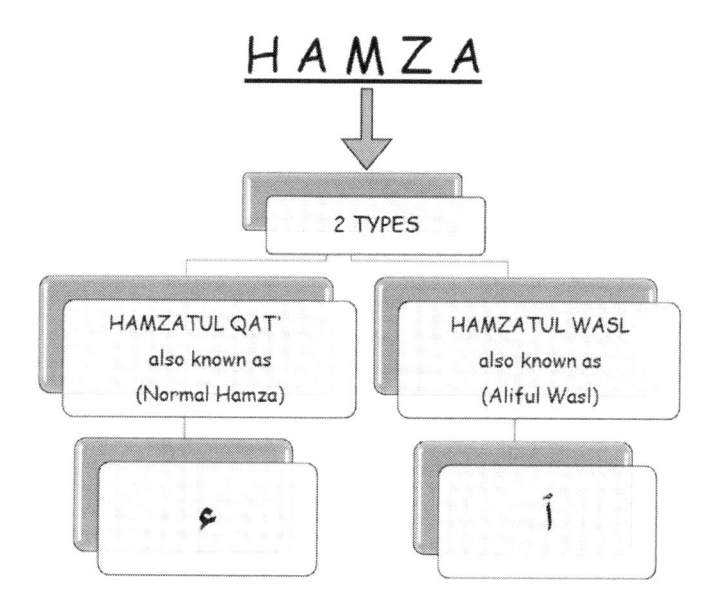

HAMZA

HAMZA

↓

2 TYPES

- **HAMZATUL QAT'**
  also known as
  (Normal Hamza)

  ء

- **HAMZATUL WASL**
  also known as
  (Aliful Wasl)

  أ

HAMZA

2 Types of Hamza in the Holy Qur'an
Both are read and treated differently

HAMZATUL QAT'
also known as
(Normal Hamza or cutting Hamza)

ء أ إ ؤ ئ لأَ لإ

The Head of the letter Ayn which can appear alone or above or below certain letters

1) Appears in many forms

2) Can appear in the beginning, middle or the end of words

3) Can carry vowels of Fat-ha, Kasra, Dhamma, Sukun and sometimes Tanween

4) It is always pronounced as a Hamza, even if it is sitting on another letter or even if it has a Sukun

HAMZATUL WASL
also known as
(Aliful Wasl or Connecting Hamza)

ٱ

Alif with a Half Saad (fish shape) on top

1) Appears as only One form. Sometimes appears as a bare Alif without the Saad.

2) Appears only in the beginning of words

3) Has no vowels in **written** form. We will discuss further on how it can be read with the Fat-ha, Kasra & Dhamma.

4) Is not always pronounced and certain rules are applied to its pronounciation

HAMZATUL QAT' ء

HamzatulQat'aa looks like the top half of the letter ع. It is sometimes referred to as the normal Hamza OR the cutting Hamza OR the dividing Hamza.

MANY FORMS OF HAMZATUL QAT' – In whichever form the HamzatulQat' appears, it is always read clearly and the sound is always 'A', 'I' or 'U', depending on the vowel (haraka) it appears with. The sound of the HamzatulQat'aa is produced by cutting off the airstream at the top of the windpipe.

ء	أ	إ	ئ
Hamza by itself	Hamza seated on top of an Alif	Hamza below the Alif (appears with the Kasra vowel)	Hamza on a Yaa (Note: This Yaa has no dots)
ئ	ؤ	لأ	لإ
Hamza in a joining format	Hamza seated on a Waw	Hamza seated on the Alif in the letter Laam Alif	Hamza under the Alif on the letter Laam Alif

HamzatulQat'aa is a regular consonant letter that in writing appears anywhere in a word, either by itself or is carried by an Alif, Ya or Waw. It can appear in any part of a word, in the beginning, in the middle or at the end.

EXAMPLE

Hamza in the beginning of a word

اكل   انعمت   AKALA   AN AMTA

Hamza in the middle of a word

را   الملاءكة   RA A   AL MALAA IKA

Hamza at the end of a word

السماء   جاء   AS SAMAA   JAA A

HAMZATUL QAT' ء

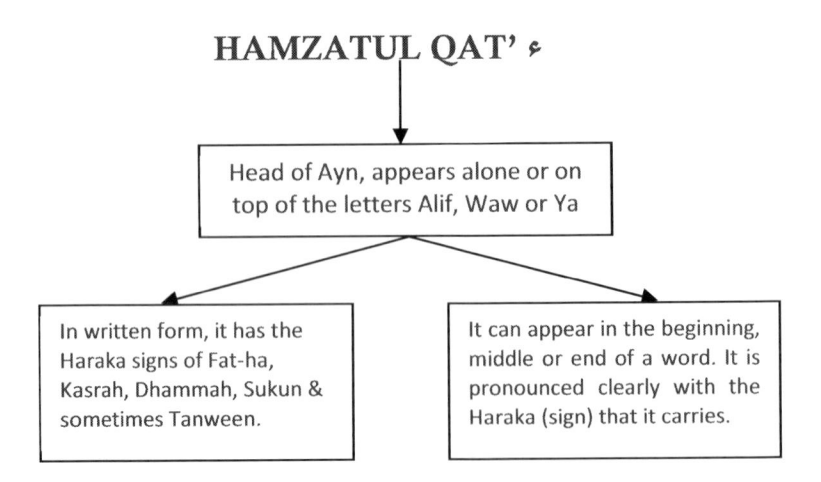

Head of Ayn, appears alone or on top of the letters Alif, Waw or Ya

- In written form, it has the Haraka signs of Fat-ha, Kasrah, Dhammah, Sukun & sometimes Tanween.
- It can appear in the beginning, middle or end of a word. It is pronounced clearly with the Haraka (sign) that it carries.

WAYS OF READING HAMZA:

When it appears with a Sukun, there is a jerking or cutting sound and it is pronounced at Half its normal length.	
موصدة	فأتوا
Mu' sadatun and not Muusadatun	Fa' tuu and not Faatuu
When 2 Hamzas' appear together, next to each other, the Hamza is pronounced clearly for both of them, continuously with no cut	
ءأنتم	ءأنت
A-antum (continuously no cutting)	A-anta (continuously no cutting)
Sometimes the Hamza is not written above the Alif, only a Sukun is written. The jerky sound (half it's normal length) will still be pronounced. **Example:**	
قرات وامر نات	

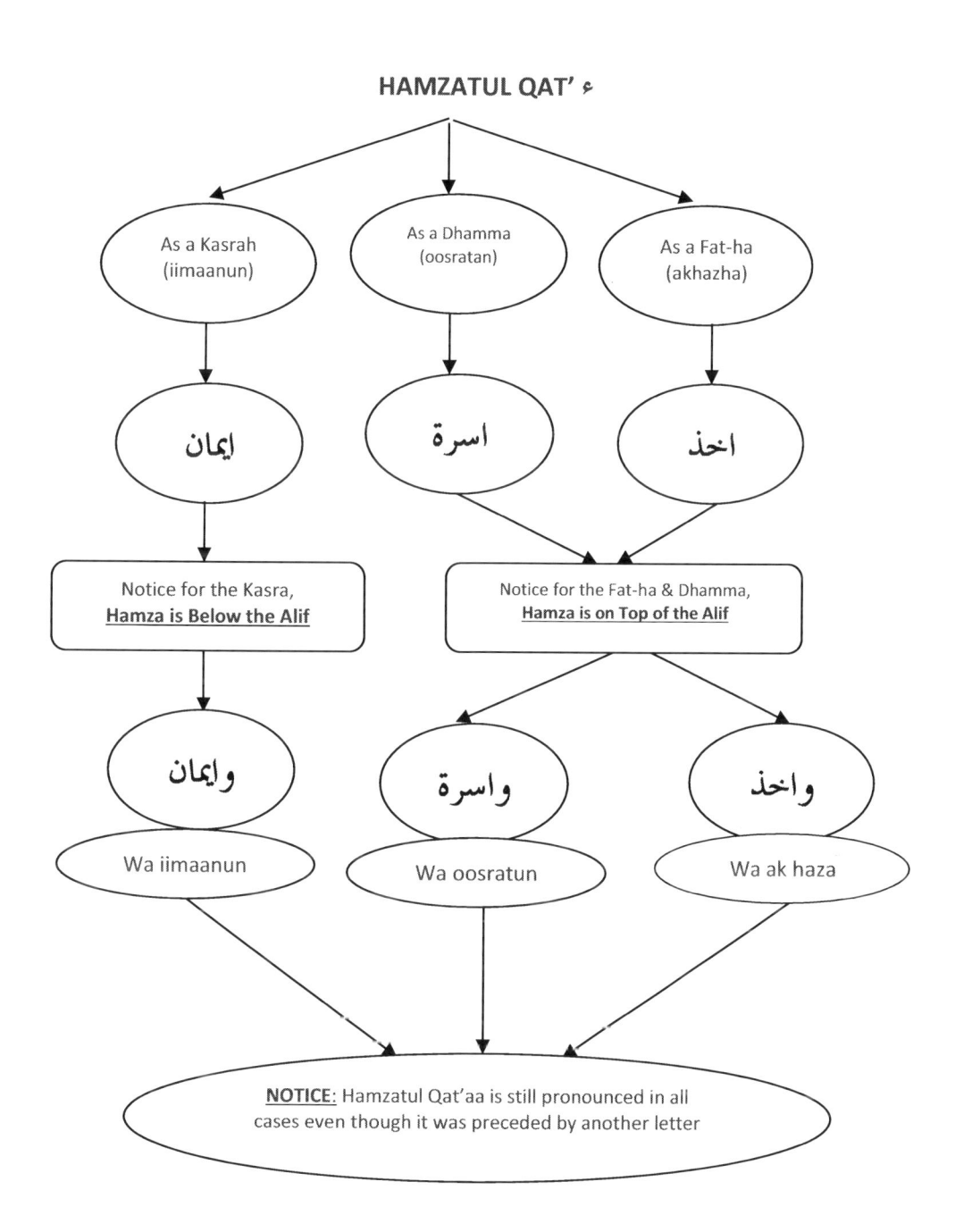

HAMZATUL QAT' ء

- As a Kasrah (iimaanun) → إيمان → **Notice for the Kasra, Hamza is Below the Alif** → وإيمان → Wa iimaanun
- As a Dhamma (oosratan) → اسرة
- As a Fat-ha (akhazha) → اخذ

Notice for the Fat-ha & Dhamma, **Hamza is on Top of the Alif** → واسرة (Wa oosratun), واخذ (Wa ak haza)

NOTICE: Hamzatul Qat'aa is still pronounced in all cases even though it was preceded by another letter

HAMZATUL WASL ﺃ

This is the connective Hamza that always appears at the beginning of nouns, verbs and prepositions. It is represented by the symbol that looks like an Alif with a half Saad ص over it, thus the name HamzatulWasl OR AlifulWasl. It occurs only at the beginning of a word and does not have any vowel on it. In some Qur'an, the Alif has no such sign over it, so it's an Empty or Bare Alif.

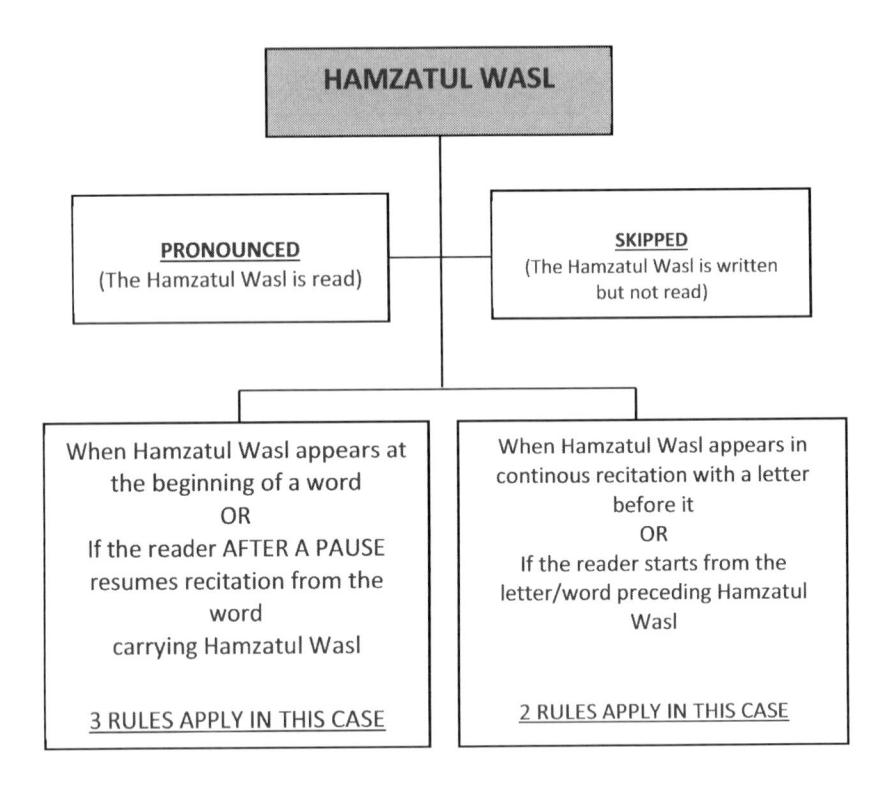

```
                    HAMZATUL WASL
                    /            \
           PRONOUNCED           SKIPPED
      (The Hamzatul Wasl      (The Hamzatul Wasl is written
           is read)               but not read)
```

PRONOUNCED:
When Hamzatul Wasl appears at the beginning of a word
OR
If the reader AFTER A PAUSE resumes recitation from the word carrying Hamzatul Wasl

3 RULES APPLY IN THIS CASE

SKIPPED:
When Hamzatul Wasl appears in continous recitation with a letter before it
OR
If the reader starts from the letter/word preceding Hamzatul Wasl

2 RULES APPLY IN THIS CASE

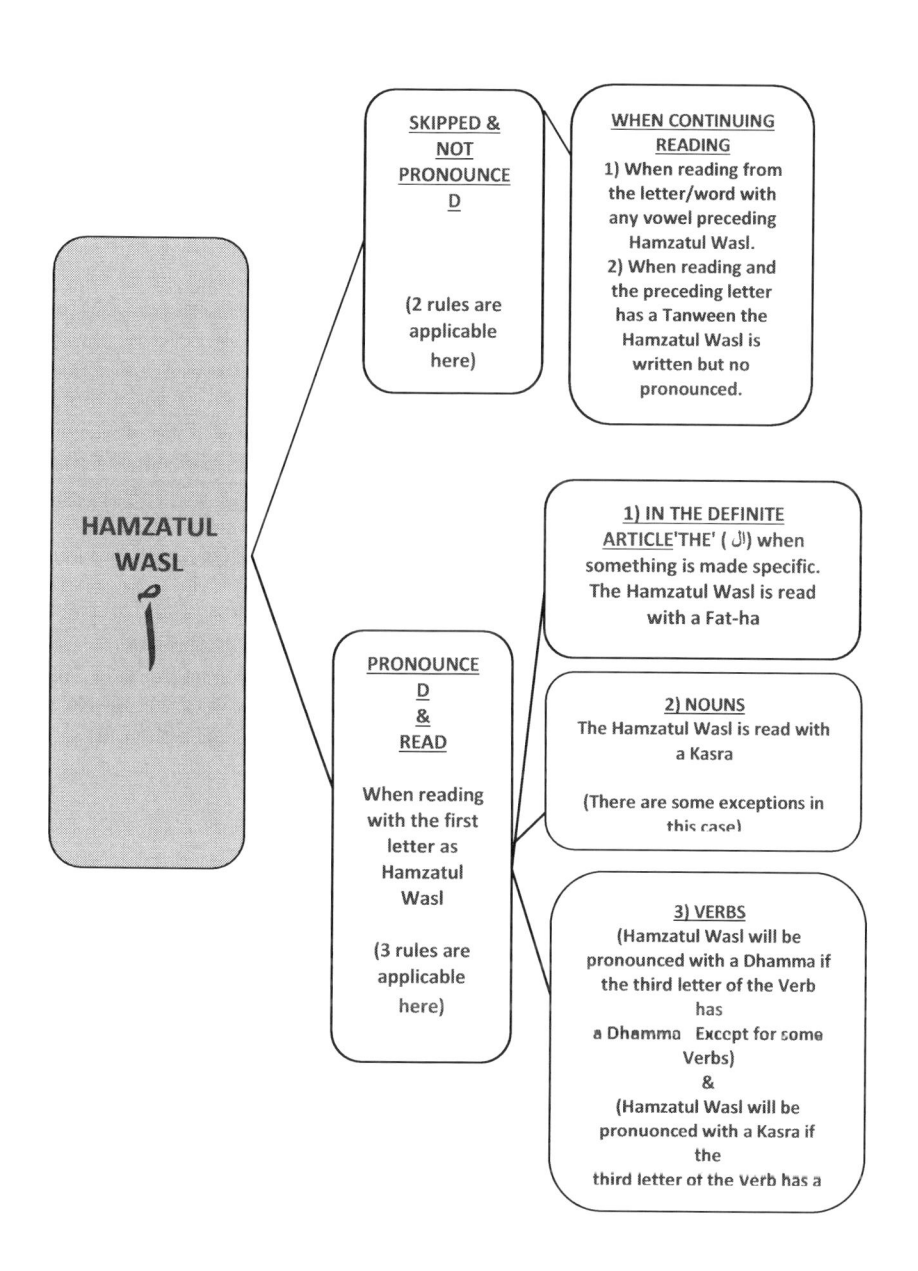

HAMZATUL WASL
ٱ

SKIPPED & NOT PRONOUNCED
(2 rules are applicable here)

WHEN CONTINUING READING
1) When reading from the letter/word with any vowel preceding Hamzatul Wasl.
2) When reading and the preceding letter has a Tanween the Hamzatul Wasl is written but no pronounced.

PRONOUNCED & READ
When reading with the first letter as Hamzatul Wasl
(3 rules are applicable here)

1) IN THE DEFINITE ARTICLE 'THE' (ال) when something is made specific. The Hamzatul Wasl is read with a Fat-ha

2) NOUNS
The Hamzatul Wasl is read with a Kasra

(There are some exceptions in this case)

3) VERBS
(Hamzatul Wasl will be pronounced with a Dhamma if the third letter of the Verb has a Dhamma Except for some Verbs)
&
(Hamzatul Wasl will be pronuonced with a Kasra if the third letter of the Verb has a

THE RULE OF HAMZATUL WASL: SKIPPED IN CONTINOUS RECITATION

The 2 rules when HamzatulWasl appears in continuous recitation with a letter before it. The HamzatulWasl is written but skipped during recitation.	
RULE 1: If the HamzatulWasl appears in continous recitation and there is no pause, and the letter preceding HamzatulWasl has a Vowel, then the HamzatulWasl is dropped and not pronounced.	RULE 2: If the HamzatulWasl appears in continous recitation and there is no pause, but the letter preceding the HamzatulWasl is a Tanween, then one harakah from the Tanween is dropped and a small Nun with Kasrah is placed under the HamzatulWasl. The Nun Kasrah connects with the next letter. This small Nun with Kasrah is called NUN QUTNI (Refer to the Chapter on Nun Qutni where this is covered in detail)
EXAMPLES Notice the HamzatulWasl is not pronounced	**EXAMPLES** Notice the HamzatulWasl has a Nun Kasrah under it, the Tanween changes to one vowel + a small Nun Kasrah
والعذاب بالمغفرة Wal adhaabaBilmaghfirati	يماذن السلم Yaw ma idhinis Salama
رب العالمين RabbilAalameen	قدير ن الذ KadeeruNilladhi
ماابتله Mabtalahu	خيرا ن الوصية KhairanilWasiyyah

THE RULE OF HAMZATUL WASL: SKIPPED IN CONTINOUS RECITATION

RULE 1: WITH A VOWEL BEFORE THE HAMZATUL WASL
Example:

وانحر (wanhar)	قل الحمد (Qulil Hamdu)
رب هذ البيت	ما القارعة	في الدنيا
Rabba Haadhal Bayti	Mal Qaari atu	Fid Dunya
والسماء	غير المغضوب	صراط الذين
Was Samaaaai	Ghairil Magh Dhoobi	Siraa Tal Ladhii na

RULE 2: WITH A TANWEEN BEFORE THE HAMZATUL WASL
Example:

Majeedi Qur'an Indo-Pak	Uthmani Qur'an	Majeedi Qur'an Indo-Pak	Uthmani Qur'an
خَيْرًا ٱلْوَصِيَّة	خَيْرًا ٱلْوَصِيَّة	يَوْمَئِذٍ ٱلْحَقُّ	يَوْمَئِذٍ ٱلْحَقُّ
Khairanil wasiyyah		Yawma izinil haqqu	
بِغُلَامٍ ٱسْمُهُ	بِغُلَامٍ ٱسْمُهُ	قَوْمًا ٱللَّهُ	قَوْمًا ٱللَّهُ
Bighulaami nismuhu		Qawmanil llahu	

1.) HAMZATUL WASL PRONOUNCED IN THE DEFINITE ARTICLE 'THE' اَلْ

In the Sun and Moon letters (HuroofulShamsiyyah and HurufulQamarriyya), the letters are preceded by the letters Alif and Laam. This combination of Alif and Laam is known as 'AL' and makes it specific. <u>Whenever the HamzatulWasl is followed by Laam, it is always pronounced as a Fat-ha</u>

Example:

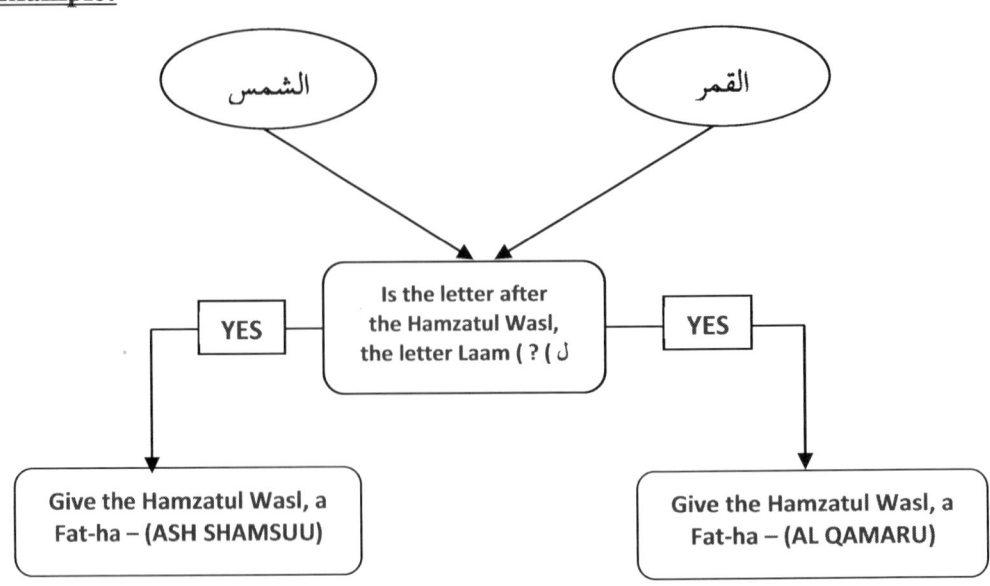

```
        الشمس                              القمر
           ↓                                  ↓
                    Is the letter after
         ← YES ←    the Hamzatul Wasl,    → YES →
                    the letter Laam ( ل ) ?
           ↓                                  ↓
   Give the Hamzatul Wasl, a       Give the Hamzatul Wasl, a
   Fat-ha – (ASH SHAMSUU)          Fat-ha – (AL QAMARU)
```

IN THE SUN LETTERS	IN THE MOON LETTERS
➢ The letter Laam of the Definite article is NOT pronounced	➢ The letter Laam of the Definite article is pronounced
➢ The Sukun shaped diacritic is NOT written on top of the Laam	➢ The Sukun shaped diacritic is written on top of the Laam
➢ The HamzatulWasl has a Fat-ha ➢ The Definite article sounds as 'a' ➢ The letter following the Laam has a Shaddah	➢ The HamzatulWasl has a Fat-ha ➢ The Definite article sounds just like its name 'AL'
Example: السماء 'as samaa'	Example : الوسيم 'al wasii mu'

2.) HAMZATUL WASL PRONOUNCED IN NOUNS – The HamzatulWasl is read with a Kasra.

Example:

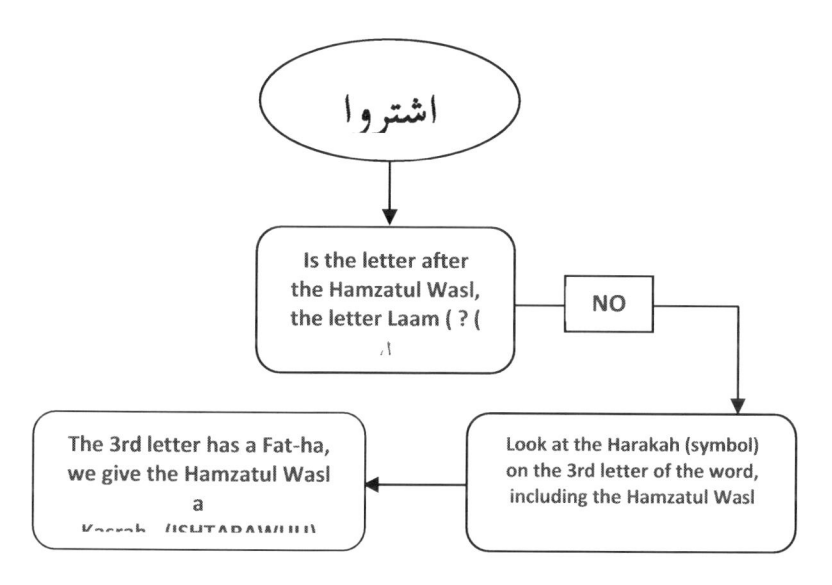

اشتروا

Is the letter after the Hamzatul Wasl, the letter Laam (ل) ? → **NO**

Look at the Harakah (symbol) on the 3rd letter of the word, including the Hamzatul Wasl

The 3rd letter has a Fat-ha, we give the Hamzatul Wasl a Kasrah. (ISHTARAWUU)

EXCEPTIONS TO THE HAMZATUL WASL

HamzatulWasl is always read with a Kasrah in the following words regardless of what is on the third letter.

VERBS and NOUNS WHERE HAMZATUL WASL IS READ WITH A KASRA

ابنوا	ابنوا	امشوا	امشوا	امضوا	امضوا
Ibnuu		Imshuu		Imdhuu	
ابن	ابن	ائتو	ائتو	اقضوا	اقضوا
Ibnun		I'tuu		Iq'dhuu	
اسمه	اسمه	ايتوا	ايتوا	امس	امس
Ismuhu		Imru oon		Imsoon	

191

3.) HAMZATUL WASL READ IN VERBS – in the beginning or after a pause

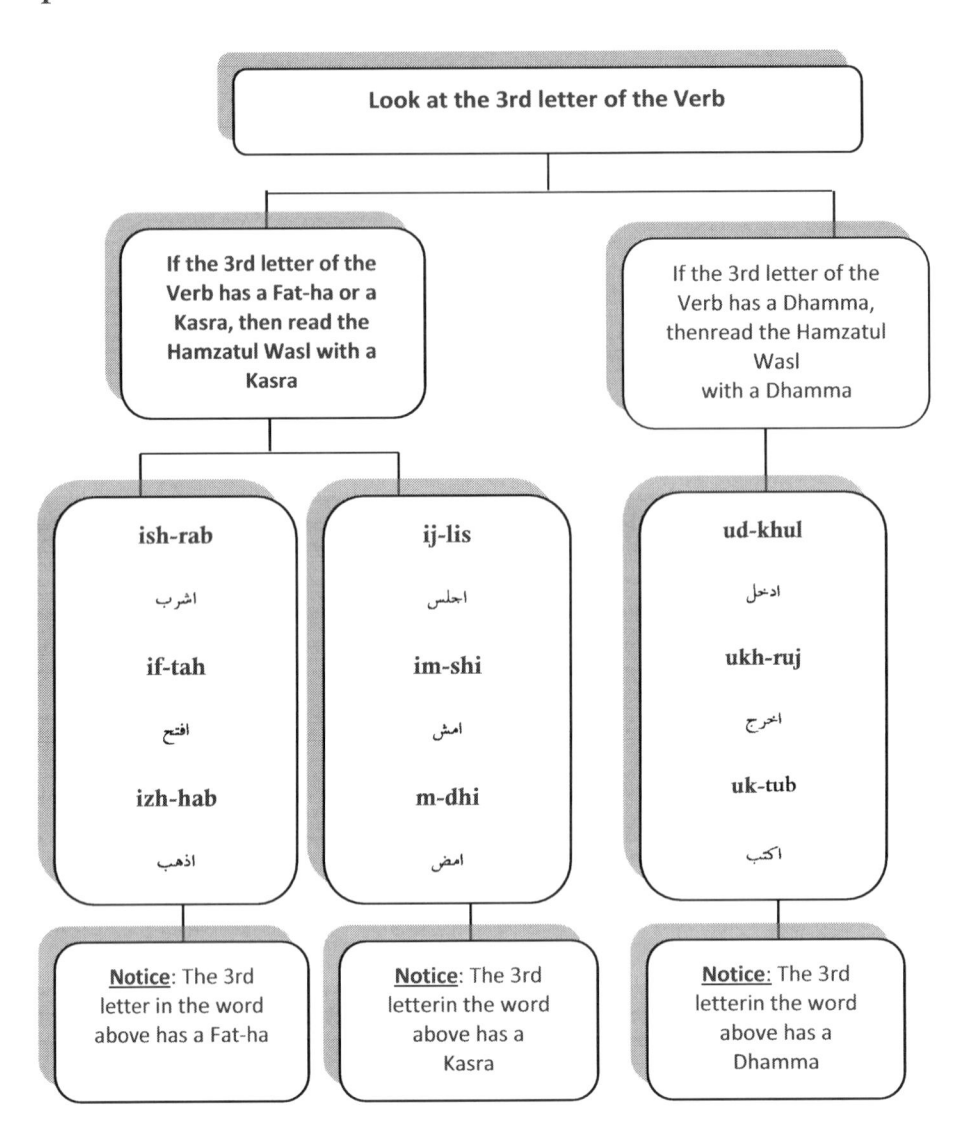

Look at the 3rd letter of the Verb

- **If the 3rd letter of the Verb has a Fat-ha or a Kasra, then read the Hamzatul Wasl with a Kasra**
- **If the 3rd letter of the Verb has a Dhamma, then read the Hamzatul Wasl with a Dhamma**

ish-rab	ij-lis	ud-khul
اشرب	اجلس	ادخل
if-tah	**im-shi**	**ukh-ruj**
افتح	امش	اخرج
izh-hab	**m-dhi**	**uk-tub**
اذهب	امض	اكتب

Notice: The 3rd letter in the word above has a Fat-ha

Notice: The 3rd letter in the word above has a Kasra

Notice: The 3rd letter in the word above has a Dhamma

HAMZATUL WASL PRONOUNCED IN VERBS – Easy to remember

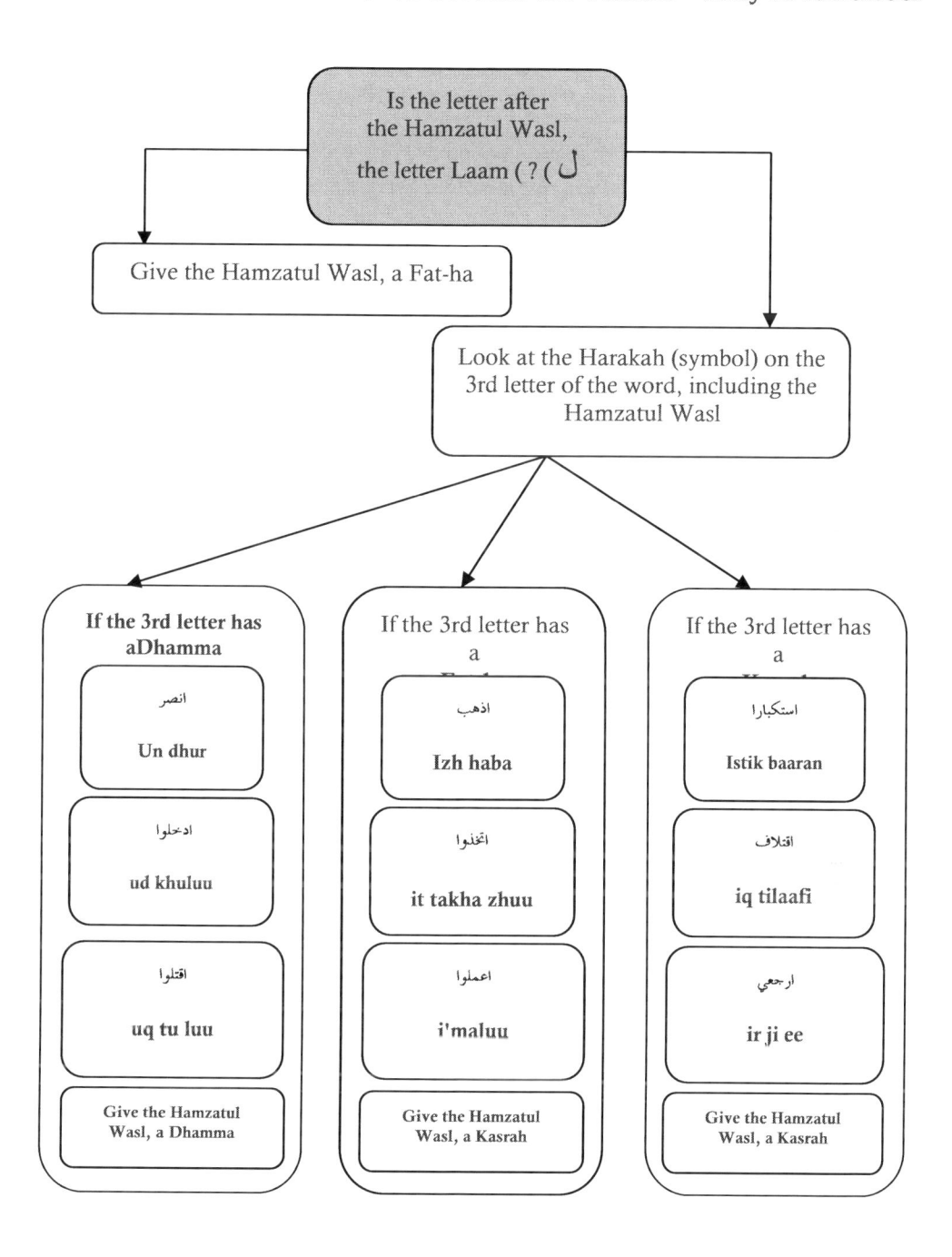

Is the letter after the Hamzatul Wasl, the letter Laam (ل) ?

→ Give the Hamzatul Wasl, a Fat-ha

→ Look at the Harakah (symbol) on the 3rd letter of the word, including the Hamzatul Wasl

If the 3rd letter has aDhamma

انصر
Un dhur

ادخلوا
ud khuluu

اقتلوا
uq tu luu

Give the Hamzatul Wasl, a Dhamma

If the 3rd letter has a Fat-ha

اذهب
Izh haba

اتخذوا
it takha zhuu

اعملوا
i'maluu

Give the Hamzatul Wasl, a Kasrah

If the 3rd letter has a Kasrah

استكبارا
Istik baaran

اقتلاف
iq tilaafi

ارجعي
ir ji ee

Give the Hamzatul Wasl, a Kasrah

HAMZATUL WASL FOLLOWED BY ANOTHER HAMZA

Step 1: We do not pronounce the 2nd Hamza (Hamza al Qat'i— أُوٓئ), rather we exchange it with the Madd letter it is sitting on.
Step 2: We give the HamzatulWasl, the matching symbol of the Huroof Madd letter.

ٱPreceded by a Dhamma, ٱpreceded by a Kasra and ٱpreceded by a Fat-ha

Step 2: The Haraka matching the Madd letter is placed on the HamzatulWasl. In this case the Haraka Dhamma matches the letter 'Waw' Read as **'UUTUMINA'**	**Step 1**: If paused and recitation starts from the HamzatulWasl, then we do not pronounce the second Hamza. We exchange for the Madd letter it is sitting on, which is the letter Waw, so we keep the letter Waw	**Alladhitumina** Read with cutting sound (If recited continuously)
Step 2: The Haraka matching the Madd letter is placed on the HamzatulWasl. In this case the HarakaKasrah matches the letter 'Ya' Read as **'EEDHAN'**	**Step 1**: If paused and recitation starts from the HamzatulWasl, then we do not pronounce the second Hamza. We exchange for the Madd letter it is sitting on, which is the letter Ya, so we keep the letter Ya	**Yakuulu' dhan** Read with cutting sound (If recited continuously)

AL-WAQF (THE STOP)

AL-WAQF The Stop	AS-SAKT The Breathless pause	AL IBTIDAA The Beginning

WAYS OF STOPPING & STARTING WHEN RECITING THE GLORIOUS QUR'AN

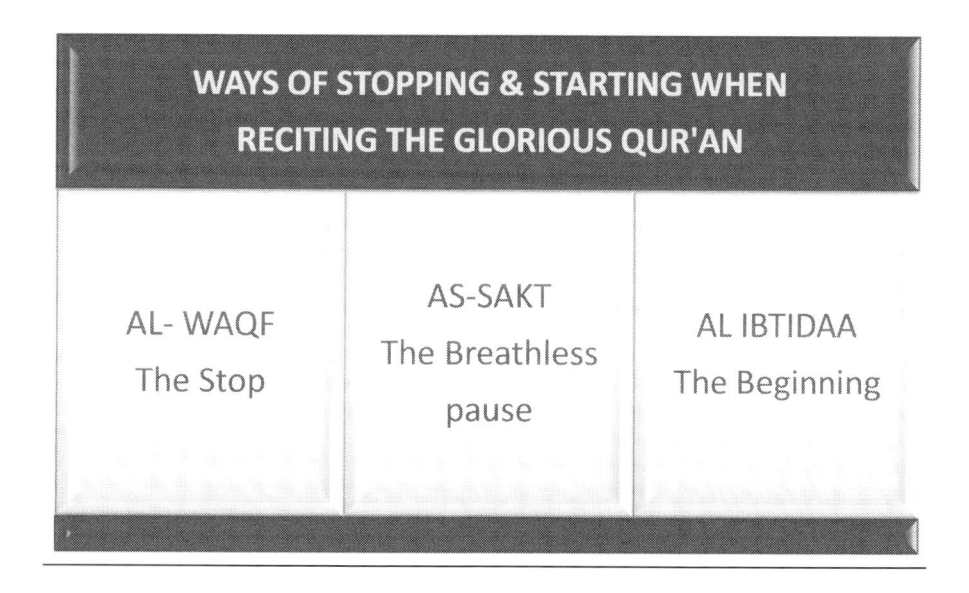

AL-WAQF – The Stop

Introduction: In Arabic, the word WAQF is singular and WUQUF is plural. Wuquf means
confinement, restriction or limitation in Tajweed. Linguistic definition of the stop: Halt and imprisonment
Applied definition of the stop: Cutting of the sound at the end of a word, usually for the period of time of breathing, with the intention of return to the recitation, not with the intention of abandoning the recital.
- The Bismillah is required after the stop when beginning a Surah
- The stop can be at the end of an Aayah, or in the middle of an Aayah
- It can never be in the middle of the word, nor in between two words that are joined in writing. One of the most important areas in the science of Tajweed is the knowledge of Al-Waqf and Al-Ibtidaa, which means the stop and the beginning. The understanding of Allāh's words cannot be realized, nor can comprehension be achieved, without this knowledge. Ali (رَضِيَ اللهُ عَنْهُ) said: "Tarteel means Tajweed of the letters and knowledge of stops." One scholar described Al-Waqf as: "The stop is sweetness of Tilawah, beautifies the reciter, an announcement of the succeeding,

understanding for the listener, pride of the scholar, and through it one knows the difference between two different meanings...."

DIVISIONS OF THE STOP

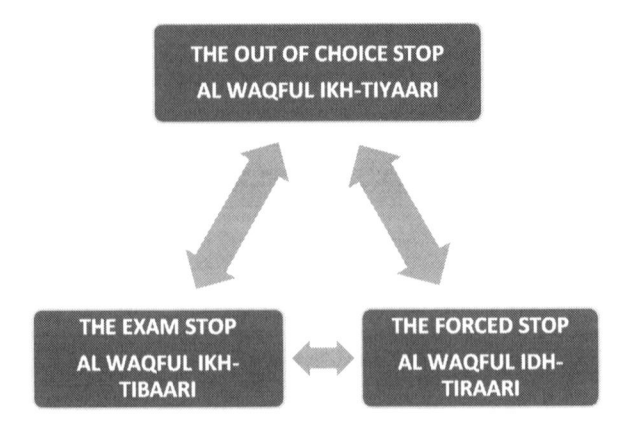

```
            THE OUT OF CHOICE STOP
            AL WAQFUL IKH-TIYAARI

   THE EXAM STOP              THE FORCED STOP
   AL WAQFUL IKH-             AL WAQFUL IDH-
   TIBAARI                    TIRAARI
```

DIVISIONS OF THE STOP

1.) **THE EXAM or TEST STOP – AL WAQFUL IKH-TIBAARI** – Occurs when a student is being examined by a teacher. The student stops when instructed to or when a mistake is being corrected.

2.) **THE FORCED or COMPELLED STOP – AL WAQFUL IDH-TIRAARI** – Occurs when a reader has to stop due to shortness of breath, sneezing, coughing, disability, forgetfulness, etc. In this case, it is allowed to stop on the end of the word, even if the meaning is not complete. The reader then starts with the word stopped on, and then joins it with what follows if it is a sound beginning; if not, the reader then should start back one or two or more words, until they can start with what is sound for a beginning.

3.) **THE OPTIONAL STOP or OUT OF CHOICE STOP – AL WAQFUL IKH-TIYAARI** – Occurs when the reciter chooses to stop by his own choice, without any outside reasons. This is the Stop that needs to be studied and applied in the correct way by the reciter of the Qur'an. The out of choice stop has been divided into four categories:

   - **The complete stop – Taam**– it is the stop on a Qur'anic word complete in meaningand not attached to what follows it in grammatical expression or in meaning. **RULE**:Best to stop on the word that is a complete stop, then start on what follows it.
   - **The sufficient stop – Kaaf** – it is the stop on a Qur'anic word that is complete inmeaning, and is attached to what follows it in meaning, but NOT in grammar. It canbe at the end of a verse, or in the middle of a verse. **RULE**: It is advisable to stopon it and start with that which follows, just as in the complete stop (Taam).
   - **The good stop – Hasn**– it is the stop on a Qur'anic word, complete in its meaning,but is attached to what follows it grammatically and in meaning. **RULE**: It is allowedto stop on it, but not allowed to start on what follows it due to its attachment towhat follows grammatically and in meaning, except on the end of an aayah. Stoppingon the end of an aayah is Sunnah.
   - **The repulsive (ugly) stop – Kabeeh**– it is the stop what does not give a correct orintended meaning, since whatever comes after it has a strong connection in meaningand grammar. **RULE**: Not allowed to stop intentionally. In case one stops due toshortness of breath or sneezing or forgetting, then the reader must repeat one, twoor more words, as necessary to convey the correct and sound meaning.

THE SYMBOLS OF WUQUF

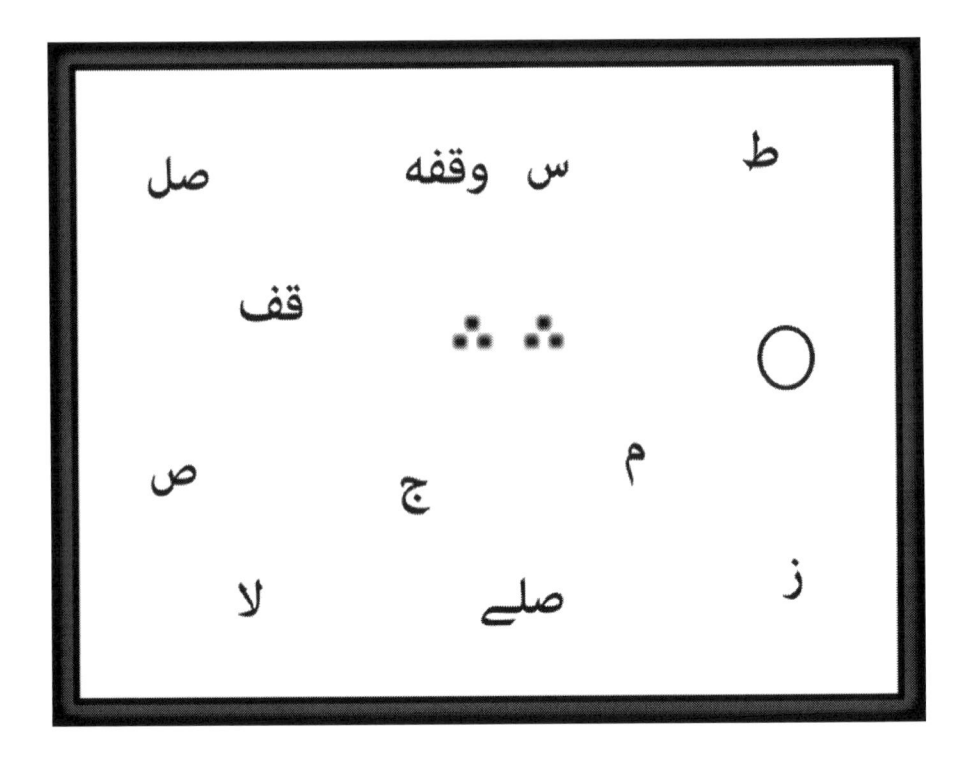

ط	س وقفه	صل
قف	࿓ ࿓	○
ص	ج	م
لا	صلے	ز

THE SYMBOLS OF WUQUF

Knowledge of the rules and of the places of Waqf is critical in preventing errors that may lead to ambiguities in the intended meaning of the verse. The correct recitation of the Holy Qur'an requires a complete familiarity with the rules of punctuation and the places
where one can pause. To assist the reader with this aspect of recitation, the Qur'an contains an elaborate system of abbreviations that identify the places and types of Waqf. These are found in the middle or the end of the ayaat and give us an indication whether stopping/pausing is permitted or not. Whenever more than one sign are found together, the reciter should follow the sign that is above all (on top of) the others. The most commonly found signs are:

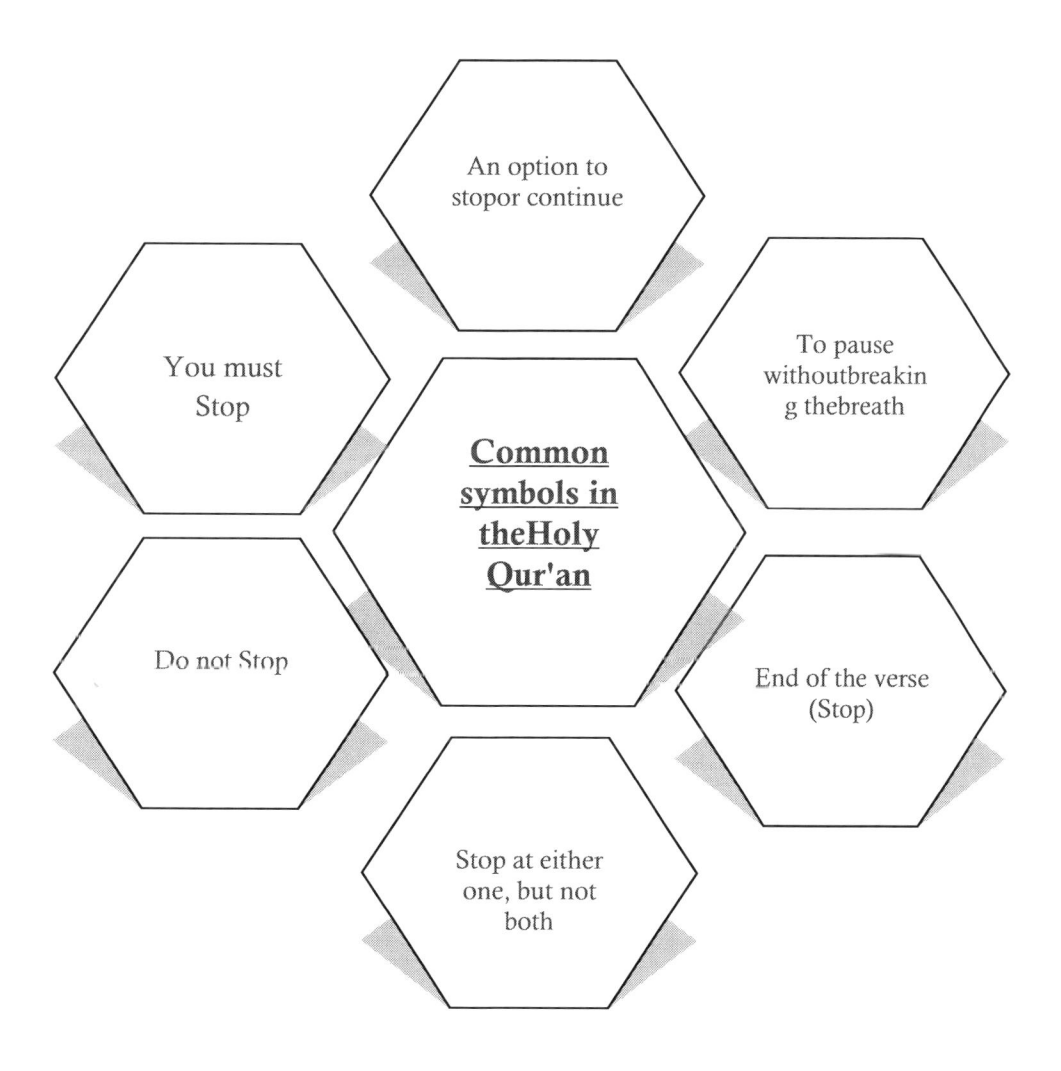

Common symbols in the Holy Qur'an:

- An option to stop or continue
- To pause without breaking the breath
- End of the verse (Stop)
- Stop at either one, but not both
- Do not Stop
- You must Stop

SUMMARY OF THE SYMBOLS OF WUQUF

SYMBOL	NAME	WHAT TO DO
م	Waqf al-Laazim (The Compulsory stop)	It is necessary to stop here and take a pause; otherwise, one can change the meaning of the verse
ط	Waqf al-Muttlaq (The Absolute pause)	It is better to stop and take a gap in reciting the long passage by taking breath. After the break the recitation should continue from the next word. It helps in making the reading process easier by fully grasping the meaning of the already read text.
لا	Waqf al-Mamnu	If this sign is at the end of verse with the circle, one can stop or continue. If it appears in the middle of a verse, it is **prohibited** to stop, as it would change the meaning of the Ayah completely.
ج	Waqf Jaa'iz (The Permissible stop)	It is better to pause at this sign but it is also permissible to continue. It points towards the completion of the matter discussed in that fragment of the Ayah, so as to absorb the meaning discussed in the previous part, and get ready to know about new matter in the following part of the same verse.
ز	Waqf Mujawwaz (Continue reading)	It is better not to pause at this sign. The reciting process can continue, although there is no prohibition in stopping here.
ص	Waqf Murakh-khas(The Licensed pause)	This symbol permits the reader to take a break and take a breath in case if getting tired only, but it is highly advisable to carry on reading.
صلى	AlwasluAwlaa (Preference for continuation)	This means that it is better to continue, with no need to stop.

ق	Qila Alayhil Waqf (Better not to stop)	Not recommended to stop at this sign, but one can pause
قف	Qif (The Anticipation mark)	This is an order to pause, and one should stop at this sign. The sign is used at all places where the reciter would otherwise have continued without pausing.
س السكت	Saktah (The Silence symbol)	Here one should have a short pause in such a way that the breath is not broken. Brief pause and continue recitation. A breathless pause.
وقفت	The Longer pause	Here the pause is longer than Saktah. The pause is done without breaking the breath. Longer pause and continue recitation.
مع مع	Waqf al-Mu'anaqah (The Embracing Stop)	When these signs appear close to each other, a pause at the first place makes a pause at the second prohibited, because the meaning of the verse is incomplete. **One must pause at any one of the signs, but not both.**
صل	QadYusal (The Permissible pause)	Permission to continue reading, although one could stop here.
قلا	Qila La Waqf Alayh	It is better to continue the recital at this sign
ك	Kadhalik (Means 'Like that')	This sign means that the punctuation to be followed is the same action as the preceding symbol.
ْ	The Perfect Stop	This indicates the end of the verse. The reciter has to stop here and take a breath before continuing to read further.
ع		This indicates the end of a paragraph.

THE RULES OF WUQUF

Besides learning the Wuquf signs, it is equally important to know how to pause at a Waqf. There are several rules of Tajweed that apply on the last letter of the word onwhich Waqf occurs. These rules need to be observed to correctly recite the Qur'an. These rules have been categorised by the Diacritics found on the last letter of the word on which the Waqf is exercised.

Definition of Diacritic– A mark, or a sign, or a phonetic character, which, when written above or below a letter indicates a difference in pronunciation from the same letter when unmarked or differently marked.

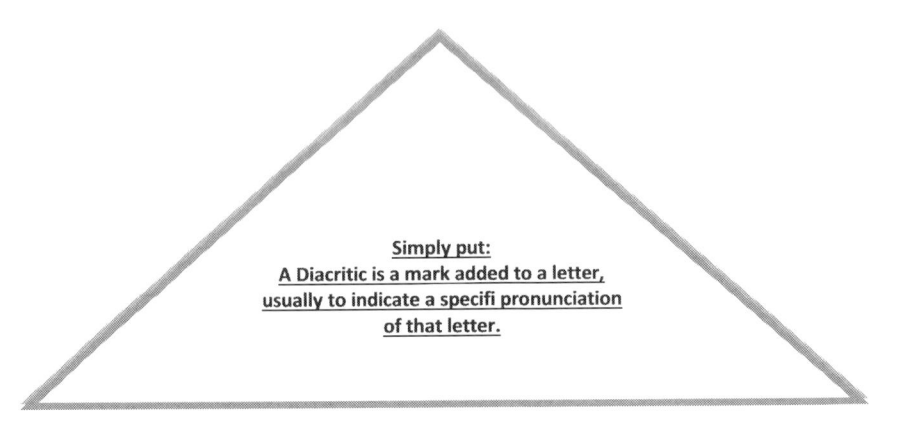

Simply put:
A Diacritic is a mark added to a letter, usually to indicate a specifi pronunciation of that letter.

Arabic Diacritics include:
  a.) Harakah – These are the short vowels of Fat-ha, Kasra and Dhamma.
  b.) Sukun – The Hicup sound.
  c.) Tanween – The Nunation sounds of Fat-hateen, Kasrateen and Dhammateen.
  d.) Shaddah – The double letter

The **Signs** of Wuquf give us a guideline on where to stop, pause or continue, whereas the **Rules** of Wuquf guide us on how to stop when various Diacritics appear at the end of an Ayah

RULES OF WAQF (STOPPING RULES)

1.) The general rule of Waqf is to remove the harakah of the last letter and replace it with a Sukun / Jazm. The harakah can be a Fat-ha, Kasrah, Dhamma or a Kasratain or a Dhammatain (Not Fat-hatain)

Written as / Read as						
	دَلْوَهٌ	غَيْرُهُ	فَلَقٌ	كَسَبَ	رُسُلُ	لَهَبٌ	أَحَدٌ
⇓	⇓	⇓	⇓	⇓	⇓	⇓
	دَلْوَهْ	غَيْرُهْ	فَلَقْ	كَسَبْ	رُسُلْ	لَهَبْ	أَحَدْ

2.) If the last letter has a Fat-hatain, take out one Fat-ha and read with the Alif after it (If there isn't an Alif after it, then add one)

Written as / Read as						
	جَزَاءً	نِدَاءً	نَشْرًا	قَلِيلًا	حِسَابًا	يُسْرًا	حَمِيمًا
⇓	⇓	⇓	⇓	⇓	⇓	⇓
	جَزَاءَا	نِدَاءَا	نَشْرَا	قَلِيلَا	حِسَابَا	يُسْرَا	حَمِيمَا

3.) If the last letter is a round Taa (ة), change it to a small Haa (ه), and put a Sukun / Jazm on it.

	بَقَرَةٌ	حَامِيَةٌ	عَالِيَةٌ	تَذْكِرَةٌ	رَاجِفَةٌ	غَاشِيَةٌ	جَنَّةٌ
	⇓	⇓	⇓	⇓	⇓	⇓	⇓
	بَقَرَهْ	حَامِيَهْ	عَالِيَهْ	تَذْكِرَهْ	رَاجِفَهْ	غَاشِيَهْ	جَنَّهْ

Written as / Read as

4.) To read as it is. No change will take place when stopping: a) if the last letter is an Alif with a Fat-ha before it; b) if the last letter has a Sukun/Jazm; c) if the last letter has a standing Fat-ha

Written as / Read as						
	قَلَى	سَجَى	حُشِرَتْ	سُيِّرَتْ	دَسَّاهَا	بَنَاهَا	تَلَاهَا
⇓	⇓	⇓	⇓	⇓	⇓	⇓
	قَلَى	سَجَى	حُشِرَتْ	سُيِّرَتْ	دَسَّاهَا	بَنَاهَا	تَلَاهَا

5.) If either Alif, Waw or Yaa (Maddah letters) come before the last letter, then pull slightly when making Waqf

قُرَيْشٌ	خَوْفٌ	نَسْتَعِينَ	شَكُورٌ	بَيَانٌ	اَلرَّحْمٰنُ
⇩	⇩	⇩	⇩	⇩	⇩
قُرَيْشْ	خَوْفْ	نَسْتَعِيْنْ	شَكُوْرْ	بَيَآنْ	اَلرَّحْمٰنْ

Written as
Read as

6.) If the last letter has a Tashdeed, pull a little when making Waqf

Written as
Read as

مَفَرُّ	جَانٌّ	حَجُّ	مُضَآرٌّ	مَسٌّ	فَطَلٌّ	تَبَّ
⇩	⇩	⇩	⇩	⇩	⇩	⇩
مَفَرُّ	جَانٌّ	حَجُّ	مُضَآرٌّ	مَسٌّ	فَطَلٌّ	تَبَّ

EXAMPLES FOR RULES OF WAQF (STOPPING RULES)

When there is a single harakah of Fat-ha, Kasrah or Dhamma at the end of a verse, then replace it with a Sukun
أَحَدْ ۞ حِسَابْ ۞ عَلِيمْ ۞ ← أَحَدٌ ۞ حِسَابٌ ۞ عَلِيمٌ ۞
When there is a Kasratain, Dhammatain or Sukun at the end of a word, then read as a Sukun on the last letter.
مَسَدْ ۞ شَدِيدْ ۞ يُولَدْ ۞ ← مَسَدٍ ۞ شَدِيدٌ ۞ يُولَدْ ۞
When there is a Fat-hatain at the end of a verse, whether there is an Alif attached to the word or not, take one Fat-ha off and read with an Alif.
أَنۡوَاجَا ۞ طُوَىٰ ۞ ← أَنۡوَاجًا ۞ طُوًى ۞
When you stop on a word that ends with Alif or Standing Fat-ha, then read as it is written, NO change will take place.
يَغۡشَىٰهَا ۞ وَالضُّحَىٰ ۞ طٰهٰ ۞ ← يَغۡشَىٰهَا ۞ وَالضُّحَىٰ ۞ طٰهٰ ۞
If you see a round Taa ۃ or Haa ه with any harakah on it, then end it as Haa Sukun ۡه ل, except for the Haa that has a Standing Fat-ha
حُطَمَهۡ ۞ يَرَهۡ ۞ بِهۡ ۞ ← حُطَمَةٌ ۞ يَرَهُۥ ۞ بِهِۦ ۞

Stopping at the End of Words

- At the end of a verse, if the word ends with any Harakah, other than Fat-hatain - then change the Harakah into Sukun on the last letter.

- At the end of a verse, words ending with a Mushaddad letter
  - If the letter is any letter other than Meem or Nun or Qalqalah letters - then stop with a Sukun on both identical letters with a small jerk (Nabr) in the reader's voice
  - If the letter is Meem or Nun Mushaddad - then stop with NO Harakah and make Ghunnah for 2 beats
  - If the letter is a Qalqalah letter - then Stop with Strong Qalqalah

- At the end of a verse, if the word ends with Taa Marbutah - then change it into Haa Sakin (For this change — any Harakah can be on the Taa Marbuta, except for the Haa with a Standing Fat-ha)

- Words ending with Sakin letter or with Madd letters of Alif, Ya or Waw - THERE IS NO CHANGE - READ AS IS

- At the end of a verse, if the word ends with Fat-hatain - then change it into one Fat-ha + an Alif (if there is no Alif at the end)

AS – SAKT (ARABIC) or س (The Breathless Pause)

Literally meaning: Prevention

Technically means: Cutting the sound on the last letter of a Qur'anic word for a short time (the duration of two harakaat), without taking a breath to continue the recitation immediately. The symbols:

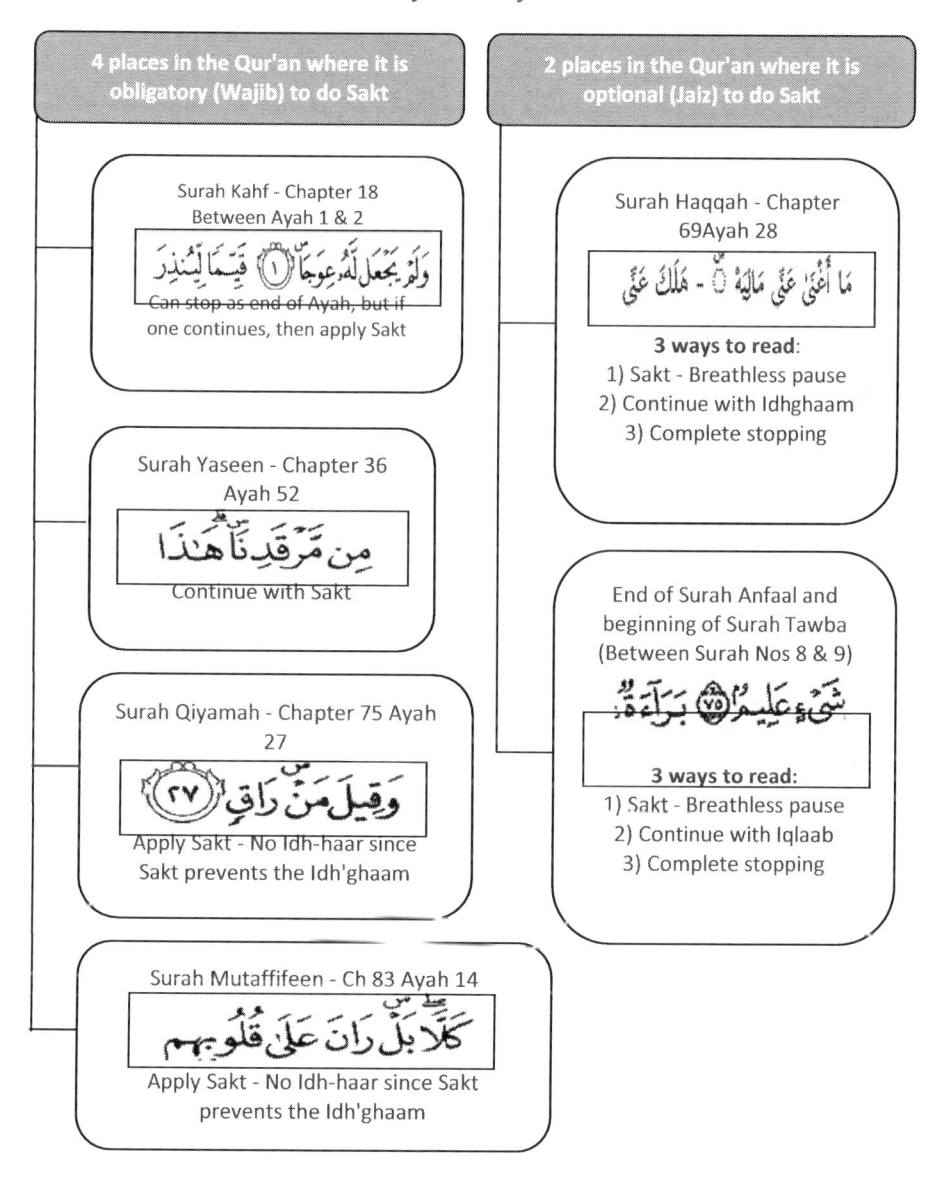

4 places in the Qur'an where it is obligatory (Wajib) to do Sakt

- Surah Kahf - Chapter 18 Between Ayah 1 & 2
  Can stop as end of Ayah, but if one continues, then apply Sakt

- Surah Yaseen - Chapter 36 Ayah 52
  Continue with Sakt

- Surah Qiyamah - Chapter 75 Ayah 27
  Apply Sakt - No Idh-haar since Sakt prevents the Idh'ghaam

- Surah Mutaffifeen - Ch 83 Ayah 14
  Apply Sakt - No Idh-haar since Sakt prevents the Idh'ghaam

2 places in the Qur'an where it is optional (Jaiz) to do Sakt

- Surah Haqqah - Chapter 69 Ayah 28
  3 ways to read:
  1) Sakt - Breathless pause
  2) Continue with Idhghaam
  3) Complete stopping

- End of Surah Anfaal and beginning of Surah Tawba (Between Surah Nos 8 & 9)
  3 ways to read:
  1) Sakt - Breathless pause
  2) Continue with Iqlaab
  3) Complete stopping

AL-IBTIDAA (The Beginning or Starting)

Technically it means: To commence reading after one has stopped reading due to one reason or another. If one stopped due to cutting the recitation and turning away from it, then one must observe the rules of Isti'aadha and the Bismillah. If one simply applied a stop then there is no need to observe the Isti'aadha and the Bismillah, since the stop was only done for rest and to take a breath.

Al-Ibtidaa is the "resumption in recitation" after a pause. Resuming of recitation always occurs on voweled letters. Since HamzatulWasl occurs without a vowel, one needs to be mindful of the several rules that govern the application of particular vowels on it, in order to determine the most suitable to use.

AL WAQF WITH HAMZATUL WASL

There are two types of Hamzah

a.) HamzatulQat'aa – This is the regular consonant letter that in writing appears anywhere in a word, either by itself or is carried by Alif, Ya or Waw. It is always read clearly with the sounds A, I and U, depending on the harakah it appears with.

Example:

انعمت	الأسماء	يؤاخذ
An amta	As maa i	Yu Aakhidhhu

b.) HamzatulWasl also known as AlifulWasl – This is the conjuctive or connective Hamzah that always appears at the beginning of nouns, verbs and prepositions. This Hamzah is always represented by the symbol that looks like an Alif with a small Saad over it, in the Qur'an that is printed in Arab countries (Uthmani Script Qur'an).

In other countries like India & Pakistan (Majeedi Script Qur'an), it is simply written as an Alif. It is pronounced when starting with a word and dropped when continuing the recitation, when joining the word that begins with it, with the one that precedes it.

NOTE: These rules have been discussed extensively on the chapter of HamzatulQat'aa and HamzatulWasl and the chapter on Nun Qutni, but we will briefly touch on them in this chapter.

AL-WAQF WITH HAMZATUL WASL

1.) Continuing recitation with words beginning with HamzatulWasl

RULE 1: If the HamzatulWasl appears in continous recitation and there is no pause, then the HamzatulWasl is dropped and not pronounced. <u>Example:</u>

Wal adhaabaBilmaghfirati (Notice the HamzatulWasl is not pronounced)	والعذاب بالمغفرة

RULE 2: If the HamzatulWasl appears in continous recitation and there is no pause, but the letter preceding the HamzatulWasl is a Tanween, then one harakah from the Tanween is dropped and a small Nun with Kasrah is placed under the HamzatulWasl. The Nun Kasrah connects with the next letter. This small Nun with Kasrah (Nun Maksur) is called NUN QUTNI.
<u>Example:</u>

KadeeruNilladhi Notice the HamzatulWasl has a Nun Kasrah under it, the Tanween changes to one vowel + a small Nun Kasrah	قدير الذي

In copies of Qur'an printed in Arab countries, this Nun Qutni is not present. However, the rule still applies.

2.) <u>How to resume recitation with a word that starts with HamzatulWasl after a pause</u>

RULE 1: HamzatulWasl is **always read with a Fat-ha** if a Laam follows HamzatulWasl in the same word or a word starts with ال(Rule related to Sun and Moon letters)

RULE 2: HamzatulWasl is **read with a Dhamma** if the third letter of the word bears a Dhamma (Rule related to Nouns)

RULE 3: HamzatulWasl is **read with a Kasrah** if the third letter of the word (verb) bears a Fat-ha or Kasrah (Rule related to Verbs) Detailed explanations and examples for all the above are discussed elsewhere in this book in the Chapters on Nun Qutni, HamzatulQat'aa and HamzatulWasl.

SOME EXCEPTIONS FOUND IN THE HOLY QUR'AN

SOME EXCEPTIONS IN THE HOLY QUR'AN

1) In some words a small and light س is found written above the ص

Examples in the Holy Qur'an (small س above the ص)
وَٱللَّهُ يَقْبِضُ وَيَبْصُۜطُ
Surah Al-Baqarah – Chapter 2 – Ayah 245 (Read with the س)
خَلَفَآءَ مِنْ بَعْدِ قَوْمِ نُوحٍ وَزَادَكُمْ فِى ٱلْخَلْقِ بَصْۜطَةً فَٱذْكُرُوٓاْ ءَالَآءَ ٱللَّهِ لَعَلَّكُمْ تُفْلِحُونَ
Surah Al-A'raaf - Chapter 7 - Ayah 69 (Read with the س)
أَمْ عِندَهُمْ خَزَآئِنُ رَبِّكَ أَمْ هُمُ ٱلْمُصَۣيْطِرُونَ
Surah At-Tur - Chapter 52 - Ayah 37 (can be read with the س or the ص Preferred to be read with a ص)
لَّسْتَ عَلَيْهِم بِمُصَۜيْطِرٍ
Surah Al-Ghaashiyah - Chapter 88 - Ayah 22 (Read with the ص) in some Qur'an, the س appears under the ص

2) The word انا is always read as أَنْ The second Alif is not read ان This is covered in detail on the topic of the '7 Alifaat' elsewhere in this book.

3) Wherever the word ملائه is written, the Alif is not pronounced. Some copies of the Qur'an have the Alif which is not to be read marked with a prominent circle. ملايه   ملءه

4) The 'yaa' without a vowel at the end of some words is called an 'alif maqsurah' or shortened alif. At this stage, it may be conveniently ignored in pronunciation.
5) The letters Laam and Ra are also known as Idh'gham letters but are read without a Ghunnah. If after Nun Sakin or Tanween, you see the letters Laam or Ra then you will merge the Nun Sakin or Tanween with the Laam or Ra but there will be no Ghunnah.
6) If you see a Ra Mushaddad (Ra with a Shaddah) bearing a Fat-ha or Dhamma on it then it will be read with full mouth
7) If you see a Ra Mushaddad with a Kasra on it then it will be read with empty mouth.

منشر	ليس البر	يسرون
Example to be read empty mouth	Example to be read full mouth	

8) If you are going to stop on a Ra and before it there is a Ya Sakin, then read the Ra with empty mouth (light Ra).

خير	قدير	بعير
All these will be read with an empty mouth		

9) If after a Ra Sakin which has a Kasra before if, you see one of the 7 full mouth letters then this will be read with a full mouth (heavy Ra – read with a rattling sound RRRR).

قرطاس	مرصاد
These examples will be read with a full mouth	

10) The 'alif' in the word **(ARABIC)** (meaning 'a hundred') is written but not pronounced.
11) The 'alif' at the end of certain forms of verbs is written but not pronounced. Example:

امنوا		رضوا
aamanuu		radhuu

12) The letter(s) coming between a vowel and a letter with a sukun on it are not pronounced. Example:

Read as 'mal qaa ri a tu' and not as 'maal qa ri a tu'	مَاالْقَارِعَة

In the above example, the two alifs between the 'meem' and 'laam' are not pronounced. The first 'alif' does not lengthen the 'meem'.

13) The 'waw' in the words and is written but not pronounced

SOME EXAMPLES FOR PRACTICE

Apart from the 'alif' used for lengthening the vowel 'a', as a general rule at this stage, do not pronounce letters without vowels or signs.

فهدى	اوى	الى	على
ماءة وانا	ترضى	يحيى	اغنى
مالقارعة	امنوا	رضوا	من الاولى
انا	وانحر	فانصب	بالغيب
زكوة	۲لوة	هدى	طوى

14) The following Seven words are pronounced differently when stopping at them compared to when joining them with the next word.

  ❖ When they are joined to the next word, the last letter is pronounced with Fat-ha.

  ❖ When stopping at them, the last letter is pronounced with the long vowel of Alif.

The Word	When Joining	When Stopping
أنا	ان	أنا
Several places in the Holy Qur'an		
لكنا	لكن	لكنا
Surah Al-Kahf : Verse 38		
الظنونا	الظنون	الظنونا
Surah Al-Ahzaab : Verse 10		
الرسولا	الرسول	الرسولا
Surah Al-Ahzaab : Verse 66		

السبيلا	السبيل	السبيلا

Surah Al-Ahzaab : Verse 67

سلا	سل	سلا

Surah Al-Insaan : Verse 4

قواريرا	قوارير	قواريرا

Surah Al-Insaan : Verse 15
This word occurs twice in the same Surah. The one mentioned above isthe first one, because the second one is in Ayah 16, and is pronouncedwithout the long vowel of Alif either way.

15) **ISHMAM** – You show with your lips that you are pronouncing a Dhamma but you don't actually make the dhamma sound. Keeping the lips in the position of Waw, while articulating the letter Nun.

This appears in the Holy Qur'an in Surah Yusuf, Chapter 12 – Ayah 11. Sometimes there is a diamond shape on the word and sometimes it appears without the diamond shape.

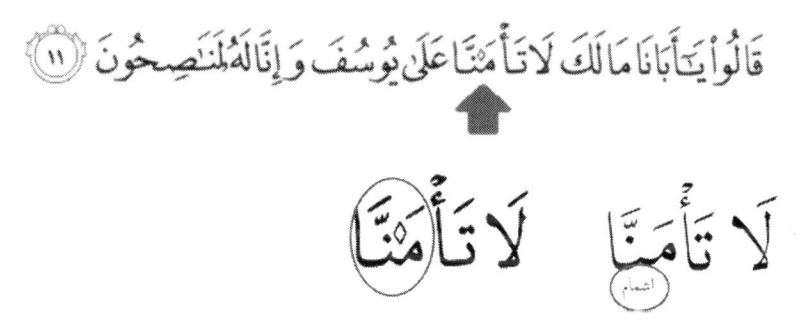

قَالُوا۟ يَٰٓأَبَانَا مَا لَكَ لَا تَأْمَنَّا عَلَىٰ يُوسُفَ وَإِنَّا لَهُۥ لَنَٰصِحُونَ ﴿١١﴾

لَا تَأْمَنَّا   لَا تَأْمَنَّا

Note: When you hear a person reciting this Ayah, you will not be aware of the Ishmam, but when you see the person reciting the Ayah, you will see them forming the shape of Waw on the lips, without pronouncing the Dhamma sound.

16) **IMAALAH** – To produce a sound which is between the Alif and the Yaa. Its not an Alif (aa) or a Yaa (ii), rather it is in-between (e)

This appears in the Holy Qur'an in Surah Hud, Chapter 11 – Ayah 41. Sometimes there is a diamond shape on the word and sometimes it appears without the diamond shape.

$$\text{وَقَالَ ٱرْكَبُوا۟ فِيهَا بِسْمِ ٱللَّهِ مَجْر۪ىٰهَا وَمُرْسَىٰهَآ إِنَّ رَبِّى لَغَفُورٌ رَّحِيمٌ}$$

$$\text{وَقَالَ ارْكَبُوا فِيْهَا بِسْمِ اللهِ مَجْرٰىهَا وَمُرْسٰهَا}$$
اِمَالَة

This word is not read as Majraahaa, nor is it read as Majriihaa. **It is read as Majrehaa**

17) In some words a superfluous tooth (an extra line like a Be ب without the dot) is written after the standing fat-ha. Like empty letters, this tooth is also only written, but is not read.

اتكم
Aataaku
m

احداهما
ihdaahumaa

ادراكم
Adraaku
m

هدانا
hadaanaa

مثواه
Mathwaah
u

نجواهم
najwaahum

TERMINOLOGY FREQUENTLY USED IN TAJWEED

TRANSLITERATION	ENGLISH MEANING
Ayah	A verse of the Qur'an
Ruku(Plural: Rukuat or Arkaan)	A paragraph or section of the Qur'an, containing 7 – 12 ayaat. One paragraph is called a Ruku
Surah	A chapter of the Qur'an (Total – 114 Surahs) A division of the Holy Qur'an into 30 equal parts. This allows the reciter to complete recitation of the Whole Qur'an in one month.
Juz - Part (Plural: Ajza) - Rub ¼ part - Nisf ½ part - Thalatha ¾ part	A division of the Holy Qur'an into 7 parts. This allows the reciter to complete recitation of the Whole Qur'an in one Week.
Manzil (Plural: Manaazil)	A division of the Holy Qur'an into 7 parts. This allows the reciter to complete recitation of the Whole Qur'an in one Week.
Mus-haf	The Arabic volume of the Holy Qur'an
Tilawah	A Qur'anic recitation
Tajweed (Root word: Jawada)	To improve or make better or beautify something. To give every letter it's right with description and origination.
Levels of speed in Qur'an Recitation	Tahqeeq – Reciting slowly with concentration Tahdeer – Swift with speed recitation Tadweer – Average and medium recitation
Tarteel or Murattal	Applicable to all the above speeds of recitation. In Tarteel, each letter is pronounced individually and clearly with due observance to the rules of Wuqoof
Istiaadha or Ta'awwudh	I seek refuge in Allāh from the rejected Shaitaan – The phrase recited before the Bismillah, at the time of beginning the Qur'an recitation
Bismillah or Tasmiyya	'In the name of Allāh, The Beneficient, The Merciful' – The

	opening phrase when reciting the Holy Qur'an. Applicable to all the Surahs of the Qur'an except Surah At-Tawbah
Lahn	Mistakes in Qur'an reading
Al-LahnulJalee	Clear mistakes in Qur'an recitation
Al-LahnulKhafee	Hidden mistakes in Qur'an recitation
Muqatta'aat Letters	Separate letters in the beginning of a few Surah
Harf	A letter of the Alphabet
Huroof	Letters
HuroofulIsmat	Silent Letters
Al-Huroof Al Qamariyyah	The Moon (Lunar) Letters
Al-Huroof Al Shamsiyyah	The Sun (Solar) Letters
Harakaat – Symbols	Short Vowels (Fat-ha, Kasra & Dhamma)
Mutaharrik	Letter that carries a vowel
Fat-ha or Zabar	Short vowel marked by a small line written above the letter pronounced "a" (symbol:
Maftooh	A letter carrying a Fat-ha
Kasra or Zair	A short diagonal stroke written below a letter. It represents a short vowel "i" (symbol:)
Maksoor	A letter carrying a Kasra
Dhamma or Paish	A small apostrophe-like shape written above a letter. It represents a short vowel "o" (like the 'u' sound in 'who' but only stretched for 1 count) (symbol:)
Madhmoom	A letter carrying Dhamma
Tanween	Double Vowels that produce "nn" sound immediately after it (Double Fat-ha, double Kasra and double Dhamma). In other words, it is Nunnation, duplication sound of letter "Noon".
Fat-hateen	The two Fat-ha (symbol:)
Kasrateen	The two Kasra (symbol:)
Dhammateen	The two Dhamma (symbol:)
Sukoon / Jazm	A circle or semi-circle above a letter denoting that it has no haraka (non-vowelled) (symbol: or)
Saakinah	A letter bearing a Sukoon is known as a Sakin letter

Shaddah / Tashdeed	A small 'w' (symbol:) written above a letter. This doubles the sound of the letter so that it is stressed.
Mushaddad	A letter bearing a Shaddah is a Mushaddad letter
Makharij Al-Huroof: **They are five:** Al-Halq Al-Lisaan Al-Jawf Ash-Shafataan (Shafawi) Al-Khayshoom	(short form: Makhraj) The emission point or Place of origin or point of articulation from which each of the 28 letters of Arabic are pronounced. The Throat The Tongue The interior or the empty area of the Mouth The Two Lips The Nasal Passage
Sifah	Quality or Characteristic of a letter
SifaatulHuroof: **With Opposites:** Hams – Jahr Shiddah–Tawassut–Rakhawah Isti'laa – Istifaal Itbaq – Infitaah Idhlaq – Ismaat **Without Opposites:** Safeer Qalqalah Leen Inhiraf Takrir Tafashshee	How the letters are pronounced and how they change according to the situation. If not pronounced correctly with its characteristic, then the letter can change into another letter. Continuation – Stoppage of breath Strong stoppage, in-between stoppage & continuation of sound Pronounced heavily – pronounced lightly Covered - Open Read with effort – Read with ease Whistling – Sound like a bird Echoing/vibration – Breaking of tension or release Softness – pronounced without difficulty Inclination – Move makharij of one into another Repetition – Prounouncing the letter more than once Spreading around the sound of the word in the mouth

Istitaalah	Prolongation – Stretching sound over entire tongue
Ghunnah	Nasal Sound – Comes from the Nasal passage
Nabrah – Related to Hamza:	Command and Sharpness, the heaviest of all letters
Tas-heel	To make easy / soft
Tabdeel	To change 2nd Hamza to the long vowel of Alif
Hathf	To Eliminate – Omitting Hamza from the **word**
Tarqeeq	Giving the quality of lightness or thinness
Tafkheem	Giving the quality of heaviness or thickness
Taghleedth	To make the sound thick or heavy only in the name of Allāh
Hukum (Plural Ahkaam)	Ruling or Rules
4 Types of LaamSaakin	
Laam At-Ta'reef	When LaamSakin appears in the beginning of a Noun
Laam Al-Fi'il	When LaamSakin appear at the end of a Verb
Laam Al-Harf	When a word ends with LaamSakin (Hal and Bal)
Laam Al-Lafdhil Jalali	When LaamSakin appears only in the name of Allāh
Nun Sakin&Tanween	
Idh'haar	To recite clearly, make apparent the pronunciation
Idh'ghaam	To merge or assimilate two letters
Iqlaab	To turn or convert, the letter Nun into Meem
Ikhfaa	To hide or to conceal the sound of a letter
Meem Sakin	
Idh'haarShafawi	To recite clearly (Meem sakin followed by any of the 26 letters – apart from Ba and Meem)
Idh'ghaamShafawi	To merge or join (Meem Sakin followed another Meem)
IkhfaaShafawi	To hide or conceal (Meem Sakin followed by the letter Ba)

Idh'gham – Merging	Idh'gham Al-Kaamil – Complete Merging Idh'gham Al-Naaqis – Incomplete Merging
Other Types of Idh'gham	**Idh'ghamMutamaathilayn**– Merging of Identical letters (Same letters, same Makharij and Sifat) **Idh'ghamMutajaanisayn**– Merging of related letters (Same Makharij but different Sifat) **Idh'ghamMutaqaaribayn**– Merging of similar letters (Close to each other in Makharij and Sifat) **Idh'ghamMutabaa'idain**– Letters far from each other therefore no Idh'gham between 2 distant letters.
Nun Qutni	Small Nun
RaaTafkheem	Raa pronounced heavily with a full mouth
RaaTarqeeq	Raa pronounced lightly with an empty mouth
Maddah – 9 Types 1) Madd ulAsliyya Madd caused by other factors 2) Madd ul Badal 3) Madd ulSilah 4) Madd ulEwad Madd caused by Hamza 5) Madd ulMuttasil 6) Madd ulMunfasil Madd caused by Sukun 7) Madd ulLaazim 8) Madd ul Lin 9) Madd ul Arid Lis Sukun	The prolongation or elongation of the sound of a vowel Also known as Madd utTabee – The Original Madd The Substitute Madd The Connecting Madd The Replacement Madd The Connected Madd The Detached Madd The Compulsory Madd The Gentle Madd The Abrupt Stop Madd
Haa HaaThathee	The Essential Haa

HaaSakt HaaDhameer	The Consonant Haa The Pronoun Haa
HamzatulQat'aa HamzatulWasl	The Normal or Cutting or Dividing Hamza Also known as AlifulWasl – The Connective Hamza
Saktah or Sakt	A breathless pause.
Waqf	To pause or to make a stop by breaking off the breath at the end of the word
Wasl	The opposite of waqf. The joining of verses / sentences without stopping

Printed in Great Britain
by Amazon